D0985250

Public Sector Transparency and Accountability: Making it Happen

OECD

ORGANISATION FOR ECONOMIC CO-OPERATION AND DEVELOPMENT

ORGANISATION FOR ECONOMIC CO-OPERATION AND DEVELOPMENT

Pursuant to Article 1 of the Convention signed in Paris on 14th December 1960, and which came into force on 30th September 1961, the Organisation for Economic Co-operation and Development (OECD) shall promote policies designed:

- to achieve the highest sustainable economic growth and employment and a rising standard of living in Member countries, while maintaining financial stability, and thus to contribute to the development of the world economy;

- to contribute to sound economic expansion in Member as well as non-member countries in the process of economic development; and

- to contribute to the expansion of world trade on a multilateral, non-discriminatory basis in accordance with international obligations.

The original Member countries of the OECD are Austria, Belgium, Canada, Denmark, France, Germany, Greece, Iceland, Ireland, Italy, Luxembourg, the Netherlands, Norway, Portugal, Spain, Sweden, Switzerland, Turkey, the United Kingdom and the United States. The following countries became Members subsequently through accession at the dates indicated hereafter: Japan (28th April 1964), Finland (28th January 1969), Australia (7th June 1971), New Zealand (29th May 1973), Mexico (18th May 1994), the Czech Republic (21st December 1995), Hungary (7th May 1996), Poland (22nd November 1996), Korea (12th December 1996) and the Slovak Republic (14th December 2000). The Commission of the European Communities takes part in the work of the OECD (Article 13 of the OECD Convention).

© OECD 2002

Permission to reproduce a portion of this work for non-commercial purposes or classroom use should be obtained through the Centre français d'exploitation du droit de copie (CFC), 20, rue des Grands-Augustins, 75006 Paris, France, tel. (33-1) 44 07 47 70, fax (33-1) 46 34 67 19, for every country except the United States. In the United States permission should be obtained through the Copyright Clearance Center, Customer Service, (508)750-8400, 222 Rosewood Drive, Danvers, MA 01923 USA, or CCC Online: *www.copyright.com*. All other applications for permission to reproduce or translate all or part of this book should be made to OECD Publications, 2, rue André-Pascal, 75775 Paris Cedex 16, France.

FOREWORD

This publication presents the papers discussed at the Latin American Forum on Ensuring Transparency and Accountability in the Public Sector held on 5-6 December 2001. This joint OECD/OAS Forum brought together more than 450 ministers, senators, senior government officials, business leaders, and representatives of international organisations, non-government organisations and the media from OECD countries, Latin America and the Caribbean. The Vice President of Brazil, Marco Maciel, opened the Forum together with Seiichi Kondo, Deputy Secretary-General of the OECD, and César Gaviria, Secretary-General of the OAS.

The Forum achieved a breakthrough in the implementation of the Inter-American Convention against Corruption by elaborating policy recommendations for supporting the preventive measures defined by the Convention. These policy recommendations reflect the shared experience of Member countries of the OECD and the Organization of American States and list key principles and crucial factors in the three following key areas of good governance:

- Ensuring impartiality in the decision-making process by a credible conflict-of-interest policy.

- Increasing transparency in the preparation and execution of the budget.

- Promoting freedom of information, consultation and participation of citizens in the formulation and implementation of public policies.

In addition, country papers provide practical solutions adapted to their particular administrative environments for policy-makers and a demanding civil society.

This publication was prepared by János Bertók of the OECD Public Management Service, and is published on the responsibility of the Secretary-General of the OECD.

TABLE OF CONTENTS

Annexes: OECD Policies and Best Practices

FOSTERING DIALOGUE TO STRENGTHEN GOOD GOVERNANCE

by

Seiichi Kondo
Deputy Secretary-General of the OECD

Introduction

The theme, Ensuring Accountability and Transparency in the Public Sector, is important to all countries. Consequently, the Organisation for Economic Co-operation and Development (OECD) together with the Organization of American States (OAS) organised a Forum in Brasilia, Brazil on 5-6 December 2001, as an occasion for policy dialogue between member countries of the OECD and the OAS, who share the common aim of building accountable and transparent public administrations that serve their citizens' needs.

The OECD uses the term "governance" -- and public governance in particular -- to describe how authority is distributed in the governmental system and how those who hold such authority are held to account. When it comes to the notion of good governance, we recognise a number of generally agreed principles, including:

- *Accountability*, meaning that it is possible to identify and hold public officials to account for their actions.

- *Transparency,* meaning that reliable, relevant and timely information about the activities of government is available to the public.

- *Openness,* meaning governments that listen to citizens and businesses, and take their suggestions into account when designing and implementing public policies.

While challenges are similar across countries, and principles of good governance are widely accepted, there is plenty of room for different approaches, national priorities and institutional solutions to achieve transparent, accountable and open government.

The OECD/OAS Forum is designed to help policy-makers to consider measures appropriate to their political, administrative and cultural environments. It also aims to support implementation of the Inter-American Convention against Corruption and the follow-up mechanisms agreed to in June 2001.

This chapter outlines some of the experiences and lessons, which OECD countries have gained through recent work in fostering good public governance in three key areas that were subjects of the Forum:

- Promoting sound ethics management.

- Ensuring fiscal transparency.

- Strengthening access to information and public participation.

In addition, it highlights the need to harness the potential of e-government, as a new, powerful tool for fighting corruption and strengthening citizen participation in government.

Promoting sound ethics management in the public sector

High standards of public governance are seen by all OECD member countries as the essential foundation for achieving sustainable economic growth, social cohesion and a healthy environment. Without high standards, there can be no trust or confidence in the integrity of public institutions or indeed in the value of democratic processes in promoting and protecting the interests and well being of citizens. Left unchecked, corruption weakens economies, discourages trade and investment, creates huge inequalities and undermines the very foundations of democratic government. The absence of high standards leads to instability and unpredictability; under such conditions neither business nor citizens can prosper.

Putting it bluntly, good governance means clean government. There are other important aspects: respect for laws, responsiveness to citizens and sound budgetary management, for example. But probity and integrity in the public service and in public life generally are central to the proper functioning of public administration. It is not only a matter of fraud or financial misappropriation. Essentially, it is a question of applying the principle of honesty in all areas where governments, whether national or local, act.

All OECD countries reject bribery and have strict laws and rules applying to their public officials. Along those lines, all OECD countries, as well as four non-member countries including Argentina, Brazil and Chile, have committed to abide by the OECD Convention on Combating Bribery of Foreign Public Officials in International Business Transactions. The OECD Convention, which entered into force in February 1999, makes it a crime to offer, promise or give a bribe to a foreign public official in order to obtain or retain international business transactions. Thirty of those countries that have ratified the Convention have already undergone a peer review process regarding its implementation.

Most OECD countries also have codes of conduct to encourage honesty. But it is not just a question of laws, rules and codes, nor even of enforcement, important though that is. Achieving high standards requires a comprehensive approach to establishing a culture in which high expectations of good conduct are the norm. This requires strong leadership; training can help but encouragement and example from the top are even more powerful in setting the right cultural framework. It also requires the setting of clear standards for the acceptance of gifts and hospitality and for the conduct of private affairs, backed as necessary by disclosure. Achieving high standards involves reviewing systems for public appointments, recruitment, and promotion within the public service to ensure that these processes are open and fair. It means establishing clear lines of accountability and reporting supported by transparent and audible financial management procedures. It means open procurement processes and much more. And, not least, it means dealing with citizens in an open, fair and objective way.

What OECD countries have learned from their experiences has enabled the OECD to draw up a checklist and set of principles against which administrations can review their systems. This was reflected in the "Recommendation on Improving Ethical Conduct in the Public Service[1]" adopted by the OECD Council, by which the member countries have committed themselves to review regularly their policies, procedures and practices.

Ensuring fiscal transparency

The OECD is keenly interested in the relationship between good governance and better economic and social outcomes. Transparency, as a key element of good governance, includes ensuring openness about policy intentions, formulation and implementation. A nation's budget is the single most important policy document of governments, where policy objectives across the spectrum of economic, social and environmental interests are reconciled and implemented in concrete terms. Therefore, transparency in the budget process is of paramount importance.

Budget transparency is defined as the full disclosure of all relevant fiscal information in a timely and systematic manner. The OECD has recently published *Best Practices for Fiscal Transparency*[2]. These are compiled from the practices of OECD Members and are intended to help countries evaluate and improve their budget reporting system. These are not intended to create a standard by which countries are to be judged; rather, different countries will have different reporting regimes and may select to focus on transparency in specific areas for analysis and possibly improvement.

The best practices are a comprehensive list of reports as well as specific disclosures and processes. The Best Practices begin with suggestions on how to construct the budget. A key recommendation is that the budget be comprehensive, encompassing all government revenue and expenditures. The recommended reports on the state of the budget range from pre-budget release of economic assumptions and a picture of fiscal health, to a mid-year assessment of implementation, and finally an end-of-year report. The best practices recommend special reports including pre-election reports, and long-term assessments of budget policy. The list includes specific disclosures like economic assumptions and tax expenditures. Finally there are processes and systems that are crucial in aiding transparency, including the role of the legislature, the audit office and the public.

Strengthening public access to information and participation in policy-making

A third important aspect of good governance involves public access to information and participation in policy-making. Transparency in the public administration is enhanced by strong public scrutiny based on solid legal provisions for access to information. Strengthening relations with citizens is a sound investment in better policy-making and a core element of good governance. Investing in openness allows governments to tap new sources of policy-relevant ideas, information and resources when making decisions. Equally important, it contributes to building public trust in government, raising the quality of democracy and strengthening civic capacity. Active engagement of citizens can help to ensure that policies are supported or at least understood by the public in ways that also contribute to their effective implementation.

In strengthening *public access to information and participation:*

- Governments must ensure that information is complete, objective, reliable, relevant, easy to find and to understand.

- They should see to it that consultation has clear goals and rules defining the limits of the exercise and the government's obligation to account for its use of citizens' input.

- Governments must ensure that the process provides sufficient time and flexibility to allow for the emergence of new ideas and proposals by citizens, as well as means by which they may be integrated into government policy-making processes.

A recent OECD report and policy brief on *Citizens as Partners*[3] suggests guiding principles for governments everywhere. To engage people effectively in policy-making, governments must invest adequate time and resources in building robust legal, policy and institutional frameworks. They must develop and use appropriate tools. But without leadership at the highest levels and commitment throughout the public administration, even the best policies will do little to ensure that citizens can have a voice and that their views are heard.

Harnessing the potential of e-government

The use of new Information and Communication Technologies (ICTs) are transforming relations between governments and citizens in many fields. The communiqué of the Third Global Forum held in Naples in March 2001, which built on the previous year's Global Forum on Governance held here in Brasilia, acknowledged that: "nothing is more powerful in combating corruption than conducting transactions openly and with public knowledge of the rules and criteria to be applied...[and] ICT can be a powerful tool for good governance."

ICTs are being used increasingly to combat corruption. Provided the right procedures are in place, they can be used to make financial and administrative transactions traceable and open to challenge. ICTs facilitate publishing of rules and criteria governing decisions and entitlements. Those responsible for particular decisions or activities can be readily identified. And by providing enhanced accounting, monitoring and auditing systems, they ensure that public finances are fully open to senior managerial and external scrutiny. More generally, the power of ICTs as a vehicle for information and consultation means that citizens can be more fully involved in all aspects of government including policy-making, thus reinforcing the creation of a culture of trust and mutual interest.

Conclusions – Fostering dialogue to strengthen good governance

To conclude, two key points are worth emphasising:

- First, the success of public governance will ultimately be judged not by governments or international organisations, but by *citizens*. It is citizens who are demanding greater transparency and accountability from government as well as greater public participation in shaping policies that affect their lives. For that reason, it is encouraging to see that representatives of civil society have played an important role in the programme of the Forum.

- Second, good governance and the fight against corruption should not be just catchwords in international co-operation. They represent the keys for successful reform and for equitable and sustainable development. Opportunities for *policy dialogue* and direct exchange -- such as that offered by the OECD/OAS Forum -- are of major importance in this shared endeavour. The OECD therefore will continue to work together with representatives of governments, private enterprises and civil society to promote good governance around the world.

NOTES

1. The OECD Recommendation on Improving Ethical Conduct in the Public Service is available in Annex 1. The OECD Public Management Policy Brief on Building Public Trust: Ethics Measures in OECD Countries outlines the main findings of the OECD survey on the implementation of this Recommendation in Annex 2.

2. The OECD Best Practices for Budget Transparency can be found in Annex 3.

3. The OECD Public Management Policy Brief on Engaging Citizens in Policy-making: Information, Consultation and Public Participation can be found in Annex 4.

PREVENTING CORRUPTION IN THE AMERICAS

by

César Gaviria
Secretary-General of the OAS

As I had the opportunity to express during the opening ceremony, I wish to state for the record our recognition of the Federal Government of Brazil for the decided and effective support they have offered regarding this initiative. Likewise, I wish to express our gratitude to the OECD for facilitating this opportunity to work together in the organisation of this event with respect to issues in which, without a doubt, the Member States of both organisations may be able to learn a lot from each other and for which the co-operation of our institutions, makes sense.

The Brasilia Forum circulated around three large thematic areas that are referred to in the Inter-American Convention against Corruption. It was conceived as a stage for strengthening the exchange of information, experience and best practices in regard to each area, between the representatives of the OECD and OAS Member States.

In putting into context the content and scope of this Forum and its results, I wish to briefly mention the progress made within the OAS framework in regard to the issue of the fight against corruption, signal some of the challenges that still lie ahead in this field and highlight the importance of the conclusions of this event as part of the collective action taken by the countries of the Americas in this field.

A road map for collective action in the fight against corruption in the Americas

The fight against corruption has been a constant concern in the Americas. Within the OAS framework, we were at the forefront in adopting the first Convention on this subject, during a time when there was still a discussion of whether or not the fight against this phenomenon could be the object of an international treaty. I believe that with this step we were able to dismantle the arguments of those who were opposed to the negotiation of a treaty dealing with transnational bribery within the OECD.

The OAS Convention also expresses an integral and comprehensive vision of how this problem should be addressed. In accordance with said Convention, corruption must be understood, first, as a systemic problem and not simply one of corrupt individuals. In this sense, it is not enough to strengthen co-operation efforts for putting some corrupt people in prison without solving the structural causes that generate this problem, since other individuals shall appear and replace them. That is why the OAS Convention contains provisions that strengthen judicial co-operation in areas such as extradition, exchange of evidence, bank secrecy and measures for recuperating the proceeds of acts of corruption. However, just as equally, the Convention provides measures that the states obligate themselves to implement in order to avoid the occurrence of acts of corruption, and that have to do with the subject matter that were considered in the Brasilia Forum. They were oriented towards the modernisation of public institutions and ensuring the transparency, efficiency and accountability of governments.

Second, the OAS Convention expresses that combating corruption must be a permanent process and not simply the result of isolated or occasional actions. In accordance with this vision, just as it is not possible to pinpoint one instant or action in which corruption arises or was consolidated, neither is it possible to imagine that it will end in a single moment, with one act or decision. As such, of the Convention it is inferred that many decisions are required, on different levels and with different orientations.

Third, the Convention understands the fight against this evil as a process in which all of us have responsibilities: countries, the private sector, civil society and the international community; each one of them at their own level and with different orientations and scopes, but all of them responding to the same purpose and strategy of eliminating corruption.

Bearing in mind this vision, from the start it was clear that the Convention was not the finish line, but the first big step towards collectively confronting this disease.

The path travelled

Based on the Convention and having as a framework a Program of Co-operation adopted by our General Assembly, in the OAS we have continued our work in this field:

- We have supported and will continue to support numerous Member States in the adjustment of their legislation to the Convention.

- We developed a pilot program for the Central American sub-region on the implementation of some of the preventive measures that are provided by the Convention, including those related to the prevention of conflict of interests, access to information and participation of civil society in the prevention of corruption.

- We created an information database and information exchange network on the Internet to strengthen co-operation in the fight against corruption.

- We have begun the functioning of a Network on Mutual Legal Assistance as a result of the decisions adopted by the Ministers of Justice and Attorneys General of the Americas (REMJA).

- We sponsored a training program for journalists of the Americas on investigative journalism along with the Trust of the Americas.

Additionally, the Member States have continued to collectively adopt decisions, within the framework of our Organization, of great significance for strengthening mutual co-operation in this field. The most recent and important decision is the adoption and launch of the Mechanism for Follow-up on the Implementation of the Convention by the States Parties. This mechanism has self-evaluation and peer review characteristics, similar to those existing in the monitoring mechanisms in relation with the OECD Convention and within the Council of Europe. But it also has its own singularities, especially in regard to the emphasis placed on the nature of this exercise as an instrument for strengthening mutual co-operation among our countries in combating corruption.

Likewise, during the last few months and in development of the mandates of the Quebec Summit of the Americas, important progress has been made in also addressing private sector responsibility in the fight against corruption. As the private sector is part of the problem, it must also be part of the solution. The deliberations within our Organisation and in an international conference jointly co-sponsored by the Inter-American Development Bank (IDB) and the OAS on corporate social responsibility will allow us to move forward in the definition of specific actions that we must promote or consolidate in this field.

Some future challenges

Notwithstanding the previous, in the Americas we have begun a process that we understand must be a permanent collective effort. As such, we are aware that we still have many challenges ahead. I would like to highlight some of those challenges, which in my opinion are of significance.

First, in many countries of the Americas we need to make significant progress in reforming our institutions. A modern state is the best barrier against corruption. And when I refer to the state, I do so in its widest sense, including all the branches of government, oversight bodies and the diverse administrative-political levels. I do not think this affirmation incites any discussion. However, the real problem that we have here is how do we make the public sector institutions function well. This is a question that has still not been answered satisfactorily. It is there where we have one of our largest collective challenges.

Second, in obtaining this purpose it is necessary that we progress in becoming more knowledgeable of institutional problems. Much more investigation is needed as well as involving a wider group of citizens in order to effectively strengthen our institutions.

Third, in Latin America we have an even greater challenge: the modernisation of our political systems and the modalities of political action. In the last fifteen years we have witnessed a process without precedent regarding the consolidation of democracy. But it is also true that this process is far from definitive and finalised, that we still have blunders and setbacks, that there are countries with vulnerable institutions and that there are still systems that need to strengthen their checks and balances, and their institutions for citizen participation.

Fourth, we must improve mutual legal and judicial co-operation mechanisms at the international level. The Inter-American Convention against Corruption is a basic instrument in this field. The decisions adopted by the Ministers of Justice and Attorneys General of the Americas within the framework of their hemispheric meetings have all advanced these mechanisms. With the same orientation, progress must be made in combating the other links in the chain of corruption such as money laundering and ensuring that financial institutions comply with standards that prevent criminals from hiding behind bank secrecy regulations.

Fifth, it is necessary to move forward on the exchange of information, experiences and technical co-operation among our countries. In this sense, initiatives such as the Forum that this publication records are of great utility.

Sixth, it is necessary that the private sector assume its obligations in the fight against this disease. That is why we must work closely with institutions such as chambers of commerce and business associations in generating a greater commitment from them on self-regulation and in the development and implementation of codes of conduct.

Finally, I wish to highlight the role of civil society organisations. A great deal of the progress made during the last few years in regard to the awareness on the severity of this problem is owed to them. I have said on various occasions that there is a false dichotomy, that some pretend to establish between governmental institutions and civil society organisations. On the contrary, I am convinced that their joint action is absolutely necessary. In this sense, I believe that in the Americas we should create more bridges that will allow us to combine our efforts and work as a team with those committed civil society organisations, seriously, objectively and responsibly, in the fight against corruption.

Contribution of the Forum results

The results of the Brasilia Forum on Ensuring Accountability and Transparency in the Public Sector are of great utility for the process that has been developing in the Americas in strengthening collective action and mutual co-operation for combating corruption.

Prevention is, without a doubt, the best way to combat this phenomenon. As such, justifiably, the OAS Convention puts great emphasis on the types of measures that must be adopted in advancing the purpose of consolidating modern states, in which they should be effective, efficient and transparent, in order to create the best barrier against corruption.

That is why it is very crucial and useful to strengthen co-operation and the exchange of information and best practices among the countries of the Americas and the other regions of the world in this field. In this sense, the three thematic areas considered in the Brasilia Forum and its results are of great significance and importance for the countries of the Americas. This is confirmed by the fact that they are directly related to the measures selected by the Committee of Experts of the Mechanism for Follow-up on the Implementation of the Inter-American Convention against Corruption within the framework of its first round of review that has recently begun.

In closing, this also demonstrates the importance of continuing these policy dialogues between the members of the OECD and OAS in matters such as those that were the object of our discussions at the Brasilia Forum.

INSTITUTIONS OF INTEGRITY IN THE UNITED STATES

by

Stuart C. Gilman, Ph.D.
President, Ethics Resource Center, Washington, D.C.
Former Director of Strategic Development
Treasury Inspector General for Tax Administration
United States Department of Treasury

The vices of democracy are immediately apparent. Its advantages only become clear in the long run. There is therefore at the bottom of democratic institutions some hidden tendency, which often makes men promote the general prosperity, in spite of their vices and their mistakes, whereas in aristocratic institutions there is sometimes a secret bias which, in spite of talents and virtues leads men to contribute to the afflictions of their fellows. In this way it may come about that under aristocratic governments public men do evil without intending it, and in democracies they bring about good results of which they have never thought.

(Alexis de Tocqueville, *Democracy in America*, Volume I, Part II, Chapter 6)

The essence of anticorruption laws and systems in democracies is that they serve to assure the public that government is working in the public's interest. This paper will focus on the manifold anticorruption systems the United States has developed to retain the confidence of its people in governmental institutions. It will highlight the fundamental interfaces and tensions between the various institutions that have been created, and how conflicts over responsibilities are resolved. The paper will primarily focus on the institutional and legal fabric of the federal (or national) level in the United States.

Although only brief mention will be made of the anticorruption activities at the state and local levels of government in the US, it is important to recognise their role in American government. US states are often referred to as laboratories of democracy and, in fact, many of the most profound innovations at the federal level have begun as initiatives in one or more states. Significantly, states in the US have far greater autonomy compared to most other federal systems. The US Constitution actually reserves powers to the states and those powers are often totally independent of the federal executive function. For this reason almost any treatment of the anticorruption systems throughout the United States is incomplete, because one would have to treat the various (and complex) federal entities, the fifty different state approaches, and local – mostly large city governments – that have been given autonomy to create their own institutional structures to fight corruption.

Nonetheless the history, development and implementation of anticorruption regimes in the United States -- even at the federal level -- are important and instructive. No nation would be wise to try to exactly duplicate the anticorruption laws and institutions in the US. However, it is worthwhile reflecting on the problems and solutions America confronted and resolved, and therefore understand the questions that all governments must address if they are to have effective national anticorruption institutions. The US has accomplished many things in the battle against corruption, but it has also experienced disappointing failures. How some of the latter were overcome, as well as the continuing challenges still facing American institutions, are all parts of this story.

Historical background

Before entering into the main argument of this paper, it is valuable to set the historical context for anticorruption in the United States. In August of 1838, Samuel Swartwout, the federal Customs Collector for the Port of New York 1 disembarked on a schooner for London with two black satchels. Within them he took more than five percent of the entire treasury of the United States. In the proceedings against him, at least four employees admitted knowing about the embezzlement from the beginning. About their conduct, Joshua Phillips, Assistant Cashier, explained "I was Mr. Swartwout's clerk, and would not betray the secret of my employer we clerks of the custom-house consider ourselves as in the service of the collector, and not in the service of the United States."[1] There was no extradition treaty with England. Neither Mr. Swartwout nor the money were ever recovered.

In reaction to the massive corruption in his administration, President Andrew Jackson empowered his Post Master General, Amos Kendall, to fundamentally redesign the Post Office Department, and his fellow cabinet members followed Kendall's model in reorganising governmental institutions. Instead of relying on men of character, as Presidents since Washington had done, Kendall designed a system of redundancy of signatures in order to spend money on behalf of the United States. Additionally, he developed the first "transparent" procurement and contracting systems, and even developed "Rules of Conduct" for public employees.

A young French nobleman, Alexis de Tocqueville, in comparing the French and American systems, needing a word to describe this new "system of government," coined the term *bureaucracy*. These new bureaucracies were designed to minimise corruption in governmental systems and were added to on a regular basis to account for every fresh scandal. It is certainly true that these systems were also viewed as mechanisms for greater efficiency – something especially ironic today.

As the executive and legislative branches of government struggled to cope with newly arising forms of corruption, no one was ever made responsible to oversee what had come before – much less how new laws and orders would integrate with what had been implemented previously. The result was that systems of anticorruption tools were built upon older systems, often with no logical integration between them, and often with contradictory requirements. The layering of integrity systems became so pervasive that bureaucracies learned to operate independently of many legislative or executive controls, often through voluminous regulation, resulting in a "priesthood" of expertise in the government department.

The impact of bureaucratic minutiae in order to prevent corruption was summed up by Michael Nelson as one of the ironies of American bureaucracy: "*agencies organised to avoid evil became that much less able to do good.*"[2] In other words the burdens of doing things the "right" way can actually prevent an organisation from accomplishing its mission. This observation is truism that extends to all countries, not only the US. Unfortunately, most contemporary academic research in public administration starts with the premise that compliance systems to prevent corruption are inherently bad.[3] This misses the obvious point: what is to replace them? There is often a pathetically naïve notion that once these systems are done away with all of the problems they were created to resolve will disappear with them. So some governments have done away with anticorruption commissions (e.g. the

18

Heath Commission in South Africa) concluding with the bizarre notion that when anticorruption systems are done away with the corruption that they were uncovering also disappears.

The issue that all countries must come to grips with is how to have adequate accountability, due diligence in oversight and at the same time allow governmental institutions to function effectively. In other words, how do we determine an appropriate balance between effective anticorruption systems and effective governmental institutions?

Compliance versus integrity systems

The anticorruption literature in public administration focuses on the distinction between compliance and integrity based systems.[4] For example, the recent overviews of government ethics programs by the OECD, *Ethics in the Public Service* and *Trust in Government*, focused on this distinction. Yet in many ways this difference is a straw man. Compliance based systems are supposed to be only rule or law based with little room for individual conscience or decision. Integrity based systems are designed to increase human autonomy through aspirational goals avoiding rule structures. Perhaps these concepts can be framed as ideal types. But, the empirical reality is that they are ends of a continuum. For that reason, a more informed discussion should look at the social psychological dynamic of this process.

Compliance based rule systems at their worst degrade into a system of casuistry governed by a priesthood, often of attorneys or personnel specialists. They exercise sole authority in providing authoritative interpretations of rules in more and more narrowly defined circumstances. Casuistry is not always negative, as many bioethics experts have recently noted; however, to be effective such a system must remain open for interactive communication. Any system in which an elite simply hands down edicts becomes more and more isolated from the daily processes of government.

Integrity based systems at their worst become systems of wishful thinking. These become general, very abstract guides of performance with no enforcement and no method for receiving advice or education. Empowerment of public officials in such a setting can be a recipe for disaster.

Empowering ethically or morally bankrupt people simply leads to corruption more quickly.

Modern anticorruption programs must balance integrity and compliance, multiple programs, intersecting laws and authorities, and institutional responsibilities. There is no perfect balance. At the federal level of the US the "national" anticorruption regime is divided into four major parts, each of which have significant subparts. They can be roughly defined as institutions of *prevention, investigation, prosecution and protection*. The lines between these four elements are often blurred in day-to-day practice, but the distinctions are useful ways to organise the institutional frameworks and their responsibilities.

The institutional embodiment of these four anticorruption elements occurred after the Watergate crisis in the United States, because of the institutions Congress created trying to prevent a repeat of the abuses of the Watergate era. For that reason we can clearly define the beginning of the modern epoch of anticorruption systems in the US as 1978.[5] It was the year the Ethics in Government Act was passed creating the Office of Government Ethics and the Independent Counsel. The Federal Election Commission was created to oversee the American electoral process. Laws were also passed creating the first domestic Inspectors General and the Office of Special Counsel -- responsible for protecting whistle blowers.[6]

What follows then is the anticorruption approach of the executive branch of the federal government of the United States.

Prevention

The Office of Government Ethics (OGE)[7] has the predominant responsibility for writing ethics and conflict of interest regulations, and interpreting conflicts of interest law. OGE was created in 1978, in order to deter corrupt activities before they could occur. From its inception the hallmark of OGE was the prevention of conflicts of interest in the executive branch. Prevention is OGE's central mission. It accomplishes this by setting standards, counselling and education. OGE does not generally investigate or prosecute instances of individual misconduct.

OGE sets standards by both interpreting the law and writing regulations. For example, President George H.W. Bush issued Executive Order 12674, which provided 14 principles of conduct for federal employees. OGE was charged with writing regulations interpreting these, and issued a detailed set of Standards of Conduct in 1993. These Standards (5 CFR 2635) provided detailed guidance on the most common ethical and conflict of interest problems most government employees confront. In addition, OGE issues Informal Advisory Opinions when issues arise that are not covered by the Standards yet are broadly applicable. These are published regularly and are available to everyone on OGE's Web site.[8] Since 1979, OGE has issued well over 1,000 advisory opinions that make up, for all intents and purposes, a body of law.

Like most other federal anticorruption systems OGE is decentralised. OGE has the responsibility for setting the ethics policy for the executive branch of government. The actual management of the ethics program, however, is accomplished by each individual agency. The head of each agency is responsible for the ethics program of that agency and the conduct of its work force. The agency head exercises that responsibility by appointing a Designated Agency Ethics Official, or DAEO, who takes care of the day-to-day management of the program. This is the way in which the executive branch ethics program is decentralised.

Like most other anticorruption bodies at the federal level OGE is considered independent in the executive branch. Independence does not mean that it functions as a fourth branch of government (e.g. the Independent Commission Against Corruption (ICAC) in Hong Kong), but rather that it takes advantage of the separation of powers in the Constitution to ensure that no single institution (the President or Congress) can dictate to it. For example, OGE derives its budget directly through the Office of Management and Budget, but its budget is approved and overseen by committees in both the House and the Senate. Second, the Director of OGE is a Presidential appointee who must be confirmed by the Senate and serves for a fixed five-year term. The vast majority of the remaining OGE staff are career federal employees.

OGE fulfils its preventive mission in a variety of ways. It issues executive branch wide regulations dealing with standards of conduct, financial disclosure, conflict of interest waivers, post-employment restrictions, and ethics training; OGE provides guidance and interpretation to agencies, including providing informal oral advice and publishing selected written opinions annually; OGE oversees both the public and confidential financial disclosure systems (transparency systems) and reviews the financial disclosure reports of Presidential nominees in the confirmation process. In fact, the Senate of the United States will generally not hold a confirmation hearing for a political appointee until the Director of the Office of Government Ethics certifies that the candidate has no conflicts of interest with their new government position.

OGE provides leadership in ethics training, by producing training courses, pamphlets, videos and even computer games. The primary focus is to train trainers in the various ethics offices. OGE also regularly reviews agency ethics programs to ensure that these programs maintain their effectiveness, and has the authority to order corrective actions, as well as additional steps to ensure that all agencies comport with their ethical obligations.

Investigation

Until 1978, the investigation of corruption at the national level was carried out primarily by the Federal Bureau of Investigation, and -- in certain other cases -- by other entities in the Justice Department and the General Accounting Office. With the advent of domestic Inspectors Generals (IG) the vast majority of corruption investigations are now undertaken by the IGs. However, the notion of "investigation" is really far more expansive within the IG function. The Act requires IGs to prevent and detect "waste, fraud and abuse in government" while at the same time encourage "economy and efficiency." For this reason, investigation not only refers to initiating criminal and administrative investigations, but also to the use of financial and management audits to detect corruption and misfeasance, as well as identifying ineffective or inefficient programs.

Although the original IG Act created only a handful of IG offices, the numbers have grown so that almost every federal agency has an Inspector General. Currently, there are 64 Inspector General offices. Some of these IGs have only three or four employees, and others have over 1,000 employees. They are assigned to have oversight over only their agency. In the largest 30 IG offices, the Inspector General is appointed by the President and confirmed by the Senate. He or she is viewed as independent and, although they may be removed by the President, an explanation must be sent to the relevant committees in Congress. All other Inspectors General area appointed by the head of the agency, but are expected to exercise independence in investigations and to follow the Government-wide *Yellow Book*[9] standards governing all federal agencies. The vast majority of employees in each IG office are career government employees.

The typical Inspector General Office has three substantive components: Investigations, Audits and Evaluation (or Inspection). As originally envisioned in the IG Act, these units work in concert with each other. In fact, they generally are discrete functions within each IG office. Investigations offices are comprised of "sworn officers"; a term referring to individuals with the authority to request warrants to seize pertinent documents and materials as well as detaining individuals. Most of the leads for investigators originate from complaints or "whistle blower hotlines." The latter are well-advertised telephone numbers that receive complaints, some of which are anonymous. It is the IGs discretion to determine whether there is enough of a fact basis to proceed with an investigation based on these allegations.

The Audit function within each IG is responsible for certain mandatory financial audits as well as independent audits of Agency programs. Mandatory audits are usually requested of the IG by Congress. For example, Congress recently mandated an audit of each agencies financial statement. In this role, the IG plays an independent, internal auditor role allowing Congress to determine whether the agency has comported with the norms of government accounting standards (usually the GAO *Yellow Book*). Sometimes Congress will also request special audits of programs that they suspect of misfeasance or malfeasance. However, the vast majority of financial or program audits are undertaken independently by the IG under his or her responsibility to prevent waste, fraud and abuse.

The Evaluation function (sometimes referred to as the Inspection function) is the only one of the three major areas not mandated by law. Many IGs have found the Inspections functions very useful.

This function allows an IG the flexibility, outside of a time consuming audit, to quickly look at potential problems or issues within their agency. Evaluation units generally look at programmatic data and decide whether there is a long, term justification for the program, and whether resources could be better spent elsewhere. For example, a waste water program might expend $100 million to eliminate 99.1% of pollution in a particular area, but the last 0.1% of removal might cost the government an additional $1 billion. The role of the Evaluation unit is to examine whether it is reasonable to expend such funds and what the alternatives are.

As was mentioned above, the IGs are responsible for only their own agencies. It is obvious that some issues cut across normal agency parameters, and might actually involve the entire government. For that reason, in the early 1980s the President's Council on Integrity and Efficiency (PCIE) was created. It was institutionalised (along with the Executive Council for Integrity and Efficiency, for the non-Presidentially appointed Inspectors General) in law in the early 1990s. This Council is chaired by the Deputy Director for Management at the Office of Management and Budget, with a Vice Chair selected from the IGs. The role of the PCIE has grown with time, but its primary mandate is to facilitate investigations, audits and evaluations that cross normal agency lines. (For a more complete discussion of the PCIE, its role and responsibilities, see Annex of this chapter.)

The PCIE's committee structure reflects the major IG responsibilities, e.g. investigation, audit, and evaluation.[10] However, there are several other committees as well. Perhaps, the most interesting is the Integrity Committee. Chaired by the Deputy Director of the FBI, it is comprised of the Director of the Office of Government Ethics, the Special Counsel to the Office of Special Council, the head of the Public Integrity Section of the FBI and three Inspectors General. Its primarily role is to answer the ages old Platonic question: Who watches the watchdogs? The Integrity Committee only entertains, and investigates, accusations made directly against the Inspectors General and their Deputies.

Prosecution

Although the Department of Justice is responsible for all federal prosecutions for corruption (and some state and local prosecutions as well), the reality of who does what within the department of Justice is far more complex. Primary responsibility for prosecuting corruption falls to federal US attorneys who are found in 102 regional offices throughout the United States.[11] These "local" federal prosecutors are the main source of prosecutions for public corruption. Investigators (and sometimes auditors) must convince an Assistant US Attorney to prosecute. In the majority of cases, the US Attorney has the right to decline cases that they believe are either not warranted by the evidence or the dedication of resources. Since each of the 102 districts are headed by a US attorney appointed by the President, it might be suggested that they could hold up prosecution of "politically sensitive" cases. However, such a desire, even if it were present, is dampened by the reality that the vast majority of their staffs are career civil servants.

A further blurring between the lines occurs, because a US attorney (or the Department of Justice) can request the opening of an investigation and can use either the FBI or an Inspector General to gather evidence to be used in a federal prosecution.

In sensitive cases or cases involving conflicts of interest, some US attorneys will defer to a special section in the Department of Justice. The Public Integrity Section of Justice was created in the aftermath of scandals in the Department of Justice during the Truman administration. The Public Integrity takes responsibility for many of the most sensitive political cases. Traditionally, it is lead by a very senior civil servant. Often this individual is on the "hot seat" because the Attorney General usually relies on their advice as to whether to open a case or not. For example, during the last term of the Clinton administration the head of public integrity, Jerry McDowell, incurred the ire of many Republicans in Congress for not opening an investigation of then Vice President Al Gore's fund raising activities involving international contributions to the 1996 Presidential campaign.

Aside from these high profile political cases, the Public Integrity Section handles hundreds of other public corruption cases per year. Some involve billions of dollars in fraud, while others involve abuse of government position. Because the Public Integrity section is comprised of entirely career attorneys, its independence is widely respected throughout the government. Having this kind of special office has had a profound, positive effect on combating corruption in the United States.

It is important to mention that a decision not to prosecute (a declination) does not necessarily end a case. Mirroring the majority of criminal violations, are administrative regulations that prescribe administrative penalties for acts that do not rise to the level of criminality. Usually these cases will be sent back to the agency -- usually the agency General Counsel -- to handle. Administrative violations have a lesser standard of guilt (preponderance of evidence) as compared to criminal laws (beyond a reasonable doubt). And the penalties are different. Administrative penalties can vary from a reprimand in one's personnel file, time off without pay, demotion in grade, to being removed from federal service.

Protection of whistle-blowers

After 1978, Congress was especially sensitive to protecting whistle-blowers. The term "whistle-blower" was coined in the 1970s and generally refers to someone who reports illegal or illicit government actions through the non-regular government channels or the media. These government channels might be Congressional Committees or Inspector General offices. Congress was most concerned with protecting individuals from reprisals in agencies for reporting these abuses. The history of these reprisals appalled many in Congress. Reprisals have taken many forms: from firing people for doing "the right thing" to putting them in rooms with no windows, and absolutely nothing to do. More subtle discriminations from threats, to denial of promotion or training were also common.

In this context, the Office of Special Counsel (OSC) was created.[12] Its primary job is to protect government employees who feel that reprisals have been taken against them for reporting illicit activities. The OSC has a variety of authorities: They can investigate cases, obtain agency records and take sworn statements; they can seek injunctions in court to prevent agencies from following through with actions such as firing, demoting or transferring an employee. The OSC has responsibility, like the Office of Government Ethics, across the entire federal government. Unlike OGE they are not decentralised and have no officials in any other federal agency.

The Special Counsel is also a Presidential appointee who must be confirmed by the Senate. She or he serves a fixed term of five years, and no special counsel has ever been removed before the term has expired. It is common for both the Special Counsel, the Director of the Office of Government Ethics, and the Inspectors General to serve across presidential terms. For example, although it is traditional for a President to ask for the resignation of all presidential appointees during a transition, no such letter was sent to the IGs, the Director of OGE, or the Special Counsel. Generally, these entities, because of their anticorruption work, are viewed above the political fray.

Conclusion

The US does not have a perfect system. We still prosecute for corruption -- firing people and then putting them in jail. We fine employees and take administrative actions against them. Yet, with all of this, I believe the system in the US has achieved reasonable success in managing the risks of corruption. The few number of prosecutions and actions, as a percentage of the total number of employees is strong testament to the success of corruption management. By and large the systems in place control corruption, and do a reasonable job of anticipating new avenues of corruption created by technology or human inventiveness. Both in reality and perception, corruption is incidental in the United States and only the most extreme press view the US as having huge corruption problems.

That is not to suggest that we do not have unresolved issues. The most notable example is in the electoral process. Although it is difficult to support the claim that the system of privately financing elections actually corrupts individual politicians, it is impossible to argue that it doesn't have a negative impact on the perception of voters. Just as difficult to discount is the claim that the price of the election discourages good candidates putting themselves forward for office. Therefore, the Federal Election Commission – also a product of the Watergate reform – appears to be the least successful in resolving the public perception of corruption in the processes for which it is responsible. Some of this criticism is unfair because of the highly active institutional role of the FEC at all levels of government. But it is impossible to argue that the American people perceive this success.

A new area that has barely been touched by anticorruption efforts has been the huge expansion of contractor employees in government. At the US federal level the mandate to contract out and privatise services has been ongoing for almost twenty years. This has led one critic, Paul Light, to argue that the shadow government is now almost ten times the size of the federal work force. Few of these private sector government entities have or abide by an ethics code or the Federal conflict of interest laws governing federal employees. There is no consistent oversight of their activities and their employees, with very few exceptions, have no whistle-blower protections. Yet this shadow government carries out much of the US government's work.

For these and many other reasons, as advanced as US anticorruption laws and institutions might be, they are still a work in progress. Many nations are discouraged because of the difficulties in fighting corruption. There is a broad recognition of the costs of corruption in both its economic and political sense.[13] Yet there is a tendency to be complacent, almost accepting, that corruption is part of the reality of politics. When contemplating how hard this fight is, it is useful to remember the words of George McGovern, former US Senator and Presidential Candidate:

> *It is simply untrue that all our institutions are evil, that all politicians are mere opportunists, that all aspects of life are corrupt. Having discovered an illness, it's not terribly useful to prescribe death as a cure.*

ANNEX

Introduction to the Inspector General Community

The Inspectors General: How were we created?

The Inspector General Act of 1978, as amended, established the duties, responsibilities, and authorities of a federal Inspector General (IG). Over the years, the Act has been amended to increase the number of agencies with statutory IGs and establish IGs in smaller, independent agencies. Currently, 57 statutory IGs provide oversight to 59 federal agencies.

Who are we?

IGs are appointed on the basis of their personal integrity and expertise in accounting, auditing, financial analysis, law, management analysis, public administration, or investigations. IGs serving at the cabinet-level departments and major sub-cabinet agencies are nominated by the President and confirmed by the Senate. IGs at smaller independent agencies, corporations, and other designated federal entities are appointed by the heads of those entities.

What do we do?

- Conduct independent and objective audits, investigations, inspections, and evaluations.

- Promote economy, efficiency, and effectiveness.

- Prevent and detect fraud, waste, and abuse.

- Review pending legislation and regulation; and

- Keep the agency head and the Congress fully and currently informed.

What are our authorities and responsibilities?

- Have access to records and information of the agency,

- Conduct audits and investigations and issue reports as the IG deems appropriate,

- Issue court documents requesting information from outside the agency,

- Administer oaths for taking testimony, and

- Hire and manage our staff and contract resources.

How do we contribute to good government?

- Offer analysis and advice on critical government-wide initiatives, such as computer security, Results Act, and financial management.

- Look independently at problems and recommend possible solutions;

- Issue fact-filled reports based on professional audit, investigative, and inspection standards;

- Perform independent investigation of allegations;

- Provide technical and/or consultative advice as new plans are developed; and

- Maintain hotlines for employees and others to report confidential information regarding allegations of fraud and abuse.

What are some of our recent accomplishments?

The IG community continues to be a positive force in the federal government for recommending improvements and detecting fraud, waste, and abuse. Each year billions of dollars are returned to the federal government or better spent based on IG recommendations. Our FY 2000 results include:

- Potential savings of USD 9.5 billion.

- Recoveries of almost USD 5.5 billion.

- More than 5,500 successful prosecutions.

- Suspensions or debarments of nearly 7,000 individuals or businesses.

- More than 2,600 civil or personnel actions, and

- More than 120 testimonies before the Congress on issues of national interest.

How can you contact us?

The official Web site for the IG community is IGnet. It can be accessed at *www.ignet.gov*. The Web site provides information such as:

- The history, organisation, mission, reports, and activities of the community.

- Frequently asked questions about the IGs.

- A directory of IGs and links to their home pages.

- Vacancy announcements; and

- A feedback function to provide comments and suggestions.

What are the PCIE and ECIE?

The President's Council on Integrity and Efficiency (PCIE) was created by Executive Order dated March 26 1981, to co-ordinate and enhance governmental efforts to promote integrity and efficiency and to detect and prevent fraud, waste, and abuse in federal programs. Executive Order 12805, signed on May 11 1992, created the Executive Council on Integrity and Efficiency (ECIE) to perform this same mission among the designated federal entities. This 1992, Executive Order also updated the responsibilities of the PCIE.

Who are the members of the PCIE and ECIE?

- Presidentially-appointed IGs make up the PCIE; agency head-appointed IGs make up the ECIE.

- The Deputy Director for Management of the Office of Management and Budget is the chair for both Councils.

- Each Council has a Vice Chair who manages the Council's day-to-day activities. The Vice Chairs are recommended by their respective Council members and approved by the Chair.

- The following are members of both Councils:

    - Controller of OMB's Office of Federal Financial Management,

    - Assistant Director for Investigations for the Federal Bureau of Investigation,

    - Director of the Office of Government Ethics,

    - Special Counsel of the Office of Special Counsel, and

    - Deputy Director of the Office of Personnel Management.

How do the Councils function?

Six standing PCIE committees, listed below, conduct the business of the Councils. ECIE representatives serve as members on each committee.

- Audit Committee.

- Improves audit quality, co-ordinates government-wide audits, and enhances audit professionalism.

- Inspection and Evaluation Committee.

- Shares best practices and provides training to improve inspection and evaluation techniques.

- Investigations Committee.

- Addresses crosscutting investigative issues and shares best practices.

- Legislation Committee.

- Keeps community abreast of congressional areas of interest.

- Human Resources Committee.

- Leads the creation of innovative and effective human resources management programs.

- Integrity Committee.

- Ensures that administrative allegations against IGs are appropriately and expeditiously investigated and resolved.

Where are we headed?

A *Strategic Framework*, adopted by the PCIE and ECIE in May 2001, outlines the IG community's goals and objectives. The overall mission is to independently anticipate and communicate the weaknesses and vulnerabilities of the federal government, facilitate solutions, and identify opportunities for improved performance.

In line with this mission, the Councils will pursue the following Strategic Goals over the next 3 years:

1. Improve federal programs and operations.

2. Communicate reliable and timely information.

3. Implement human resource programs to recruit and retain highly skilled and well-trained staff.

4. Foster and advance the professional image and effectiveness of the OIG community.

Offices of Inspector General

Agency for International Development

Appalachian Regional Commission

Commodity Futures Trading Commission

Corporation for Community & National Service

Department of Agriculture

Department of Defense

Department of Energy

Department of Housing & Urban Development

Department of Labor

Department of the Interior

Department of Transportation

Environmental Protection Agency

Farm Credit Administration

Federal Deposit Insurance Corporation

Federal Emergency Management Agency

Federal Labor Relations Authority

Federal Reserve Board

General Services Administration

Legal Services Corporation

National Archives and Records Administration

National Endowment for the Arts

National Labor Relations Board

Nuclear Regulatory Commission

Peace Corps

Railroad Retirement Board

Small Business Administration

Social Security Administration

Treasury Inspector General for Tax Administration

United States Postal Service

Amtrak

Central Intelligence Agency

Consumer Product Safety Commission

Corporation for Public Broadcasting

Department of Commerce

Department of Education

Department of Health and Human Services

Department of Justice

Department of State and Broadcasting Board of Governors

Department of the Treasury

Department of Veterans Affairs

Equal Employment Opportunity Commission

Federal Communications Commission

Federal Election Commission

Federal Housing Finance Board

Federal Maritime Commission

Federal Trade Commission

Government Printing Office

National Aeronautics & Space Administration

National Credit Union Administration

National Endowment for the Humanities

National Science Foundation

Office of Personnel Management

Pension Benefit Guaranty Corporation

Securities and Exchange Commission

Smithsonian Institution

Tennessee Valley Authority

US International Trade Commission

NOTES

1. Quoted in Leonard White, The Jacksonians: *A Study in Administrative History*, NY: Macmillian, 1954, p. 427.

2. Michael Nelson, "A Short, Ironic History of American National Bureaucracy," *The Journal of Politics*, Vol. 44, 1982, p. 763.

3. Frank Anechiarico and James B. Jacobs, *The Pursuit of Absolute Integrity: How Corruption Control Makes Government Ineffective*, Chicago: University of Chicago Press, 1998. See also Robert D. Behn, *Rethinking Democratic Accountability*, Washington, Brookings, 2001.

4. E.g., Terry Cooper, *The Responsible Administrator*; Carol Lewis, *Ethics in Public Service*; John Rohr, *Ethics for Bureaucrats*.

5. However, it would be an error to assume that US anticorruption laws and institutions began in 1978. In fact, many of the laws -- an in some cases institutions -- were in place more than 150 years ago. See Robert Roberts, *White House Ethics*, N.Y: Greenwood Press, 1988.

6. The term "whistle-blower" was coined in the 1970s and generally refers to someone who reports illegal or illicit government actions through the non-regular government channels or the media.

7. It is important to emphasise that OGE has responsibility only for the executive branch of government -- more than 3 million people. In the legislative branch the House and Senate have separate committees that deal with ethics, as does the judiciary.

8. *www.usoge.gov*

9. See the Publications Section, *Yellow Book at http://www.gao.gov*

10. See: *http://www.ignet.gov*

11. See: *http://www.usdoj.gov/usao/eousa/contact/usalist.html*

12. See the Office of Special Counsel Web site: *http://www.osc.gov*

13. See Susan Rose-Ackerman, *Corruption and Government*, Boston: Cambridge, 1999.

TRANSPARENCY AND ACCOUNTABILITY IN COLOMBIA

by

Humberto De La Calle
Former Vice President of Colombia

This chapter describes three experiments relating to transparency and accountability in Colombia with which the author was directly involved.[1] One failed, another partially succeeded, and the third was a complete success.

General background

It might be useful to begin by briefly describing a few of Colombia's cultural and political characteristics. In recent years, the quest for transparency and the establishment of accountability procedures in the public sector have acquired increasing importance. This is one of the keys to understanding Colombia's political development -- one could say *the key*, were it not for the persistence of a long-running internal armed conflict. However, despite the formulation and implementation of a large and growing number of policies, the public believes that corruption has increased. In fact, it is impossible to know whether it is corruption itself that has increased or merely public awareness of it. First, there is the difficulty of obtaining reliable statistics, especially in relation to the past. Secondly, because corruption is arousing greater interest, the media are giving it wider coverage, and the information mechanisms at society's disposal are becoming more extensive and steadily more effective.

The public perception of increasing corruption has deep cultural roots. According to a 1995 Gallup poll, while Colombians consider themselves to be cheerful (87%), intelligent (83%) and enterprising (79%), a mere 28% think citizens are law-abiding and only 30% feel certain they are honest. This sort of environment has bred a very low level of political legitimacy with respect to Colombia's institutions. In fact, according to a 1999 poll carried out by the *Centro Nacional de Consultoría*, whereas 62% of those polled trusted private enterprise and 54% television, only 8% trusted the parties, 16% Congress, and a worryingly low 33% trusted the police.

An additional consideration, which follows from the above, is that over 60% of Colombians think that politics is a dishonest business. Most distressingly, within this group the percentage reached 82% among educators and 66% among judges. At the same time, the whole notion of party allegiance is taking an alarming turn. Almost every member of Congress is seeking election on a separate list, playing on the weaknesses of the electoral system. As a result, intra-party ties are now very feeble. This has the effect of personalising relations with the executive power, thereby fostering corruption and weakening the ability of Congress to exercise political control over the government. Moreover, members of Congress are acting as mediators between the state services and the needs of the population, a situation which creates a framework of patronage that affects political activity. In turn, the public service sector is divided, since a sizeable proportion of officials do as they are instructed by political leaders. It is hardly surprising, then, that public distrust should have increased.

This also explains why, especially since the adoption of the 1991 Constitution, succeeding governments have embarked on the path of reform, trying to identify the weak spots in the political system in order to strengthen its legitimacy. These efforts have, as stated above, led to mixed results. The three initiatives outlined here are:

(a) An attempt to hold a constitutional referendum to establish mechanisms for fighting political corruption, which failed.

(b) Several efforts to modernise the public service and eliminate red tape, which yielded partially satisfactory results.

(c) A successful anti-corruption measure, namely the establishment of the *Fiscalía General de la Nación* (Office of the Attorney General of the Nation).

The 2000 constitutional referendum

Against the background described above, a huge corruption scandal exploded involving members of the leadership of the Chamber of Representatives, who are now in prison. Faced with a powerful wave of popular dissatisfaction, the government proposed a programme of constitutional reform. This had previously failed to win the approval of Congress when introduced in the usual way, and so it was decided to resort to a constitutional referendum.

The seventeen-point initiative sought, among other things, to reduce the size of Congress; to abolish the local electoral colleges -- expensive, inefficient and sometimes corrupt -- and replace them with purely administrative bodies; to adopt new and stringent rules on unfitness for public office and government procurement; to extend significantly the grounds for loss of elected office; to establish a Court of Public Ethics with broad powers, some discretionary, for hearing cases relating to state property or electoral integrity; to adopt a new set of rules for the financing of election campaigns that would ensure tighter control and greater transparency; to counteract the Balkanisation of the parties; to abolish congressional perks; and to hand over the supervisory bodies to the opposition party.

Under the Constitution, 5% of citizens could propose a constitutional reform initiative to Congress. If Congress rejected it, then 10% could override that refusal and order the electoral body to convene the electors to decide by secret ballot on a fixed date.

Popular acceptance of the government proposal was immediate and overwhelming. The media, civil society and the business community prepared to promote the collection of signatures in solid support of the government's initiative. Although Congress viewed the proposals with distaste (and in some cases frank hostility), the avalanche of support forced it to keep silent. A minority of members even supported the proposals.

However, in formulating the proposal, the government had included one additional item: the calling of new elections for Congress, even though at that point the congressional term had three more years to run.[2] This led to the main opposition party (which had a majority in Congress and enjoyed a high level of support among the traditional political class), together with some members of Congress from the governing coalition (*Gran Alianza por el Cambio*), to launch a bitter anti-referendum campaign.

The situation became critical when the opposition party announced that it would begin collecting signatures to initiate a second referendum (the so-called social referendum), which included ending the presidential term and immediately calling a general election.

The political crisis was accompanied by a weakening of the country's external financial position. This led, following the mediation of several important personages, to a compromise that involved discarding the idea of early elections, both presidential and congressional.

At the same time, in principle, it was understood that Congress would continue to study the government proposal in relation to the other issues. In fact the debate languished and Congress finally rejected the entire proposal.

Lessons to be learned

When the executive wishes to place itself at the head of a reform movement that is provoking resistance in Congress but nevertheless requires the latter's approval, it is preferable to make use of the initial honeymoon period normally granted to every administration. In the present case, the government had already tried to introduce similar reforms through the ordinary channels, and these had been thrown out by Congress.

By the time it resorted to the exceptional procedure of a referendum, after a certain process of natural wear and tear in the exercise of its mandate, the risks were very high -- particularly as Congress -- called upon to rule on the proposal in the first instance, saw its interests seriously threatened.

If, on the other hand, there is recourse to ordinary channels, it is essential to carefully cultivate a political consensus, which will certainly mean less audacious reforms but also a more effective approval procedure.

As will be seen in other cases, it is not enough to have a broad margin of public support at a given time; it is necessary to go further. It is desirable to form citizens' groups responsible for sustaining the information campaign and keeping the idea alive in the face of the confusion that will inevitably arise in connection with debate on such delicate matters.

The engagement of the media can also be decisive.

Eliminating red tape

The second example concerns various initiatives taken in 1995 and 1999, with a view to cutting back the accumulated mass of administrative formalities and bureaucratic requirements characteristic of the Colombian public service. An effort was made to stress the observance of ethical principles (since excessive bureaucracy is known to breed corruption), greater efficiency, cost savings and administrative dispatch, as well as to leave real room for the constitutional principle of good faith.

The first phase was based on Law 190 of 1995, whose general aim was to maintain ethical standards in the civil service and facilitate relations between the state and its citizens. Article 83 of that law granted the government exceptional powers (enabling it to issue decrees with the force of law) to abolish or reform unnecessary procedures, regulations and formalities. Under this authority it issued Decree 2150 of 1995. In the main its provisions have survived, although a few were rejected by the Constitutional Court; meanwhile, custom has led to revival of some of the abolished formalities.

Subsequently, in a second phase, Congress passed Law 489 of 1998. This also granted additional powers to the government, on the basis of which it issued Decree 1122 of 1999, abolishing certain formalities and improving the effectiveness and efficiency of the public service. On procedural grounds, the Constitutional Court set aside both the law and the implementing decree.

For this reason, a new law -- Law No. 573 of 2000 -- was passed, with a view to reviving the annulled Decree 1122. The supreme constitutional body again found defects and set the law aside.

Again, a new draft law was submitted. As expected, Congress responded positively and approved the necessary legal framework. Public opinion welcomed the initiatives, although the degree of enthusiasm was less than anticipated.

The worst setbacks occurred when the courts had to hear complaints against the legislation. The Constitutional Court found defects that brought down some of the initiatives. Certain formalities that had been eliminated were slowly, almost imperceptibly reappearing. The legalistic tradition was so entrenched that often the public itself was demanding certificates that had been abolished -- people felt more at ease with a public authority confirming the facts.

The result is that, in spite of some progress, the setbacks have obliged the government to submit a proposal for new powers for Congress in order to continue consolidating the original ideas.

Lessons to be learned

There are various reasons why reforms of this type may prove unsuccessful, or at least fail to achieve all the expected results.

There are institutional problems linked to particular cultural environments. In the case described, as already noted, the legalistic tradition is deeply entrenched, especially among officials but also within society as a whole.

Public support should not be taken for granted. It is essential to learn to communicate better, to organise social groups to defend the reforms and empower the respective communities.

There is an aphorism: "Protect me from my friends and I will protect myself from my enemies" Indeed, in this case, the enemy is within. Every formality has its ready mourner. For every requirement, there is someone within the state apparatus who benefits. Some of these benefits relate to the corruption inherent in certain forms of red tape. However, this is not always the case. The benefits can be more subtle: justification of the need for a post or recognition of a hierarchical structure which confers the ability to take decisions and the power that entails, both within the service and over the public.

When the reforms have such a broad field of application, ultimately no one is willing to do the job. In this particular instance, the procedures of almost every administrative department were affected. It would require a powerful body at the heart of central government to carry on with the daily task of implementing, evaluating and defending the changes. Glossy presentation is not enough. The process demands persistence, trial and error, follow-up, and the cultivation of a spirit of apprenticeship.

Establishment of the Attorney General's Office: A successful move against white collar crime

In 1991, the government of the day, invoking exceptional procedures, convened a Constituent Assembly which adopted the Constitution currently in force. This established the Office of the Attorney General of the Nation for the purpose of ensuring that the law was rigorously enforced, especially in connection with organised crime -- in particular, drug trafficking and administrative corruption. Up to then, the investigation of more serious crimes had been entrusted to examining magistrates who operated in a somewhat disorganised fashion, which led to their becoming isolated and increasingly vulnerable in the face of new rackets operated by highly dangerous gangs of criminals. At the same time, it was becoming clear that organised crime was beginning to penetrate the political establishment, acquiring power that could threaten the state. Shortly before 1991, it openly opted for terrorist methods. As far as political corruption was concerned, the individual magistrates, in their isolation, were incapable of defeating the white collar criminals who had considerable influence in society and the public service. To combat organised crime, it was also necessary to organise the law enforcement agencies. Finally, the Attorney General's Office had to operate under the adversarial system to ensure that crime policy, formulated by a single authority, was properly implemented.

What the country experienced can be described by examining the situation's various stages of evolution.

In the first stage, there was a certain amount of permissiveness with regard to the activities of the drug traffickers. Later, they began to organise themselves and attack -- through intimidation or bribery, or both -- anyone who dared oppose their schemes. There followed a period of violence during which journalists, politicians, policemen and even presidential candidates perished. To consolidate their power, the traffickers decided to exploit their connections within the political class by financing the campaigns of various congressmen. When the current rules on extradition began to be applied, they turned to systematic use of terrorism -- and this was the point at which, as it was said, the viability of the state came to be at stake.

Around 1994, the Attorney General of the time realised that his first task should be to cut the links between organised crime and the political establishment. The financial networks of groups on the fringes of the law were investigated and charges of unlawful enrichment were brought against those who had profited from crime. About thirty members of Congress were investigated and of these, no fewer than twenty were convicted and are now serving their sentences.

After that, the new Attorney General carried on the good work without faltering. About 30,000 cheques issued by the so-called Cali cartel and confiscated by the authorities were investigated.[3] Society learned its lesson. Now in Colombia there is no longer indifference to the drug traffickers. It is understood that the threat they pose goes beyond mere illicit drug smuggling. Extradition has been re-established and is now regularly applied. An expropriation law has been passed to deprive the bosses of their fortunes. Immense progress has been made. The destruction of the large cartels does not mean that the flow of drugs has dried up, but the danger to the state has been averted.

Some crime still goes unpunished in Colombia, but the success of the agency's struggle against the drug trafficking gangs and high-level corruption is undeniable. Convictions have been won against prominent persons ranging from ministers and governors to the heads of regulatory bodies. Between July 1997, and March 2001, the Attorney General's Office achieved the following results: 23 065 preliminary investigations, 22 729 cases prepared for trial, 7 398 preventive detention measures or the like, 8 952 *estoppels*, 9 086 orders of stay of proceedings and 4 939 indictments.[4]

Lessons to be learned

Implementation of public policies can eventually change the public's perception of a situation. In Colombia's case, the media played a vital role. There were attempts to set back the clean-up process undertaken by the Attorney General's Office -- by suddenly approving laws that favoured the bosses, by trying to remove the Attorney General from office, by filing legal objections to his election and by appealing to nationalism to prevent extradition -- but these attempts were thwarted by timely exposure in the press.

It is never too late to respond to a serious crisis -- but the quicker the response, the lower the social costs.

It is essential to cut the links that organised crime forms with society and, especially, the political establishment. Drugs now have much less influence. No concessions can be made to terrorism.

Finally, the co-operation of the international community is an essential part of the fight against transnational organised crime.

NOTES

1.   The author was Vice-President of Colombia when the process of elimination of formalities to which this conference relates first began. The task has since been taken on by the Council for the Modernisation of the State, which reports to the Office of the Vice-President. The author was also twice Minister of the Interior. The 1991 Constitution creating the Office of the Prosecutor General was drawn up during his first term, and his second came at the end of the political crisis that led to the referendum on political corruption.

2.   At this point it should be recalled that Colombia operates under a presidential regime with no provision for the dissolution of Congress. For his part, the President is elected directly by the citizens.

3.   The number of cheques confiscated totalled 37 090. Of these, 26 692 were investigated. The other 8 735 were for smaller amounts or had been drawn on non-Mafia accounts. See *Informe de Gestión. Fiscalia General de la Nación, 1997-2001.*

4.   The Attorney General's Office takes the case to the trial stage, thus placing it in the hands of the judge. These figures have been taken from *Informe de Gestión. Fiscalía General de la Nación, 1997-2001.*

MAKING IT HAPPEN: DEVELOPING POLICY GUIDELINES FOR ACCOUNTABILITY AND TRANSPARENCY

by

János Bertók, Joanne Caddy and Michael Ruffner[1]
OECD Public Management Service

Creating a forum for policy dialogue

The General Assembly of the Organisation of American States held in Costa Rica on 3-5 June 2001 was a turning point for anti-corruption efforts on the American continent. On this occasion, the States Parties of the Inter-American Convention against Corruption officially adopted the follow-up mechanism defined by 18 delegations in Buenos Aires in May 2001. This Convention was the first multilateral instrument of its kind to combine obligations for the States Parties related to the criminalisation of corruption and bribery of foreign public officials, procedures for mutual legal assistance and extradition with respect to corruption offences, and a series of anti-corruption preventive measures that the Parties agree to consider establishing. The signature of the Convention in 1996 helped to bring the problem of corruption to an unprecedented degree of discussion and scrutiny in the region, and provided a general international legal framework for remedial action.

Member countries of the Organisation for Economic Co-operation and Development consider the dialogue with non-members a crucial instrument for sharing experience and jointly developing solutions that take into account the specific features of the given country environment. The Final Communiqué of the OECD Council at Ministerial level on 17 May 2001 declares that

> *"strengthening effective and coherent public governance remains a priority on the policy*
> *agenda. The effective performance of democratic institutions, including legislatures, and*
> *the fight against corruption, are central elements of good governance. Enhanced*
> *openness, transparency and accountability must become guiding principles for*
> *governments within OECD's membership and beyond. OECD should continue to make a*
> *vital contribution through its dialogue on public governance with non-members."*

This mandate is the third in a series of mandates that were handed down to the OECD by ministers to address governance questions in a policy dialogue with non-members. They are an expression of an emerging consensus on governance issues among OECD countries and non-members alike and the hosting of the Forum on Ensuring Accountability and Transparency in the Public Sector[2] on 5-6 December 2001 was considered as a welcome sign of the importance that Brazil attaches to the issue. The primary audience consisted of senior policy-makers and high-level officials from OAS and OECD countries responsible for the creation and management of measures to increase transparency and accountability in the public sector. Representatives of business, media and NGO communities, through their regional and national associations, were also involved, in order to facilitate deeper understanding as well as co-operation and alliances among the many stakeholders in the implementation of these measures.

The Forum was organised jointly by the Organisation for Economic Co-operation and Development and the Organisation of American States to provide an opportunity for a policy dialogue based on the experience of OECD countries in order to help OAS countries to prepare and implement of their public administration reform measures. In particular, the Forum:

- Supported the creation of an informal network of policy-makers and high-level officials facing comparable problems linked to the implementation of preventive measures, as agreed in Article III of the Inter-American Convention against Corruption.

- Examined existing solutions to find out how they work in their national environment.

- Worked out policy guidelines to give options for solutions in the implementation of preventive measures of the Convention.

The Forum provided a unique opportunity to analyse reform measures from their design to their implementation. Particular emphasis was given to reviewing concrete examples:

- What approaches have been used to find solutions to problems?

- Why were certain measures successful while others not, and why did they produce the expected results, or why did they fail?

Presentations of case studies on recent or ongoing reform efforts in both OECD and OAS countries introduced interactive discussions in three parallel focus groups where participants examined these concrete examples and reviewed their specific approaches and measures to find out how they could be relevant to their own national environment. The debate also explored what follow-up measures could be taken to review the design and implementation of these policies, with a view to increasing transparency and accountability, as requested by the preventive measures of the Inter-American Convention.

Exchanging experiences

The Forum was opened by Marcus Marcel, Vice-President of Brazil and addressed by Martus Tavares, Minister of Planning, Budget and Management of Brazil, César Gaviria, Secretary-General of the OAS and Seiichi Kondo, Deputy Secretary-General of the OECD. Several ministers and vice-ministers played an active role in the sessions, which were attended by more than 450 participants, including senators, senior government officials and business leaders as well as representatives of international organisations and non-governmental organisations from OECD countries and Latin America.

The first plenary session started with taking stock of the challenges countries are facing and their recent efforts in designing and implementing transparency measures. In his keynote speech, Jules Muis, Director-General, Internal Auditor of the European Commission, provided a comparative review of reform efforts in the European Commission and measures taken by countries in Latin America. He emphasised the importance of brave visionary leaders and radical steps that are necessary to manage modernisation of whole systems. He argued that critical review of existing situations and courageous measures are the right steps in these situations: "please do throw away the bathwater from time to time, there is not always a child in it"

The reform itself has become the political priority in the European Commission. The White Paper on Reforming the Commission was centred on the core principles of openness, participation, accountability, effectiveness and coherence in order to further enhance democracy at the European level. Key measures included a new personnel policy to attract and retain fresh resources -- the best and the brightest -- as well as the modernisation of financial management and a new system of strategic planning. "Directors report on plans, activities, achievements and governance dynamics of each Directorate-General..." in their activity reports. The management of annual assurance statements is another important measure in the housekeeping reform of the European Union to provide "... reasonable assurance ... that money has been used for purposes intended, ... efficiently and effectively in accordance with sound management principles".

While the keynote address highlighted the main issues of the forum, a panel of discussants launched the general discussion with an overview of the challenges faced by OECD and OAS countries. Experiences of both OECD and OAS countries have shown that effective implementation of important policy measures requires strategic management of reforms. A presentation by Humberto De la Calle, former Vice-President of Colombia, outlined recent efforts in core policy areas to enhance transparency in the administration and also reviewed the key factors for success and reasons for failure. These examples encouraged participants to share their views and own experiences on

- Analysing strengths and weaknesses in the preparation of decisions.

- Combining a comprehensive strategy with a realistic but "selective radical" action plan.

- Adequate sequencing to seize opportunities.

- Developing ownership of reform measures.

Stuart C. Gilman, Director of Strategic Development at the Office of the Inspector-General of the US Treasury Department, outlined the mechanisms for fighting against corruption and promoting integrity in the United States and stressed the importance of a comprehensive approach when preparing national measures for implementing the Inter-American Convention against Corruption. Dr. Gilman underlined that "modern anticorruption programmes must balance integrity and compliance, multiple programmes, intersecting laws and authorities and institutional responsibilities -- nonetheless, we know that all anticorruption regimes must have institutions of prevention, investigation, prosecution and protection.

The opening plenary session was followed by three parallel Focus Groups that discussed lessons learned from the design and management of reform measures in three key administrative areas, namely:

- Preventing conflicts of interest.

- Establishing transparent and efficient budget management.

- Accompanying mechanisms for public scrutiny and access to information.

Discussions in the three parallel Focus Groups not only provided for an exchange of experience but also developed policy guidelines to provide tools for decision-makers in the design and implementation of preventive measures. These policy guidelines contain principles of good practices that take into consideration the particularities of OAS countries. At the final plenary session of the Forum, the conclusions of the discussions at the three focus groups together with the policy guidelines were presented by the Rapporteur General, Evelyn Levy, Secretary for Management, Ministry of Planning, Budget and Public Management, Brazil. Ensuing discussions focused on the application of the policy guidelines and on how the agreed policy guidelines can be applied to take into consideration the conditions in the national environment.

At the closing plenary session, participants also started a debate on possible follow-up measures to review efforts and progress. Marilyn Yakowitz, Head of South America Programme of the OECD and Jorge Garcia-González, Director, Department of Legal Co-operation of the OAS outlined the future measures for follow-up and explained the role of agreed policy guidelines in the follow-up mechanisms.

Managing conflicts of interest

Growing concern among the public has forced governments to ensure that the private interests of public officials do not influence the integrity of official decision-making. Serving the public interest is the mission of public institutions. Citizens expect public officials to perform their duties in a fair and unbiased way. The first session of Focus Group 1, chaired by Hélène Gadriot-Renard, Head of Governance and the Role of State Division of the OECD Public Management Service, examined the challenges countries have been facing in identifying and resolving conflicting situations. Over hundred and fifty participants reviewed the main sources of potential conflicts and the possible approaches to prevent conflicts of interest.

The public sector has developed an increasingly intimate relationship with the business and not-for-profit sectors, especially in those countries that have introduced private sector methods in the modernisation of their public services. However, maintaining public confidence is particularly important in this new public management environment, where deregulation and devolution have created a situation in which citizens' compliance with crucial laws is directly related to their trust in their administration. It is particularly important in key areas, such as taxation, licensing and registrations, and benefits administration. Countries have put more and more emphasis on establishing public trust in government institutions by delineating core principles and standards and/or introducing strict regulations for redefining conflicts of interest situations in the public service.

Howard R. Wilson, Ethics Counsellor, Government of Canada outlined the main elements of a principles-based approach and described how it fits into the social-political-administrative environment of Canada. This integrity-based system combines a set of principles, stating what is expected of those in public life, and a limited set of procedures and rules. Core principles include:

- *Ethical Standards* -- public office holders shall act with honesty and uphold the highest ethical standards so that public confidence and trust in the integrity, objectivity and impartiality of government are conserved and enhanced.

- *Public Scrutiny* -- public office holders shall perform official duties and arrange private affairs in a manner that will bear the closest public scrutiny, an obligation that goes beyond simply acting within the law.

- *Public Interest* -- public office holders shall arrange private affairs in a way that will prevent real, potential or apparent conflicts of interest from arising.

The Canadian Conflict of Interest and Post-Employment Code covers the top 1,300 full-time and 2,000 part-time public office holders -- ministers, political staff and senior officials (deputy ministers, heads of agencies and tribunals, etc.). They are obliged to complete a confidential disclosure on assets, investments, debts, outside activities, gifts and benefits valued at CAD 200 or more. In the latter case gifts and benefits are acceptable if they arise out of official duties and are a normal expression of hospitality. Certain activities are prohibited, such as practising a profession, managing a business, being a director or officer in a corporation, holding office in a union or a professional association or being a paid as a consultant, while memberships, directorships or offices are permissible in organisations which are philanthropic, charitable, or non-commercial. Special attention is paid to post-employment in order to avoid the use of insider information, for example, in the case of direct and significant official dealings where a one-year limitation is used for:

- Accepting employment or directorships.

- Lobbying back to government institutions.

The proactive approach -- identifying and removing the risks in advance -- is a key feature in countries with established institutions and public service culture. However, this forward-looking strategy can also be of assistance in countries that are in the process of building a modern public service culture. João Geraldo Piquet Carneiro, President of the Public Ethics Commission at the Office of the President in Brazil, outlined the very recent steps taken to create a conflict of interest policy put into practice in Brazil. Political commitment played a significant role in the preparation of the Brazilian Code of Conduct for the Federal Administration that mainly targeted the top leaders in the executive branch. Leadership and consultations in the drafting, along with strong emphasis on training and counselling in the implementation of the Code, were the key features of the Brazilian policy.

The second session of Focus Group 1 was chaired by Shabbir Cheema, Principal Adviser and Programme Director for Governance Institutions, United Nations. Jane Ley, Deputy Director, Office of Government Ethics, USA, presented an overview of the methods used to enforce compliance with the conflicts of interest policy in the United States. From a historical perspective she outlined the series of concrete measures that were taken to elaborate the code of conduct and put it into practice at the federal level of the executive branch. The use of new technology in disclosure procedures provides new opportunities for introducing cost-effective modern tools that enhance transparency. Nicolás Raigorodsky, Senior Manager for Legal Affairs, Anti-Corruption Office, Ministry of Justice and Human Rights, Argentina, presented the recent experience of using new technologies in the collection and processing of information on financial interests. The introduction of modern technologies had not only radically lowered the cost of the procedure but also significantly improved the level of compliance.

Discussions focused on risks and key factors for success in achieving a coherent and manageable conflict of interest policy. János Bertók of the OECD and Elia Amstrong of UNDESA also talked about the experiences of other countries that have participated in the respective OECD and UN surveys, to provided further information on a range of potential solutions and put them in their political-administrative environment. Managing conflicts of interest requires a comprehensive system that clearly defines the situations that conflict significantly with the public interest and that has sufficient capacity to manage these situations. When these conflicts occur, the system should ensure that public officials disclose and manage them appropriately, so as to resolve them or to minimise their potential impact.

In order to meet the growing expectations of a demanding society, governments have introduced measures to provide more information on the private interests of public officials. Formal disclosure systems for public officials can be used as a key instrument to prevent or detect situations where the private interest of a public official is in conflict with the public interest. The higher the position of public officials, the more transparency is demanded to maintain or re-establish public trust in government institutions.

Box 1. **Focus Group 1**

Managing Conflicts of Interest

Crucial factors of a sound conflict of interest policy to ensure impartiality in carrying out public duties

- Clear and realistic *definition* of what can lead to a conflict of interest situation, namely when the private interests of a public official may be in conflict with the public interest.

- Setting unambiguous *rules* on what is expected of public employees in order to resolve this conflicting situation.

- Put stated standards into practice by:

- Socialisation -- communication, training and counselling.

- Enforcement -- disclosure system, detecting and punishing those who do not comply with the stated standards.

Policy recommendations for managing conflicts of interest

- Raise awareness of the basic concept of public service, namely public office is for serving the public interest and not for private gain.

- Involve public servants and the wider public in the development of standards in order to ensure that those standards reflect public expectations.

- Mobilise public opinion to scrutinise daily practice and ensure accountability.

- Protect those who report violations -- whistle-blowing.

- Assess the impact of conflict of interest measures -- review existing policies in order to identify risk areas.

Challenges and options for implementation

- Elaborating standards is the easy part of the work, their implementation (socialisation, enforcement and monitoring) is more difficult, not to mention to achieve real change in the culture.

- Co-ordinate prevention and enforcement measures and integrate them into a coherent institutional framework.

- Balancing contravening principles -- for example protecting privacy *versus* ensuring transparency when providing access to information on private interests.

Establishing transparent and efficient budget management

Government taxes and spending take up on average in the OECD 40 percent of GDP, with similar averages worldwide. We need only look at the macroeconomic effects of higher interest rates of the 1980's and 1990's caused by borrowing crowded out by government deficit financing to understand the importance of the budget and budget process. It is not an overstatement to say that there is a direct link between economic growth and government performance especially in a globalised world where capital flees economies with unsound governance regimes. Therefore, it is imperative to produce government services efficiently and effectively.

The relationship between good governance and better economic and social outcomes is increasingly acknowledged. Transparency -- openness about policy intentions, formulation and implementation -- is a key element of good governance. The budget is the single most important policy document of governments, where policy objectives are reconciled and implemented in concrete terms. A transparent budget contains a full disclosure of all relevant fiscal information in a timely and systematic manner. The OECD Best Practices for Budget Transparency [3] and the IMF code of budget transparency stress the need to create a comprehensive picture of all government spending so that all policy options and tradeoffs can be fairly assessed. Moreover, countries, both OECD and non-OECD alike, have modernised their budget processes to address the three levers of budget: control of the aggregates, allocative efficiency and technical efficiency. Focus Group 2 was a session devoted to looking at these two aspects: transparency and technical efficiency.

While there was not a clean distinction between both topics, the first half of the session looked at case studies of countries use of devices to promote fiscal transparency. The second half looked at a few innovative ways of enhancing the technical efficiency of the budget. Over 200 senior officials attended Focus Group 2 with presentations made by delegates from Brazil, Canada, Chile, Australia, Colombia and the OECD.

The focus group started with a presentation of the Canadian budget process by John Keay from the Department of Finance. Canada was at the forefront of developing the OECD Best Practices for Budget Transparency. Mr. Keay stressed the need for comprehensive reporting on the budget and specific reports through the fiscal year. He also emphasised the need for citizen involvement in the development of the budget and highlighted innovations in Canada on how citizens were proactively included in the budget process.

Mr. Marcelo Tokman, principal economist in the Ministry of Finance in Chile presented an overview of how the Government of Chile first created a consensus to instil fiscal discipline then use that discipline to address second generation issues like outcomes and results. Building on a successful treasury system, the first priority for Chile was to achieve a political consensus on controlling total expenditures. They then instituted a modernisation plan that gave managers freedom over budget allocations, improved reporting, implemented the use of performance indicators, instituted systemic and systematic evaluations and public sector pay reforms. Once achieved, Chile agreed to a three point plan to further the reforms of the 1990's. These included:

- Achieving a structural surplus.

- Requiring a two percent reallocation of each ministry's budget, and forcing programs to compete for central funds; and

- Better financial reporting including an innovative annual look-back at performance and budgets by the political decision-makers.

The final speaker, Tyrone Carlin, Macquarie Graduate School of Management of Australia made a presentation on the reforms in Australia and the difficulties of using non-financial performance information. Australia has historically been one of the most innovative countries in public management. Starting in the early 1980's, Australia started using modern tools and processes like accrual accounting and performance budgeting, reforms that are still only being contemplated by other countries today. One area of major transformation has been the changing technologies by which funding, reporting and monitoring for the budget dependent sector are achieved.

A recent aspect of this process of reform has been a changing central budgetary regime, and within this a shift towards the presentation of public sector budgeting information on an 'output' basis. This transition began in the mid-1990s and continues to date. These changes have been justified by their champions on the grounds that they will promote greater efficiency, transparency and accountability by governments. Yet to accept such claims at face value is to ignore the political and rhetorical aspect of public sector budgeting. Just as the adoption of accrual accounting by public sector agencies has been criticised as being the reflection of a rhetorical rather than technically neutral process, changes in budgeting process can be analysed critically. Indeed, it has been suggested that predictions of output budgeting's successes have not been matched in reality, again hinting at a strong rhetorical aspect to public sector budgeting changes in Australia.

The sessions on the second day were focused on practical changes to enhance the efficiency of the budget process. These included bringing a results focus to budgeting, and organisational structures like independent agencies to deliver services and innovative tools to make the budget transparent.

Ms. Elsa Pilichowski of the OECD made a presentation on the use of agencies -- independent or semi-autonomous bodies charged with public purposes -- and the challenges in holding these bodies to account. In the quest for modernisation and decentralisation, countries have increasingly used agencies, authorities and other more autonomous government institutions. Over time it has become evident that in some instances the operational advantages of structural innovations in government, have been off-set by a loss of whole-of government cohesion and of democratic over-sight. Some countries have also found a need to rethink their processes of control and scrutiny of bodies which have traditionally operated with degrees of autonomy. A set of common questions and key issues critical for improving distributed public governance is emerging. They are:

- Greater clarity about the differences between the various types of agencies, authorities and other government bodies, their strengths and weaknesses.

- Strengthening the capability and clarifying the roles and status of governing bodies and senior management.

- Strengthening accountability mechanisms to ministers and ministries, Parliament and civil society.

- Improving performance management of these bodies without undermining discretion and autonomy

- Improving co-ordination mechanisms.

Ms. Pilichowski then laid out a draft report on principles for distributed public governance that resulted from an OECD meeting in Bratislava. The principles are a detailed list of recommendations relating to a set of characteristics of good governance to consider when setting up agencies and holding them to account. The areas of recommendations include: a possible generic law for organisations, the main accounting and performance reports, clear key policy agreements and directives, transparent employment and remuneration policies, internal and external auditing requirements and balancing the needs of central control versus the needs for autonomy.

Mr. Guilherme Gomes-Dias, Executive-Secretary of the Ministry of Planning, Budget and Management in Brazil provided an extensive overview of the new budget process in Brazil, including passage and implementation of the new fiscal responsibility law. The budget in Brazil is moving to an output and performance focus within a medium term expenditure framework. Government managers will be held to account for performance and in return they will receive more flexibility, better cost and financial information and modern management and organisation tools.

The new fiscal responsibility law includes new requirements for fiscal targets and fiscal discipline as well as a comprehensive assessment of fiscal risks. Backed by real sanctions, one of the most important features is the transparency and reporting requirements of the new law including:

- Transparency during the preparation and broad dissemination of budgetary and accounting documents.

- Public access -- by electronic means -- to all the information of the three levels of government (PPA, LDO, LOA, rendering of accounts, preliminary audit reports and fiscal management reports).

- Bi-monthly summary reports on budget execution and four-month fiscal management reports are required.

- National Consolidation of Accounts (National Treasury Secretariat).

- Monthly dissemination by the Ministry of Finance of the listing containing the member states of the Federation which have exceeded the debt ceilings.

One of the most interesting aspects of the fiscal responsibility law is the application of the requirements to all levels of government including the independent states and municipalities.

Finally, the last presentation by Maria Ines Granado of Transparency International in Colombia centred on the integrity pacts in Colombia. Colombia has instituted a new regime for transparency on budget and public management called integrity pacts. Integrity pacts are voluntary agreements, subscribed between all the actors who take part directly in a hiring process, to promote transparency, fairness and sustainability. They are an invitation to a voluntary cultural change to accept common regulating systems, bound to allowances and sanctions over the established ones within the legal framework.

Ms. Granado made an assessment of the changes looking at the strengths and weaknesses and observed the following strengths of the new formal system:

- Constitutional guarantees for citizen control.

- Sufficient institutionalised process of control organisms.

- Transparent hiring processes.

At the same time the new law was challenged by a number of problems, institutional weaknesses and threats including:

- Little acceptance of the new law.

- Few sanctions and high impunity.

- Trading votes for local spending.

- Reluctance at the regional level to contract experts to structure the projects.

- Belief in the necessity of confidentiality in the hiring processes.

Participants generally welcomed the presentations but cautioned the presenters that for the most part it was too early to proclaim success. Delegates expressed the need that to achieve the goals, the issue of data quality was a necessity, and that most reforms would succeed or fail based on the quality of the data. Moving from a traditional hierarchical budget and management process to a modern, decentralised and results focused system would require new oversight and accountability mechanisms. Delegates thought that innovations like agencies and voluntary integrity pacts were crucial to the success of the regimes. However, there is a need for clear lines of authority with practical and enforceable sanctions and limits in return for more autonomy. In the end, the reforms need the acceptance of the public service as much or more than the consent of civil society to make a real impact. All of the changes must be built on an open process basis where the rules of the game are known to all. Finally, delegates considered the conclusions that are listed in Box 2.

Box 2. **Focus Group 2**

Establishing transparent and efficient budget management

Budgets should follow the principles of good governance: transparent, accountable, coherent, future-oriented, integrity (rule of Law).

Countries must construct a budget process to fit cultural and organisational realities

Basic Principles

- Comprehensive budget: reflect all revenues and expenditures

- Need automated/integrated system

- Good legal framework -- rules known to all

- Budgets should be based on multi-annual plan

- E-Government, internet based -- open to civil society

- Public Service must be engaged -- its values and principles are key determinants of success

- Budget reform is continual process, no silver bullet, can not rely on one process

---

Results/performance oriented (Box 2, Continued)

- Need to link inputs with product or output of government

- Outputs should relate to societal goals

- Stable, limited, timely and measurable performance indicators

- Need to know economic cost of government (accruals)

- What is "Opportunity Cost" of government activity?

Accountability

- Clear line of responsibility -- specific person responsible

- Systematic integration between goals, standards, annual budget and multi-annual plan

- Sanctions must be reasonable, but significant and enforceable

- Efficient and timely audit: audit must evaluate program effectiveness and program quality; avoid audit fatigue

- Systematic reporting on schedule; comparable over time

- Independent agencies special case - "Bratislava Principles": Granting autonomy requires:

- Need for clear governance structure and strong reporting mechanisms

- Need for strengthened capacity of central ministries and audit bodies to control and monitor semi autonomous agencies

- Need to set up a review process to assess the benefits and shortcomings of the agency system

Transparency

- There should be a role for civil society/non-governmental organisations as well as effective legislative oversight

- Cultural change and common regulatory systems

Mechanisms for public scrutiny and access to information

Efforts to build open government and improve the accountability and transparency of the public administration are enhanced by:

- Strong public scrutiny based on solid legal provisions for access to information; and

- Public participation and awareness-raising among citizens and public officials.

Starting from this perspective, Focus Group 3 on "Mechanisms for public scrutiny and access to information" examined the role of laws, institutions and tools for information in ensuring open government decision-making as well as practical measures for consultation and participation.

Over fifty practitioners, drawn mainly from government ministries, state agencies and local government in Brazil, met to discuss lessons from their own experience and those of colleagues from a wide range of countries (including Columbia, Costa Rica, Finland, Mexico, Nicaragua). The group also benefited from a rich variety of perspectives, including those of practitioners from government and civil society, which ensured a lively debate. The role of facilitator was shared by Cláudio Weber Abramo (Secretary General, TransparênciaBrasil) and Joanne Caddy (OECD), providing a concrete demonstration of the benefits of partnership between government and civil society.

Brief presentations of concrete cases by practitioners from Costa Rica, Brazil, Finland, and Mexico were followed by extensive discussion. Finland was one of the first OECD countries to adopt a law on access to information in 1951, and Katju Holkeri (Counsellor, Ministry of Finance, Finland) reviewed the country's longstanding experience as well as recent innovations included in the new 1999 Act on Openness of Government Activities. She emphasised the link between economic development and open government, citing transparency as one of the main factors in attracting foreign direct investment to Finland.

A presentation by Alfredo Chirino (Director, School of Law, Costa Rica) identified the main characteristics of a model law on access to information and stressed the crucial role of such legislation in the fight against corruption and building greater public trust in government. Fernando Castaños (Director General of Research and Analysis, Alianza Ciudadana, Office of the President, Mexico) presented recent policy initiatives in Mexico aimed at fostering greater public participation and underlined the key issues facing government reformers and civil society organisations in building effective partnerships. His presentation was complemented by a brief overview by Lucy Tacher (Deputy Director General for International Relations, Secretariat for Control and Administrative Development, Mexico) of Mexico's efforts to evaluate transparency at the municipal level which includes an active role for civil society in monitoring activities.

The challenges of providing effective public participation over a vast territory and across several levels of government in a large federal country such as Brazil, were illustrated by José Paulo da Silveira (Secretary for Planning and Strategic Investments, Ministry of Planning, Budget and Management, Brazil). He explained how Brazil meets these challenges when informing and engaging members of the public and local communities in multi-annual planning for territorial and infrastructure development, by means of public meetings, workshops and a dedicated web site.

The last hour of the Focus Group was dedicated to the joint drafting of a set of policy recommendations for decision-makers on strengthening mechanisms for public scrutiny and access to information. These policy recommendations (see Box 3 below) were the fruit of much discussion and are structured around three main questions identified by the group as crucial to success in this field, namely: *What elements do we need for an effective framework? What are the obstacles? How can we ensure real public information and participation.*

Although only a first step, the recommendations testify to a growing awareness of the crucial role that citizens and civil society can play in building open government, provided that a number of essential conditions are in place.

Box 3. **Focus Group 3**

Strengthening mechanisms for public scrutiny and access to information

What elements do we need for an effective framework?

- *Laws*: access to information and guarantees for public participation

- *Policies*: training and management; collection and analysis of information; development of indicators

- *Resources*: material, financial and human

- *Independent bodies*: for monitoring and oversight

What are the obstacles?

- Lack of awareness and education on the part of citizens

- A culture of secrecy within the public administration

- Lack of resources

- Absence of specific skills in the public sector

- Lack of an independent media

- Technological, cultural and knowledge barriers

How can we ensure real public information and participation?

- Less propaganda, more accountability

- Developing concrete methodologies

- Introducing appeals mechanisms/independent monitoring

- Fostering a proactive culture in the public service

- Building performance measurement and indicators

- Publicising success stories

- Strengthening the capacity of civil society organisations

- Building capacity and awareness in the public service

- Developing a government culture of "assured listening"

NOTES

1. János Bertók, Principal Administrator, Joanne Caddy Administrator and Michael Ruffner Administrator of the Public Management Service of the OECD were the organisers and co-rapporteurs of the three Focus Groups of the OECD/OAS Forum on Ensuring Accountability and Transparency in the Public Sector that was held on 5-6 December 2001 in Brasilia, Brazil.

2. More information on the Forum, including its agenda and news release, can be seen on the homepage of the Forum on the Internet at: www.oecd.org/oecd/pages/home/displaygeneral/0,3380,EN-document-303-9-no-20-18684-0,FF.html

3. The OECD Best Practices for Budget Transparency can be found in Annex 3.

CANADA'S PRINCIPLE-BASED APPROACH: "THE CONFLICT OF INTEREST AND POST EMPLOYMENT CODE"

by

Public Policy Forum, Ottawa, Canada

Introduction

Recent decades, public trust in government has declined steadily throughout the developed world. In Canada, polling research indicates that this decline is a complex phenomenon involving economic, social and political behaviour, as well as increased scrutiny by the media into government affairs. While declining trust is a challenge for governments in and of itself, more troublesome is the fact that it undermines the legitimacy of government and reflects how existing structures have not fully adapted and responded to the changing needs and interests of citizens.

The issue of conflict of interest is a significant factor in this situation. As governments strive toward greater transparency and accountability to the public, it is becoming increasingly important to ensure that politicians and public servants do not conduct their affairs in such a way that they receive or give to others inappropriate benefits that result from their position of power and influence.

This document provides an overview of how the Government of Canada, through the office of its Ethics Counsellor and the Conflict of Interest and Post-Employment Code for Public Office Holders (the Code), deals with issues relating to conflict of interest and ethics. Central to this are the philosophy and principles that underpin the current conflict of interest framework in Canada, and these, along with the challenges and opportunities associated with the framework, are discussed in detail in the pages that follow.

Context and history

Confidence in government is rooted in trust. In turn, it has been said that trust is fostered in government when it meets the public's expectations for fair and effective public service through ethical and transparent activities.[1] This section provides an historical overview of conflict of interest guidelines -- and their implementation -- in Canada, and demonstrates how the development of a patchwork of guidelines and initiatives over the course of more than two decades culminated in the creation of the Office of the Ethics Counsellor.

Throughout the developing world, trust in government has declined steadily over the last several decades. In Canada, research has demonstrated that only one-fifth to one-third of the public trusted the federal government to "do what is right" in the last decade, marking the lowest point since the end of the Second World War, and down from 80% in the 1960s.[2] Although these statistics reflect a troubling trend, they do not illustrate the true nature of the problem: declining trust is the culmination of a number of forces at work in public opinion. According to a recent American study, these forces include a belief that politicians are corrupt and in politics only for personal gain, a sense that government operations are frivolous and ineffective, as well as a concern that government is not in touch with -- or doesn't care about -- the citizens themselves.[3]

Of particular significance among these challenges is the issue of conflict of interest. Specifically, there is concern among the public that an increasingly intimate relationship between government and industry interests due to new public management styles, including privatisation and other forms of alternate service delivery, might result in new openings for corruption and influence peddling.[4] Some challenges associated with issues such as intersectoral partnerships and other forms of new public management are discussed in Section 6 of the present report, *Challenges and Opportunities.*

The Canadian Government began to address the issue of conflict of interest in 1973, when then Prime Minister Pierre Trudeau introduced "Conflict of Interest Guidelines for Ministers" to the House of Commons. These were matched with guidelines for public service employees and Governor in Council appointees. From the beginning, therefore, the Canadian approach has been to implement guidelines rather than legislation; Trudeau's belief was that a strict legal framework would have meant that the Prime Minister would be responsible for imposing employment conditions on public officials.[5] The Office of the Assistant Deputy Registrar General was created to provide advice to public officials to help them avoid conflicts of interest, but was not given powers to investigate transgressions or impose sanctions.

In the years that followed, a patchwork system of guidelines was implemented that gradually broadened the scope of the conflict of interest framework. In 1978, post-employment guidelines were implemented to ensure that former public officials could not take unfair advantage of their previous positions. In 1979, when the Conservatives took power from the Liberals under Joe Clark, a new set of guidelines was implemented that brought the wives and dependent children of ministers within the fold of the conflict of interest system. The Clark Government was short-lived, and so his revisions, deemed unfair by some in the House of Commons, were removed from the guidelines when the Liberals swept back into power in 1980.

The most significant federal government initiative on conflict of interest was the Sharp-Starr task force, whose report, entitled *Ethical Conduct in the Public Sector,* criticised the collage of guidelines that had been created in the 1970s as ineffective.[6] The report recommended that a single code of ethics be implemented, and that an office be created to administer and enforce it. The report was tabled shortly before a general election was called, but in spite of the fact that John Turner's Liberal Government was defeated, the new Prime Minister, Brian Mulroney, initiated a programme to examine conflict of interest issues. The new study group's report directly resulted in the creation in 1985, of the first Conflict of Interest and Post-Employment Code for Public Office Holders, to be administered by the Deputy Registrar General.

In spite of the efforts of successive federal governments to address conflict of interest, a number of major scandals came to light during the period of development of the conflict of interest guidelines.[7] An inquiry into one of these, involving allegations that the Minister of Regional Industrial Expansion had used his ministerial authority in financial dealings related to a private company within which he held interests, brought to light that the existing framework did not adequately prevent conflicts of interest from taking place. Ontario Supreme Court Chief Justice Parker, who presided over the case, recommended that a Conflict of Interest Office be created that would have the ability to undertake investigations and make rulings on conflict of interest allegations. In 1988, the Mulroney Government addressed these recommendations in a Conflict of Interest Act, and by proposing that a commission be created to administer and enforce the act. Shortly thereafter, however, a general election was called and the act was set aside; bad timing, therefore, prevented yet again the creation of a more comprehensive conflict of interest system.

In the five years that followed, small measures were implemented to help deal with declining public trust in government, by addressing the issue of conflict of interest. Foremost among these was the creation of the Lobbyists Registration Act (LRA), which would help to improve transparency by making public the names of all those who lobbied the government on behalf of private interests. The conflict of interest system remained a patchwork of guidelines, however, overseen by the Assistant Deputy Registrar General, whose authority was limited by the complicated nature of the framework and by the lack of power to enforce or implement the guidelines effectively.

In response to the continued decline in public trust in government, and using the experience gained over successive initiatives during the previous two decades in the area of conflict of interest, the newly elected Liberal Government of Prime Minister Jean Chrétien created the Office of the Ethics Counsellor in June 1994. The Ethics Counsellor, who was given all of the responsibilities previously held by the Assistant Deputy Registrar General, was appointed as part of an effort to promote public trust. During the same period, the LRA was strengthened and placed under the responsibility of the Office of the Ethics Counsellor, thus improving the transparency of legitimate lobbying, and the Conflict of Interest Code for public office holders was clarified. In addition, Parliament was asked to develop a comprehensive code of conduct for members of Parliament and Senators. The Ethics Counsellor's main responsibilities involved the two areas that had produced a number of scandals in previous years: conflict of interest and lobbying. Seven key responsibilities were identified, including:

- To investigate on behalf of the Prime Ministers allegations against minister and senior officials involving conflict of interest or lobbying.

- To administer the Conflict of Interest and Post-Employment Code for public office holders.

- To oversee the LRA.

- To consult lobbyists and undertake an initiative to develop a code of conduct for their industry.

- To offer guidance to lobbyists and their clients.

- To investigate complaints about lobbying activities; and

- To report annually to Parliament on matters related to lobbying.

In the six years following the creation of the Office of the Ethics Counsellor, the office has implemented a number of smaller-scale measures to promote openness and transparency, including the use of an Internet Web site as a public clearing house for information on lobbyists, conflict of interest issues, and positions on high-profile cases. Thus, while there remains a patchwork of guidelines and regulations to oversee conflict of interest and ethics guidelines in the federal government, over a quarter century of efforts and studies appear to have produced a system that provides a solid set of ethics guidelines for public office holders.

The principles-based philosophy

The Canadian government's approach toward conflict of interest guidelines has always been to promote integrity rather than to enforce compliance. Whereas the latter involves a series of laws -- "thou shalt nots" -- within which public office holders may operate, the former path is based on the more positive assumption that public office holders essentially want to act in an ethical and honest manner. This section discusses this principles-based approach, and the ideas that underpin it.

The Canadian public service began to emphasise the importance of values and principles in the 1990s. This occurred as the federal government endeavoured to cut costs and focus on core programmes through a re-evaluation of every aspect of its operations, which resulted in part in a 20% reduction in the ranks of the public service between 1994, and 1998. The work undertaken at mid-decade by the Task Force on Public Service Values and Ethics helped to lay the groundwork for a new mindset in the public service, in which traditional values like merit, excellence and objectivity were complemented with new values such as quality, innovation and resourcefulness. In essence, this new, more comprehensive set of values and principles was developed to meet growing public demands on public service employees for service excellence, in the face of limited resources and greater financial austerity and probity. Rather than create rules and regulations, therefore, the federal government provided principles as guidance to public servants in their professional conduct and private interests.

Conflict of interest guidelines in the federal government were developed, and are implemented, using the same approach. The Conflict of Interest and Post Employment Code for Public Office Holders (the "Code") applies to a defined cadre of officials, including Cabinet Ministers, Secretaries of State, Parliamentary Secretaries, Ministerial Staff and Governor in Council Appointees.[8] The main thrust of the Code is to proactively help these individuals ensure that any of their private interests do not threaten to put them in a situation of conflict of interest. According to the Ethics Counsellor, all of those situations that are clearly illegal are dealt with under the Criminal Code, and it is really the "grey areas" that require guidance.[9] By providing them with the guidance to "see and address problems," based on the assumption that they will want to do what is right, it is expected that those who must work under the Code will address potential conflicts of interest before they become actual conflicts.

Under the Code, public office holders are instructed to act according to ten key principles:

- *Honesty*: to act with honesty and to uphold the highest ethical standards.

- *Public scrutiny*: to perform duties and arrange private affairs in a manner that will bear public scrutiny.

- *Decision-making*: to make decisions in the public interest and with regard to the merits of each case.

- *Private interests*: to avoid having private interests that would be affected by government actions in which they participate.

- *Public interest*: to arrange private affairs in a way that will prevent real, potential or apparent conflicts of interest.

- *Gifts and benefits*: to avoid soliciting or accepting transfers of economic benefit unless the transfer is pursuant to an enforceable contract or property right.

- *Preferential treatment*: to avoid using their official roles to assist private entities or persons in their dealings with the government, where this would result in preferential treatment.

- *Insider information*: to avoid taking advantage of, or benefiting from, information that is obtained in the course of official duties.

- *Government property*: to avoid using, or allowing the use of, government property for anything other than officially approved activities; and,

- *Post-employment*: to avoid, after leaving public office, acting in such a manner as to take improper advantage of their previous office.

These principles have been translated into practical guidelines for public office holders. The Code stipulates that a confidential disclosure to the Ethics Counsellor must be made on the following five types of items:

- *Assets:* Assets include residences, recreational properties, farms, household goods, and personal goods, among others.

- *Investments*: These consist of fixed value guaranteed bonds and securities, retirement savings plans, mutual funds, etc.

- *Debts*: Any debts must be disclosed to the Ethics Counsellor, including debts to lending institutions as well as to individuals.

- *Activities*: Activities range from the practice of a profession to the operation of a business, as well as director positions in commercial operations and memberships in professional associations.

- *Gifts and benefits*: Gifts valued at CAD 200 or more must be disclosed to the Ethics Counsellor, other than gifts or hospitalities received from a family member or personal friend.

Following such disclosure, the Ethics Counsellor will guide public office holders in question as to which steps to take in order to avoid conflict of interest situations. These are outlined below.

a) *Assets and investments:* Public office holders must *declare publicly* any interests in businesses that do not contract with the government, as well as on any interests in real properties or commercial farming operations. Public office holders must *divest by sale or into blind trust* any publicly traded *shares* of corporations and *securities of* foreign governments, self-administered Registered Retirement Savings Plans composed of publicly traded securities, as well as commodities, futures and foreign currency investments. Public office holders must *divest by sale or blind management agreement* any ownership interests in corporations having dealings with the government.

b) *Prohibited activities:* Prohibited activities include the practice of a profession, the operation of a business or commercial activity, a directorship or office in a commercial or financial corporation, an office in a union or professional association, or a position as a paid consultant. Public office holders must *resign and make a public declaration* of such in order to avoid conflicts of interest.

c) *Permissible activities:* Public officials are permitted to hold memberships, directorships or offices in organisations that are charitable, non-commercial or philanthropic in nature. Public office holders must seek the *approval of the Ethics Counsellor* and make a *public declaration* of any activities deemed permissible by the Ethics Counsellor.

d) *Gifts, hospitalities and other benefits:* Public office holders must *decline any gifts and benefits which might influence their judgement,* or impact on performance of duties. On the one hand, if the gift or hospitality received is valued at less than CAD 200, and is deemed not to impact on or influence their performance of duties, then no-disclosure is required. On the other hand, gifts or benefits valued at over CAD 200 that arise out of an activity related to their official duties, and are within the normal standards of protocol, must be disclosed to the Ethics Counsellor and declared publicly.

e) *Post-employment:* Public office holders must abide by a number of *regulations following their departure from public office.* At no time are they permitted to "switch sides," to act on behalf of a person or other entity or association, in any ongoing proceeding or negotiation to which the government is a party and where the former office holder advised or acted on behalf of the government. In addition, public office holders are prohibited from using insider information to their benefit or to another organisation's benefit following the end of their tenure. For non-ministers, there is a one-year limitation on accepting employment or directorships with organisations with which they had direct dealings during their *last year of* tenure, as well as on making representations back to government. This limitation is extended to two years for ministers. The Prime Minister has the authority, when it is deemed necessary, to reduce the period of limitation from the amount set out under the Code. Decisions to do so depend on the circumstances of the termination of the public office holder's position, the desirability of a rapid transfer from government to another sector, the level of authority possessed by the public office holder, and the impact that this will have on their affairs following their departure.

In the mid-1990s, a case involving a serving Cabinet Minister highlighted the need to address the issue of ministerial dealings with quasi-judicial institutions, and so another principle was added to the slate. In Canada, quasi-judicial institutions range from the review boards that administer appeals on issues such as immigration, veterans' affairs and pensions, to licensing boards and other related agencies. In order to prevent these boards from being swayed by their "ministerial aura," it was decided that ministers could not intervene with federal quasi-judicial institutions on any matter, unless required by law.[10]

Conflict of interest framework

Because Canada's conflict of interest guidelines are principles-based, rather than rules-based, responsibility for implementing them is shared among a number of parties. This section briefly reviews the roles and responsibilities of each of the parties, and discusses how the principles-based approach is implemented.

There are three main areas of responsibility under Canada's conflict of interest guidelines, covering a number of different parties. First, the responsibility to oversee the guidelines and their implementation falls to the Ethics Counsellor. Second, responsibility to follow the guidelines and promote integrity under them falls to all those who are covered by them. Third, and most importantly, the responsibility for ensuring that public office holders remain free of conflict of interest is the obligation of the Prime

Minister as a steward of good government. Each of these areas of responsibility, and the different parties involved, is outlined below.

Overseeing and implementing guidelines: The Ethics Counsellor

The first category of responsibility is that of overseeing and implementing conflict of interest guidelines, which rests solely with the Ethics Counsellor. In addition to overseeing the LRA, the Ethics Counsellor must also provide advice to public office holders under the Code. As he noted in an address to the Australian Senate in 1999, his role does not replace that of the police and the justice system when public office holders are involved in suspected breaches of the Criminal Code. Rather, his area of chief concern is the "grey areas of potential or real conflict of interest issues that may seem broadly wrong in the eyes of citizens, without ever actually being illegal."[11]

This being said, the responsibility as an adviser on conflicts of interest translates into two slightly different roles, depending on the situation.

- *Advice to public office holders:* The Ethics Counsellor helps guide public office holders, and recently departed public office holders, through situations that may place them in conflict of interest. As a start, public office holders are given a copy of the guidelines upon assuming office, as well as a step-by-step guidebook on disclosures and responsibilities under the Code. Throughout their tenure, as well as during the limitation period that follows their departure, the Ethics Counsellor is available to provide public office holders with guidance should their situations change, or should they feel that they have fallen into a potential area of conflict of interest.

- *Advice to prime minister as Head of Government:* The Ethics Counsellor reports to the Prime Minister on issues relating to actual, potential or perceived conflict of interest among current and former public office holders. It is important to note that the Ethics Counsellor does not make "judgements" on individual "cases," but rather provides an informed opinion, based on an investigation of a given situation, and on the guidelines laid out by the Code. The Ethics Counsellor also reports directly to the Prime Minister on all other matters relating to the functions of the Office of the Ethics Counsellor, rather than to Parliament or to a parliamentary committee.

During situations of perceived or alleged conflict of interest, the Ethics Counsellor's staff considers the evidence vis-à-vis the Code, and provides recommendations to the Prime Minister on whether or not conflict of interest has taken place. At this point, the Ethics Counsellor assumes a more proactive role, developing a position on a particular case and an action plan or set of recommendations on how to remove a public official from a situation of conflict of interest. It is important to note that the Ethics Counsellor does not act as a judge in this situation, but rather as a key advisor to the Prime Minister. The responsibilities of the Prime Minister are discussed in greater detail later in this section, but it suffices to say that the Prime Minister, not the Ethics Counsellor, makes the ultimate decision on whether or not a reprimand is in order.

In an effort to increase transparency in the area of ethics, and to help bolster trust in government and public servants, the current Ethics Counsellor has committed to making the work of his office on conflict of interest issues as public as possible. This means that public declarations made by public office holders, as well as documents related to perceived or alleged conflicts of interest, are available both in hard copy from the Office of the Ethics Counsellor and via the Internet.

The Ethics Counsellor also oversees the LRA, under which lobbyists dealing with the federal government must disclose information about their lobbying activities and the clients they represent. The LRA is based on four basic principles:[12]

- Free and open access to government is an important matter of public interest.

- Lobbying public office holders is a legitimate activity.

- It is desirable that public office holders and the general public be able to know who is attempting to influence government.

- The system for the registration of paid lobbyists should not impede free and open access to government.

The current LRA dates to 1995, when the existing legislation was amended as part of the more general effort to promote public trust in government that led to the creation of the Office of Ethics Counsellor the previous year. The LRA also contains a Lobbyists Code of Conduct, which mirrors to a certain extent the principles-based approach of the Conflict of Interest and Post Employment Code for Public Office Holders. Under the LRA and Code of Conduct, however, the Ethics Counsellor tables reports in Parliament when, based on reasonable grounds, he or she believes that rules have been breached. This aspect of the LRA is the only area in which the Ethics Counsellor acts more as a parliamentary commissioner than as a counsellor.

The Act is slated for parliamentary review in 2001, and a recent Public Policy Forum study on government-industry relations demonstrates that there remain considerable tensions between the federal government and the private sector. It was noted in the study, for instance, that government representatives tend to prefer to deal with business associations. For some in government, it seems, the efforts under the LRA to improve transparency have yet to achieve success, since they still often find it difficult to identify the client for whom an individual lobbyist is working.[13]

Following guidelines and promoting integrity: public office holders

The second area of responsibility is that of following the conflict of interest guidelines and of promoting integrity. This responsibility is shared among all current and former public office holders who fall under the Code, and is central to the conflict of interest framework. As previously noted, the Canadian approach has been to assume that public office holders want to "do good," and desire at all times to act ethically in every aspect of their responsibilities. Under the Canadian system, public office holders have three main responsibilities:

- *Declaration:* Public office holders are responsible for reporting honestly and clearly to the Ethics Counsellor on all holdings, assets, and interests, as outlined in the conflict of interest guidelines. This responsibility applies to them throughout the duration of their tenure of public office, and until the end of their period of limitation following their departure.

- *Monitoring*: Public office holders are responsible for ensuring that they do not place themselves in situations of conflict of interest and, should they find themselves unable to avoid such situations, to remove themselves from them based on the guidance they receive for doing so from the Ethics Counsellor.

- *Decision-making*: Public office holders are responsible for making decisions in the public interest. Since the Ethics Counsellor can only advise them on conflict of interest prevention, it is ultimately the public office holders themselves who are accountable to the Prime Minister, or in the case of the Prime Minister to Parliament, for their actions and decisions.

Accounting for government actions

The third, and perhaps most important, area of responsibility involves accounting for the actions of the government. As stated earlier in this section, the Ethics Counsellor reports to the Prime Minister, as head of government, on issues relating to actual, potential or perceived conflict of interest among current and former public office holders. According to the Office of the Ethics Counsellor, the existing reporting relationship has been developed based on two principles. First, the fact that the Prime Minister is accountable for the actions of his or her ministers and government means that the Prime Minister's action on advice offered by the Ethics Counsellor – or the lack thereof – will ultimately be put before the scrutiny of Parliament and the voting public. Second, the fact that the Ethics Counsellor works in "grey areas" rather than within a strict legal or accountability framework, means that the main focus of his or her advice is on the appearance of conflict. That is to say that the Ethics Counsellor focuses on areas that are, so to speak, "beyond what the law requires," and require the Prime Minister to decide whether a given situation requires action.[14]

In practical terms: the conflict of interest life cycle

As noted in the previous section, the Conflict of Interest framework in the federal government of Canada involves a shared set of values, principles and responsibilities. These translate into a life cycle of actions that public office holders must undertake during their tenure. This section documents these in practical terms through a case study of a fictional Cabinet Minister.[15] It documents the different steps that must be taken by public office holders under the Code, before, during and after their tenure, and discusses a number of possible scenarios that would involve intervention by the Ethics Counsellor.

There are three phases in the conflict of interest regulations life cycle within the Code. First, there is an initial compliance phase that takes place upon assuming office, and an adjustment sub-phase during which the public office holder undertakes compliance measures whenever changes to his/her personal situation takes place. The second phase is the actual tenure of the position, which requires annual review of compliance. The third phase is the post-employment phase. The life cycle is roughly depicted in the diagram below:

The processes and measures relating to each of these three phases are documented in this section. The most intensive phase is the Phase I, or the compliance phase, during which the public office holder takes measures regarding his/her personal holdings and interests in order to comply with the conflict of interest guidelines. Phases II and III, however, or the tenure/annual review and post-employment phases, are just as important since they ensure that compliance is not simply a nominal gesture at the time of appointment, but rather is reviewed and reinforced over the entire duration of a public office holder's tenure.

Administration of the Conflict of Interest and
Post-Employment Code for Public Office Holders

Office of the Ethics Counsellor

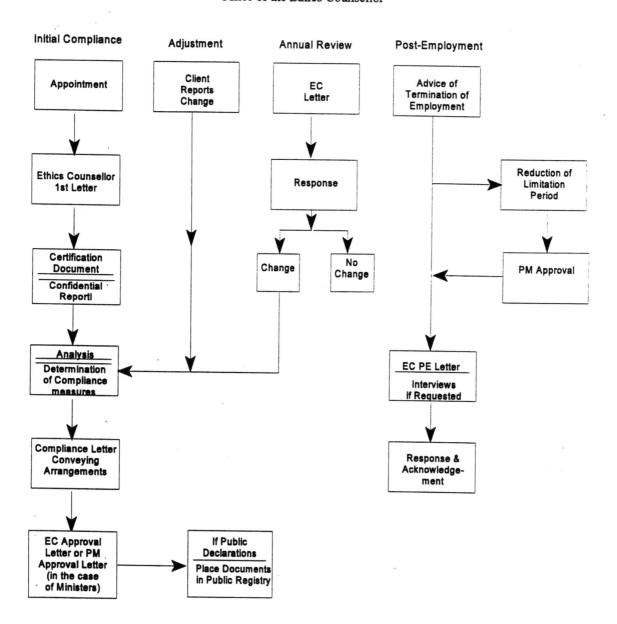

Phase I: Adjustment and compliance

Prior to assuming a new position, public office holders must, in effect, disclose their interests, holdings, and outside activities to the Ethics Counsellor. This permits the Ethics Counsellor to study their situation, and to develop a personalised report that will explain what they must do in order to prevent conflict of interest situations from occurring. Below is an explanation of each of the actions, reports and declarations that take place during this phase:

- *Introductory letter:* Upon appointment, public office holders will receive a letter explaining the role of the Ethics Counsellor, as well as the public office holder's responsibilities under the conflict of interest guidelines. This letter presents the disclosures that will need to be made. Included, therefore, are the following documents for completion by the public office holder:

    - *Certification document:* This document will allow the public office holder to declare that he or she will observe the Code.

    - *Confidential report:* The public office holder will complete this document, identifying all assets, liabilities, and interests, as required

- *Introductory meeting*: The Ethics Counsellor will meet with public office holders upon their appointment, to explain the requirements under the Code, as well as the resources available to them during their tenure.

- *Compliance measures*: Once the public office holder completes the confidential report, the Office of the Ethics Counsellor will examine the case explaining any compliance measures that they must take involving the assets, liabilities and interests disclosed. Guidance will also be provided as to any public declarations that they must make, as well as any divestments or agreements that they will need to enter into in order to avoid conflict of interest situations.

Once the confidential report has been analysed, any compliance measures recommended by the Ethics Counsellor must be acted upon. The Ethics Counsellor will provide them with any assistance or documentation that they may require to meet the stipulations of the Code. Documents and compliance measures include:

- *Public declaration of declarable assets:* Public office holders will declare all publicly declarable assets, as defined by the Code, using this document.

- *Public declaration of outside activities:* This document allows public office holders to declare any activities in which they are involved, including memberships on boards and organisations, positions in private companies, and other appointments.

- *Blind trust or blind management agreements:* The Ethics Counsellor will assist public office holders in placing their interests into blind trust or blind management agreements, and documentation attesting to such actions will be completed by the public office holder and kept by the Ethics Counsellor.

Once the public office holder has complied with the measures set out in the code, the Ethics Counsellor will review all of the documentation involved to ensure that no more steps are necessary, and will acknowledge receipt of this documentation in the form of a Summary Statement. This statement notes the compliance measures that have taken place. Once the summary statement is signed and returned by the public office holder, the Ethics Counsellor will advise the Prime Minister in writing, where a Minister is concerned, that the public office holder has made the necessary arrangements to comply with the Code.

Phase II: Tenure of office and annual review

During a public office holder's tenure, annual reviews are undertaken to ensure that the official in question remains in compliance with the Code. Following their appointment to public office, the Ethics Counsellor advises them in writing that they will remain subject to the Code throughout their tenure, and of their responsibilities under the Code. In addition, a summary of their Confidential Report is sent to them, which they must review and sign once a year. In the meantime, should there be any change to their situation, they are required to note it in the summary, and bring it to the attention of the Office of the Ethics Counsellor. All public office holders are reminded every year on or around the anniversary of their appointment that they must review their arrangements.

Phase III: post-employment

As noted earlier in this report, public office holders are subject to the Code for one year following their departure from public office. In the case of Cabinet Ministers and Secretaries of State, this period is extended to two years. The Ethics Counsellor will advise them in writing of their post-employment responsibilities under the Code immediately following the termination of their appointment. In addition, the Office of the Ethics Counsellor will offer assistance, should it be required, in ensuring that they meet the requirements of the Code following their departure. This also applies to dismantling blind trust and other divestment arrangements. In cases in which the Prime Minister decides that the period of limitation should be reduced, it is the Prime Minister's responsibility to communicate that fact in writing to the former public office holder in question.

Challenges and opportunities

Although it would be difficult to determine the overall impact of the Ethics Counsellor on government, the fact that no public office holders covered by the Code have been found to be in conflict of interest since the post was created in 1994, is testament to some degree of success. According to the Office of the Ethics Counsellor, this is due primarily to the fact that public office holders recognise that acting with integrity will help to "ensure their long-term political health," and have therefore taken full advantage of the guidance and expertise offered by the Ethics Counsellor, avoiding potential "hot spots." By contrast, however, others point to this fact as evidence of the fact that the Code may not broad enough in scope to deal with the conflict of interest issue, and that some potential conflicts of interest may have simply been "under the radar" and therefore unnoticed by the Ethics Counsellor. At the time of writing, a number of opposition-led initiatives were underway in the House of Commons, including a vote -- which was defeated -- on whether the Ethics Counsellor should report directly to Parliament.[16]

Beyond this, however, there remain a number of challenges that threaten to undermine the Canadian system, particularly in times of increased media scrutiny. During the 2000, federal election campaign, for example, Prime Minister Jean Chrétien's discussions with the head of a federal Crown corporation, on the details of a federal loan for one of his constituents, were decried by the opposition as a conflict of interest and abuse of power. Although the Ethics Counsellor determined that the Prime Minister had not contravened any of the guidelines, political opponents and the media called for a number of changes to be made to address the perception that the existing reporting relationship between the Ethics Counsellor and the Prime Minister may actually offset his effectiveness. Two opposition party political leaders even resorted to lodging formal requests with the Royal Canadian Mounted Police

(RCMP) to review the case to determine if criminal charges could be laid. The RCMP have since determined that there are no grounds for a criminal investigation.

The sections that follow discuss a number of the challenges facing Canada's conflict of interest guidelines, and touches on several important positioning opportunities that would help to improve the responsiveness of the existing system to the changing realities of Canadian Government, and would help to sustain it over the long term.

The Code of Conduct "Patchwork"

Perhaps the most significant vestige of the era that preceded the creation of the Ethics Counsellor position is the fact that conflict of interest and general conduct guidelines for all public officials are not consolidated in a single code. As illustrated earlier in this report, such codes and guidelines developed gradually over the last three decades, partly due to changing pressures on government to react to various politically charged situations. As it stands, general rules and regulations for public officials can be found in a number of places, including, but not limited to:

- The Criminal Code of Canada.

- The Parliament of Canada Act.

- The Rules of the Senate.

- The Standing Orders of the House of Commons.

- The Conflict of Interest and Post-Employment Code for Public Office Holders.

It should be noted that this concern was first raised in the 1984 report of the Task Force on Conflict of Interest, that a code of ethics should be enshrined in legislation to replace the "patchwork" of guidelines and regulations, and to expand regulations to cover all parliamentarians.[17] The task force's report noted that the patchwork of codes, guidelines and regulations translated into extensive inconsistencies in the content and administration of conflict of interest guidelines. The report recognised that, while the existing guidelines are based on sound and reasonable principles:

The rules, which have evolved gradually over the years to deal with problems as they arose, need to be reformatted to ensure consistency in content and administration and to make them simple, fair, and reasonable as possible.[18]

The task force recommended that a number of steps be taken to address the situation. These included, for instance, the creation of a Code of Ethical Conduct that was at once short and simple, yet comprehensive, that would be binding upon all public office holders, the development of standard procedures for removing public office holders from conflict of interest situations, and the creation of supplemental codes to deal with the "grey areas" of conflict of interest situations.

Possibly the most critical issue highlighted by the task force's report, that remains relevant to today's situation, was also discussed in a chapter of the 1995 report of the Auditor General of Canada. According to the Auditor General, the public's perception -- whether warranted or not -- that standards of conduct in government are on the decline, suggests a need for a comprehensive framework to address conflict of interest and standards of conduct issues. One need look no further than the inquiry into the Prime Minister's constituent affairs that caught the attention of the media during the 2000 election campaign for an example of how such a situation can impact on public perception. This would, stated the Auditor General, "provide some assurance that decisions are made impartially and objectively, and in the public interest."[19]

The 1996 Second Report of the Special Joint Committee on a Code of Conduct of the Senate and the House of Conduct noted that the existing framework is antiquated and limited in scope, since it deals primarily with specific situations. In addition, it noted that there exist no comprehensive guidelines for backbench and opposition members of Parliament, or for public service employees below the rank of Deputy Minister.[20] The Committee recommended the creation of a Code of Official Conduct that would apply to all public office holders, in response to a perceived need for action on two fronts:

- *Guiding politicians:* The Committee recognised the need for continued guidance to politicians on conflict of interest and conduct issues, just as the existing conflict of interest guidelines and the Ethics Counsellor provide guidance to a select group of public office holders.

- *Broadened scope:* The Committee noted that broadening the scope of existing conflict of interest and conduct guidelines to accommodate all parliamentarians could help to improve public perception of government.

According to the Special Committee's report, the proposed Code of Official Conduct would establish a regime that was comprehensive in scope, providing "guidance and assistance to Senators and members of the House of Commons, while assuring the public that allegations [would] be investigated and breaches dealt with. [sic]"[21] Proposed regulations would require, among others, that:

- All parliamentarians make confidential and public disclosures similar to those currently required under the current Conflict of Interest and Post-Employment Code.

- Spouses and dependants of parliamentarians disclose confidentially their assets and holdings.

- Parliamentarians disclose publicly any information on gifts received that exceed a predetermined value.

- Penalties be imposed for abuses of power.

- The existing rules regarding government contracts involving parliamentarians be reviewed.

- A *Jurisconsult* officer be appointed to receive disclosures and other such documents from parliamentarians, and provide advice on the Code of Conduct; and

- A new Joint Committee be established to oversee and implement the Code, and to determine penalties for non-compliance.

Addressing this challenge will require strong will and leadership on the part of parliamentarians and senior departmental officials. As noted in a report by a representative of the Office of the Ethics Counsellor, Canada "lags behind" other countries in rules of conduct for parliamentarians, and this is due mainly to a lack of desire to institute more comprehensive ethics, conduct and conflict of interest guidelines.[22]

Public awareness and trust

Another significant challenge facing Canada's conflict of interest framework is a lack of public awareness and understanding of conflict of interest policies and procedures, the concepts that underpin them, and the role of the Ethics Counsellor.

Although no quantitative data are available that accurately pinpoint the level of public understanding, intense media scrutiny of weaknesses or problems tends to promulgate negative public perception. This is best exemplified in research carried out by Transparency International, in its annual Corruption Perception Index (CPI).[23] The CPI reports public perceptions of the degree of corruption of government in different countries, based on surveys undertaken in each country, and then ranks countries on a scale of 0 (indicating highly corrupt) to 10 (indicating highly clean). Historical data show that, while Canada has ranked consistently among the top-10 "cleanest" countries, public perception of corruption has not improved substantially since the creation of the first Conflict of Interest and Post Employment Code in the 1980s, or the creation of the Ethics Counsellor position in 1994.[24] Some thoughts on the similarities between Canada and other "top" TI performers can be found in Section 7 of the present report, "International Context for Ethics."

Thus, the federal government has an opportunity, and an obligation, to improve understanding of the existing Code and framework, among both the public and the community of public office holders. Based on the media scrutiny of the Office of the Ethics Counsellor during the 2000 federal election campaign, there are two main areas of misinformation that could potentially impact on public opinion:

- *Counsellor vs. Commissioner:* As previously noted, the role of the Ethics Counsellor is to *counsel* the Prime Minister on situations and perceptions of conflict of interest, rather than to *report* such situations to the House. During the most recent election campaign, the media tended to portray the Ethics Counsellor as an ineffectual subordinate of the Prime Minister, ignoring the pretext of the *counsellor's* job.[25] In order to understand the actual reporting relationship, we must consider the context provided by the role of the Prime Minister, which, although it is only alluded to in the Constitution and other key documents, many scholars have noted that it has increasingly become the centre of power in government over the last five decades.[26] Within this model, the Prime Minister is perceived -- if not actually stated in the Constitution as such -- as ultimately responsible in Parliament for the actions of his or her Cabinet Ministers, and so the Ethics Counsellor's advice is intended to reinforce this accountability. One might say, therefore, that because it is primarily public perception that ascribes to the Prime Minister the ultimate accountability for the performance and actions of government, in the House of Commons and in the glare of the media, then the need for a transparent and responsive process for dealing with conflict of interest and ethical issues is raised.

- *Proactive guidance vs. reactive enforcement:* During the campaign, opposition candidates and the media complained that the primarily advisory role of the Ethics Counsellor makes his position ineffectual.[27] While the reporting relationship to the Prime Minister needs to be viewed within its constitutional context, such statements were not balanced with an explanation of the "guidance" role that the Ethics Counsellor plays. Little mention was made by the media, for instance, of the steps that public office holders must take before assuming office, or of the disclosures they must make during and after their tenure. Thus, the role of the Ethics Counsellor in providing proactive guidance rather than as a reactive enforcer of the law remains misunderstood and is frequently misrepresented.

Constituents and Cabinet Members

A third important challenge facing the existing conflict of interest framework is the fact that the guidelines facing public office holders tend to defy the traditional role of members of Parliament as constituent representatives in the House of Commons. Under Canada's constitution, Cabinet members do not interfere with the affairs of their Cabinet colleagues' portfolios or departments without their express permission or unless deemed necessary under the law. In a similar vein, the Conflict of Interest and Post-Employment Code for Public Office Holders forbids Cabinet Ministers from interfering with quasi-judicial and regulatory agencies.

In theory, prohibiting Cabinet Ministers from influencing quasi-judicial and regulatory agencies clearly prevents them from entering into a situation in which they appear to use their "ministerial aura" to influence others. In practice, however, this presents a significant challenge in the area of the minister's constituent affairs. For instance, the rule prevents Cabinet Ministers from representing their constituents' views in areas of federal regulation. Thus while the rules reduces opportunities for conflict of interest situations to occur, it could also be said that they severely constrain the ability of a minister to represent his or her constituents in government.

Perceptions of new public management

New approaches to public management, particularly in the form of public-private partnerships and alternate forms of service delivery, pose a new kind of challenge to public perceptions of conflict of interest. In a positive vein, non-traditional forms of public management allow for government to employ a more flexible approach to meeting citizens' needs. Public-private partnerships are also well positioned to leverage the expertise, resources and tools necessary to undertake projects and initiatives of many types. By contrast, however, closer service or contractual relationships between government and the private and third sectors may also contribute to a perception that government officials have "sold out" to corporate interests. As a result, the governance framework of new public management initiatives need to ensure – and demonstrate very clearly – that the public interest is safeguarded on all fronts.

It is important to consider, therefore, the scope of the existing conflict of interest framework as it applies to non-traditional forms of service, and new public management approaches. As noted earlier in this report, Cabinet Ministers, heads of agencies and heads of Crown corporations are covered by the Code, and as such need to make the same disclosures to the Office of the Ethics Counsellor upon appointment, periodically throughout their tenure and following dismissal or resignation. This underscores both a strength and a weakness inherent to the conflict of interest framework currently in place. As noted by d'Ombrain, alternate service delivery initiatives are most effective when they can produce simple and measurable results, and when the need for ministerial control or input is lower than in traditional areas of government service.[28] For example, while service kiosks to dispense licenses for motor vehicles may be a more effective and transparent means of meeting a relatively straightforward client service need, a hypothetical public-private venture for setting annual fishing quotas may pose other problems.

Based on the above example, the existing conflict of interest framework can be seen as effective due to the fact that the heads of such initiatives fall under the same conflict of interest responsibilities and guidelines as do Cabinet Ministers. As such, limited areas of responsibility traditionally held by a Cabinet Minister may be delegated to them without excessively exposing the initiative to potential conflicts of interest. In the case of the hypothetical motor vehicle license dispensing kiosk network, the responsibilities of the agency head are the same as a minister may have in overseeing the same initiative, and the client usage and satisfaction statistics are simple to measure and report.

More complex projects and organisations that do not fall under d'Ombrain's "ideal" vision for new public management initiatives pose significant obstacles to the conflict of interest process and framework. Two significant challenges emerge when the fictional intersectoral fishing quota initiative is examined, clearly illustrating the issues relating to the conflict of interest framework, public perception and confidence, and transparency.

- *Board of directors:* Many new public management and alternative service delivery initiatives are governed by a board of directors or similar body. Thus, while the conflict of interest regulations clearly stipulate that the heads of such bodies fully disclose their interests as government appointees, the rules are less clear when applied to other board members and employees. Thus, while board members may operate in good faith, the perception that they can potentially "fall through the cracks" of conflict of interest guidelines may leave the organisation exposed to a public already distrustful of government in general.

- *Public and private accountability:* A challenge that is increasingly being faced by organisations involved in partnerships with governments is related to the fact that the standards for accountability differ in the public and private sectors. Thus, while transparency in all aspects of government accounting is of the utmost importance to the public interest, non-governmental organisations and private corporations may be reticent toward opening their doors to the same standards. Given that such proprietary knowledge often forms part of a company's competitive advantage in the marketplace, this concern appears to be well-founded. Thus, new public management initiatives may be headed for an impasse over accounting standards.

Two remedies to address the former challenge are clear on the surface. First, further study needs to be undertaken to broaden the existing Code to account for contributors or employees involved in non-traditional initiatives. Care will need to be exercised, however, to prevent causing unnecessary burdens that will undermine the positive impact that new public management programs can have on government's responsiveness to its citizens. Second, governments need to be strategic in their selection of new public management programmes, and not become overly ambitious in the scope and measurability of programmes and programme outcomes. Taking this approach will help ensure that they do not find themselves overly exposed to possibilities of conflict of interest.

The challenge relating to standards of accounting is far less clear, and needs to be addressed only after all of the differences in methodology and accountability requirements are identified among and between the public, private and third sectors. As expectations for government transparency and the need for government to employ more streamlined approaches to public management increase, the tensions between the sectors can only be heightened.

International ethics and conflict of interest context

It was noted earlier in this report that, by international standards, Canada is a relatively strong performer in the area of public perceptions of corruption, frequently ranking in the "cleanest" six countries of Transparency International's (TI) Corruption Perception Index. Although it would be impossible to draw direct links between conflict of interest and ethics guidelines in the high-performing countries and public perception in each, there are some discernible trends that appear to have had a positive impact on public trust and confidence, based on the TI survey outcomes. This section briefly discusses some aspects of the public service ethics environment and framework among three of the top six performing countries of TI's 1998 survey, including Canada, Finland, Iceland and New Zealand. In particular, this section demonstrates some key differences and similarities between Canada and counterparts in how public service values and ethics are enshrined and implemented as a key step to reinforcing public confidence in government. The focus of the section is on the most prominent aspects of the Canadian conflict of interest and ethics experience detailed in the present case study, including each country's overall approach and underlying philosophy to conflict of interest and ethics, the prominence of public service values and principles, the means by which the guidelines are enshrined, and the means by which they are implemented and/or enforced.

- *Approach:* There does not appear to be a standard approach among the countries in question in the area of approach or underlying philosophy. While the governments of Canada, Finland, Iceland and New Zealand all recognise that public servants generally approach their work with the public interest at heart, only Canada and New Zealand use this assumption as the foundation for ethics and code of conduct guidelines that promote integrity rather than establish a strict legislative framework.[29] Interestingly, the Finnish constitution takes public *perception* into consideration in determining whether action is necessary, while this has not been factored explicitly into the frameworks of the other countries.[30]

- *Implementation*: Canada's Ethics Counsellor is unique among this group of countries. In Finland, the Parliamentary Ombudsman is largely responsible for the implementation of ethical and conflict of interest guidelines. The Ombudsman also has the power to recommend court action against parliamentarians, ministers and their staff, and other public servants.[31] In Iceland and New Zealand, similar functions fall under the responsibility of the Office of the Controller and Auditor General of New Zealand, and the State Audit Office in Iceland.[32] These agencies provide regular reports on government, and operate mainly as a review function for departmental activities.

- *Code*: None of the four countries in question have a centralised code for ethics and conflict of interest that applies to all members of the public service and the political sphere. The framework therefore consists of a combination of guidelines and laws. In Iceland, moreover, ethical and conflict of interest laws are more dispersed than in its "top six" counterparts. It has been stated that this is more a reflection of the fact that ethics have long been an integral element of public management in Iceland.[33]

- *Values and principles:* All but Iceland have begun to implement explicit public service values and principles statements and initiatives in recent years. As noted earlier in this report, values and principles have become a high priority in Canadian public management. By contrast, the Icelandic experience points to the fact that values and principles have long been seen as central to public management and government, possibly highlighting the existence of an implicit cultural "code" rather than an explicit statutory or other framework.

The brief comparison above demonstrates that there is no clear formula for addressing conflict of interest and ethics issues that is appropriate to all countries. For instance, while Canada and New Zealand have both chosen to take a proactive, values-based approach to addressing such challenges, there is no clear counterpart to Canada' s Ethics Counsellor in the New Zealand system. By the same token, the fact that values and principles are not explicitly stated or implemented in a framework in Iceland does not appear to have had -- by Transparency International's standards -- a negative impact on public trust and confidence. Clearly, the one conclusion that may be drawn from this comparison is the fact that ethics guidelines, as they relate to conflict of interest rules, regulations and practices, are very much a creature of history and environment, and have tended to be shaped not only through study and analysis of best practices in other jurisdictions, but also using the experiences unique to each country as a guide.

Conclusion

The Canadian Government's Conflict of Interest and Post-Employment Code for Public Office Holders, and the Office of the Ethics Counsellor, are relatively new initiatives. Thus, their overall impact on government, especially on the level of public trust in government, remains unclear. Media criticism aside, however, the system's emphasis on promoting integrity rather than on punishing bad behaviour appears to be aligned with the growing emphasis on public service values and principles throughout the federal government.

Much remains to be done to help address the key challenges outlined in this report, and to help stem and possibly reverse the declining level of trust in government in Canada. Although conflict of interest is only one facet of declining confidence in government, public awareness and information campaigns, for instance, could help remedy the lack of public understanding that plagues the Office of the Ethics Counsellor. Still greater transparency, through the Internet and official reports, should contribute to public acceptance of the Ethics Counsellor and the framework within which the office operates. Finally, there clearly is a need for a comprehensive code of conduct and conflict of interest regulations, in order to make the framework more responsive to the changing realities of the Canadian public sector and the trust and confidence test of the Canadian public.

NOTES

1.   Organisation for Economic Co-operation and Development, *Trust in Government: Ethics Measures in OECD Countries* (Paris: OECD, 2000), p. 9.

2.   Ekos Research Associates Inc., "Rethinking Government: Canadian View of Emerging Issues" (Ottawa: Ekos Research Associates Inc., 2000).

3.   These are considered in depth in Pew Research Center for The People & The Press, "Deconstructing Distrust: How Americans View Government" (Pew Charitable Trusts, 1999).

4.   A number of the governance issues related to new public *management* approaches are addressed in Nicholas d'Ombrain, "Alternative Service Delivery: Governance, Management and Practice," KPMG and Public Policy Forum, *Change, Governance and Public Management* (Ottawa: Public Policy Forum, 2000): 83-157.

5.   Pierre Lecomte, "Standards of Conduct in Canada's Federal *Government*: The Fight Against Cynicism" (Ottawa: Office of the Ethics Counsellor, 199), p. 5.

6.   Task Force on Conflict of Interest, *Ethical Conduct in the Public Sector* (Ottawa, 1984).

7.   See Lecomte, pp. 4-7 for an overview of a number of scandals *that* took place during the period 1976-1986.

8.   Unless otherwise stated, and for the purposes of this study, the term "public office holders" refers to those covered by the Code, including Cabinet Ministers, Secretaries of State, Parliamentary Secretaries, Ministerial Staff and Governor in Council Appointees.

9.   Howard Wilson, "The Common Ground between the Public *and* Private Sectors – Notes for a Presentation to the International Institute for Public Ethics Year 2000 Conference" (Ottawa: Office of the Ethics Counsellor, 2000).

10.   Howard Wilson, "Ethics and Government: The Canadian Experience" (Canberra: Australia and Parliamentary Orthodoxy and Other Lectures in the Senate Occasional Lecture Series, 1999).

11.   See Wilson, "Ethics and Government."

12.   "Lobbyists Registration Act, Annual Report for the year ended March 31, 1999" (Ottawa: Office of the Ethics Counsellor, 1999), p. 1.

13.   "Bridging Two Solitudes: Discussion paper on federal government-industry relations" (Ottawa: Public Policy Forum, 2000).

14.   More information is available from "Reporting Relationship of the Ethics Counsellor" (Ottawa: Office of the Ethics Counsellor, 1999).

15.   Much of this section has been based on Office of the Ethics Counsellor, "Implementing the Conflict of Interest Code: The Case of Jane Doe" (Ottawa: Minister of Public Works and Government Services Canada, 1996).

16.   Please see, for instance, "Two Liberals break ranks with party" *Ottawa Citizen* (14 February 2001), p. A-4.

17   Please see Task Force on Conflict of Interest, "Ethical Conduct in the Public Sector" (Ottawa: Minister of Supply and Services Canada, 1984).

18.   "Ethical Conduct," p. 269.

19.   Auditor General of Canada, "Report of the Auditor General of Canada to the House of Commons, Chapter 1: Ethics and Fraud Awareness in Government" (Ottawa: Public Works and Government Services Canada, 1995).

20.   Please see Special Joint Committee on a Code of Conduct of the Senate and the House of Commons, "Second Report" (Ottawa: March 1996); this was also noted in the 1984 "Ethical Conduct" report, p. 271.

21.   Ibid.

22.   Lecomte, "Standards of Conduct in Canada's Federal Government," pp. 15-16.

23.   Transparency International's Web site, located at *www.transparency.de*, provides summaries of each of its Corruption Perception Indices over the last decade.

24.   Transparency International, "Internet Corruption Perception Index," 1980-1999.

25.   See, for instance, "Chrétien isn't cleared where *it* matters," Globe and Mail (November 23, 2000), p. A18.

26.   See, for instance, Donald J. Savoie, *Governing from the Centre* (Toronto: University of Toronto Press, 1999).

27.   See, for instance, "You are your own ethics boss, Chrétien told in briefing," *Ottawa Citizen*, 24 November 2000, p. A1.

28.   *d'Ombrain*, p. 113.

29.   The early development of a public service code of conduct in New Zealand is addressed in OECD, *Trust in Government*, pp. 241-246.

30.   OECD, *Trust in Government*, pp. 144-146.

31.   English information on Finland's Parliamentary Ombudsman can be found at *http://www.eduskunta.fi/fakta/eoa/eoa.htm*. See also OECD, *Trust in Government*, pp. 141-146.

32.   Please see *http://www.oag.govt.nz* (New Zealand) and *http://www.rikisend.althingi.is* (Iceland) for further information on these agencies.

33.   OECD, Trust *in Government,* p. 179.

THE PUBLIC ETHICS COMMITTEE IN BRAZIL: EXPERIENCES, DEVELOPMENTS AND CHALLENGES

by

João Geraldo Piquet Carneiro
President of the Public Ethics Committee
Brazil

Introduction

The concern over public ethics has re-emerged as a high-priority item in the political and administrative agendas of developed democracies. In fact, the past two decades of the 20th century have made it clear that corruption -- the most visible breach in ethical standards of public conduct -- is no longer regarded as a mere "moral" problem but rather as a threat to economic order, administrative organisation, and even to the Rule of Law. If this is true for countries with a long tradition of democracy, what of countries in which the development of political institutions is more recent and less stable?

Nowadays it is generally held that what distinguishes nations or governments is not the existence of corruption, but the way corruption is confronted. Two basic challenges should figure prominently in the effort to promote ethics in the public sector. First, federal organisms should have effective means to achieve results that are in the public interest. Second, an effective standard of conduct that takes into account society's expectations must be established. Those expectations do not stop at a set of generic rules. Society demands concrete solutions and clear, objective rules of conduct.

The capacity to produce results was the main concern of programmes dating from the beginning of the 1980s that aimed to strengthen institutions and modernise organisation. Establishing an effective ethical standard has been a more recent concern, the result of an acknowledged need to do something about society's increasingly high levels of mistrust regarding the conduct of its public agents.

It is striking how organisations in the process of modernising have been blinkered when they are not working specifically to establish an effective model of ethical management. To reach that level of awareness, most of them went through at least four different phases. The main concern during the first phase was to *gain efficiency*, to do the same things better and more rapidly. In the second phase the emphasis shifted towards *efficacy*, getting the results desired by clients. The third phase was an acknowledgement that generating those results is impossible without *transparency*. During the fourth and final phase the conclusion reached was that transparent results are impossible to attain without an *ethical standard*.

Achieving adequate ethical standards in the public sector requires the involvement of the federal powers. Only through active government commitment can questionable, deep-rooted administrative practices be suppressed, or entrenched authoritarian cultures changed. In many cases this means overcoming a certain degree of hypocrisy that, at least in Brazil, has kept a new standard of relationship from developing between the private and public sectors.

Certainly changes this wide in scope cannot be effected instantly. Paradoxical as it may seem, it is more difficult to conceive a set of rules of conduct that are simple, easily managed, consistent and sufficient than to reach consensus on abstract rules. In addition, there must be an adequate corresponding *management structure* in which functions and responsibilities are well defined.

Background

Brazil has an institutional framework for ethics that is relatively old and characterised by a large number of rules. The Constitution establishes principles that guide the actions of the public administration in the federal, state and municipal governments, namely:

- The principles of legality, impersonality, morality, publicity, and efficiency.

- Public tender, as the rule for acquisitions of properties and services.

- Administrative probity, the violation of which can be punishable by temporary suspension of electoral rights, loss of public office, retention of properties and financial compensation.

The constitutional principles are almost always automatically applicable. In other words, their observance does not depend on other laws and regulations. Nevertheless, a number of laws prescribing punishment as well as administrative codes openly reaffirm the constitutional principles or make them clearer:

- Law 8112/90, that establishes a single judicial regime for civil servants.

- Law 9429/92, which characterises cases of impropriety.

- Law 9784/99, relating to administrative procedures.

- Law 86666/93, relating to public tender.

- Ethical codes for civil servants and members of the highest level of the executive branch.

The main subject areas covered by these laws and codes are:

- Improper use of public office.

- Illegal enrichment during office.

- Private interest sponsorship in public administration (trade of influences).

- Violation of secrecy.

- Use of privileged information.

- Rendering advice to a private entity.

- Professional activity parallel to public office.

- Hypothesis of conflict of interest.

- Limitations for professional activities after office (quarantine).

- Receiving gifts.

- Use of public resources and servants for private activities.

- Misappropriation of public funds or properties.

The entities responsible for managing ethics in the executive may be divided into three groups: those that deal with the ethics question in public service as their primary objective; those that have the ethics question among their objectives, although it is not the only one; or, that in an indirect form, reflex and subsidiary also work in this direction having control, supervision, and applying sanctions; and those in charge of qualifying and training civil servants to observe an ethical standard of conduct. They are the following:

- Ethic committees, foreseen in Decree 1171/94.

- The Union's General Office.

- Federal Court of Accounts

- Human resources and administrative bureaux.

- Entities in charge of qualifying and training, such as the ENAP (National School of Public Administration) and ESAF (School of Fiscal Administration).

- The Federal Control Bureau.

- The Union Audit Office.

- The Attorney General Office.

- Subject-related commissions from each of the houses of National Congress.

- Parliamentary commissions for inquiry.

- Federal police.

- Judiciary.

- And finally the citizens themselves, who have the constitutional right to bring suit against acts of corruption.

The law has established institutional rules of relationship and especially obligations of mutual communication. It has done so to enable bodies controlling ethical behaviour, as well as those responsible for managing ethics in some way, to take more effective action.

The main means of control available to these entities are:

- Audits, inspections and surveillance carried out by control bodies whose reports allow the administration to check aspects of legality, legitimacy and fund management.

- Disciplinary administrative procedures initiated by ad hoc groups and inquiry committees, to investigate instances of malfeasance.

- Public civil inquiry, initiated by the Attorney General Office.

- Ordinary suits for damage compensation, initiated by the Attorney General Office.

- Public civil suits for damage compensation, initiated by the Attorney General Office.

- Inquiries made by the federal police.

- Public penal suits initiated by the Attorney General Office.

- Administrative impropriety suits, initiated by the federal government and the Attorney General Office.

- Suits brought by ordinary citizens against injurious acts of corruption.

- Financial disclosure, mandatory for those holding public office, used to prevent illicit enrichment.

Although there is a large amount of regulation, the general perception of rules of conduct is that they are not effective. Among the reasons for this are:

- The disclosure of rules of conduct, mainly those from edited codes, has failed to make the rules common knowledge. If they are not known, how can they be carried out?

- There is no culture or structure to stimulate consultation, or to provide guidance as to the correct application of rules in practical cases.

- The qualifying and training programmes, as well as basic education, have only very recently begun incorporating ethics as a specific or linked subject.

- Investigations of malfeasance have only proved effective in entities whose structure is adequate for such investigations.

- The ability to apply sanctions is commensurate with the investigative capacity.

- Scarce information about assets and businesses of civil servants.

- It is against this background that the Public Ethics Committee was formed.

The beginnings of the PEC

The Public Ethics Committee (or PEC) was created by presidential decree on 26 May 1999, following a specific proposal by the State Council of Reform. This council has six members appointed by representatives of civil society. They are renowned for their knowledge and integrity; none are linked to the government.

The actions taken by the PEC have their source in three different remits:

1. From its creation on 26 May 1999, until 21 August 2000, its performance was restricted to consultation, by request of the President, regarding ethical questions.

2. From 21 August 2000 until 18 May 2001, following approval of the Federal Code of Conduct of High Administration, it also had executive functions and was responsible for the Code's implementation.

3. From 18 March 2001 on, in addition to these duties, it had the job of overseeing and co-ordinating the promotion of decentralised initiatives with the objective of ensuring adequacy and effectiveness in the ethical standards of entities and departments of the direct and indirect federal administration.

Strategy for action

For the Public Ethics Committee, to *practice* ethical management is to:

- Ensure that rules include the expectations of society with regard to what should be the standard of conduct of the public agent.

- Ensure that the rules are known and understood, which implies publicity, education, and orientation for a solution of ethical dilemmas.

- Monitor the practice of the rules.

- Apply an effective system of sanctions and be prepared to refine the rules if need be.

- Mobilise entities of civil society.

The strategy used to ensure an effective model of ethics in the federal executive branch was to develop these competencies in relation to a representative group with a high degree of public visibility, both in and out of the public sector: heads of state departments, national secretaries, presidents and directors of state companies, foundations, public companies, partnerships of mixed economies and civil associations. In the framework of this strategy the Federal Code of Conduct of High Administration, or FCCHA, was later developed. The President gave the PEC responsibility for its implementation.

The FCCHA establishes the duty to give information about assets, income, and situations that might bring about a conflict of interest. Those who have this duty are persons in the representative categories mentioned above, plus regulatory agencies and officers of State-owned companies. In addition, it imposes limits on exercising professional activities while and after (quarantine and interdiction) holding public office. Limits are also extended to acts of management of assets and investments and it is forbidden to receive favours of any nature from interested parties.

High-level employees linked to the FCCHA cannot invest in businesses of which they might have privileged knowledge of revenue, nor can they accept transportation, lodging, and other favours that might give rise to a conflict of interest.

Implementing the FCCHA

Employees linked to the FCCHA must adhere to the rules at the moment of taking office. Up to ten days later they must present to the Public Ethics Committee the "Confidential Declaration of Information -- CDI" with data about income, estates, and private interests that might bring about conflicts while in office.

In the course of office each person must inform the PEC of any changes in the information they have provided as well as sending other information, such as job proposals, participation in companies that negotiate with public powers, etc.

To help carry out its mission, the PEC counts on an Executive Bureau that has six members, the support of 135 representatives of sectors within the Federal Executive, a computerised system that helps with monitoring activities, and direct mail.

With time, new and more easily managed tools are being made available to contact PEC and employees: a Web site on the internet (*http://www.presidencia.gov.br/etica*), where useful information about the application of FCCHA can be accessed; electronic mail; and an opportunity to present the CDI electronically.

Until June 2001, PEC issued an average of 500 orientations and 50 notifications per month. By the end of September the average number of orientations remained unchanged, while there was a slight decrease in the number of notifications: about 40 per month. About 5% of authorities subject to the FCCHA still have difficulty complying with the basic FCCHA rule: handing in their CDI up to 10 days after taking office. In spite of permanent reiterations, the 5% figure has held steady, in a demonstration that the information system still needs improvement.

While most of the rules that the FCCHA establishes are in fact prohibitions, the Code nevertheless plays an important part in defending the employees linked to it. It affords them the tranquillity necessary for the full exercise of their functions, removing the risk of accusations about their private ethical conduct. There are examples to show that this second but no less important role of the FCCHA is becoming more understood and appreciated. At least three authorities from the top level of employees and several others have appealed to the PEC for a statement of position on specific conduct that was being questioned. In all of these cases, after PEC stated its position, the questioning about ethical conduct diminished.

Working with entities and departments of the federal government

On 18 May 2001, in accordance with presidential decree, the PEC established relations with all agencies and departments of the federal direct and indirect administration, and not just the top officers. This was done to reach its ultimate objective, the promotion of ethics in public administration.

Upon analyses of these entities and departments, a general picture began to emerge based on many specific ethics management initiatives and characteristics. However, there was no constant correlation between the entities that are more susceptible to ethical malfeasance and those more often involved in ethics initiatives. There is therefore wide room for short-term developments. According to the research:

- 31% of the entities and departments have specific rules to regulate the conduct of their staff.

- 26% develop educational activities for the rules of conduct that exist.

- 23% monitor how the rules of conduct are followed.

- 20% applied sanctions for transgressions in the 24 months preceding the research (which was carried out during the first half of 2001).

In September 2001, the PEC organised a meeting with representatives from the sectors of the federal executive branch. During the meeting the best measures for managing ethics, both in and outside Brazil, were discussed, and strategic recommendations promoting ethics were proposed. The papers presented during this meeting, as well as their conclusions, are available to the public on the PEC Web site.

With sector representatives now nominated in 135 entities and departments of the federal direct and indirect administration, a network of professionals has been formed. These professionals are responsible for ensuring that (above all, preventive) action is taken to promote ethics: publicising and providing orientation for the rules of conduct that must be observed, organising educational activities, monitoring, and proposing corrective measures.

The work of the PEC has relied on the help of important partners -- some of them international or non-governmental entities -- that offer aid for specific actions at no cost. These partners are:

- The UN, OECD, and Inter-American Development Bank (BID). The partnership with BID is evolving toward financial support (in addition to existing technical support), which will probably be provided following formal approval of a specific project that also involves the Union's General Office.

- The ETHOS Institute and *Transparência Brasil* (Brazil Transparency).

- About 20 voluntary workers (professionals and organisations) that systematically support the PEC and help it achieve successful diagnosis and analysis.

The PEC's next steps will be closely linked to the strategic objectives defined by the meeting with sector representatives. These are recommendations from the President himself, who determined they should be put into effect by all directors of the entities and departments of the federal direct and indirect administration.

- Improve the system of managing ethics by improving and refining rules and administrative structures, promoting education, stimulating co-operation, and creating mechanisms for protection of civil servants against persecution or discrimination related to their involvement in ethical work.

- Identify society's expectations in relation to the management of public ethics, and implement a communication plan.

- Establish mechanisms for promoting transparency.

- Implement evaluation mechanisms.

The Second Meeting of Sector Representatives with the PEC took place on 21 and 22 March 2002. That meeting evaluated the progress made in implementing the recommendations previously established.

Lessons learned from the PEC experience

- Rules will not magically alter habits and conduct if they do not have the support of society and an adequate administrative structure.

- Those who do not have an effective set of rules of conduct do not have an objective ethical reference. However, an ethical code must not be seen as useful only for the "unethical". The opposite is more likely to be true.

- The effectiveness of these rules is directly related to how well they are known and understood, as well as to political support and the commitment of leadership.

- To practice management of ethics is essentially to develop actions directed towards the understanding of rules of conduct and the spread of knowledge of how to apply them to solve ethical dilemmas.

- A great challenge in the management of ethics is to adequately balance preventive and repressive actions.

Over the next year the biggest challenge will be to lay a foundation that is strong enough in political and managerial terms so as to avoid discontinuity of the current efforts and hopefully expand them to other spheres of government.

MANAGING CONFLICTS OF INTEREST AT THE FEDERAL LEVEL IN THE UNITED STATES

by

Jane S. Ley

Deputy Director, United States Office of Government Ethics

Summary

The United States has moved from managing conflicts of interest through primarily reactive criminal prosecutions to a proactive training, education and counselling programme. The focus is on criminal, civil and administrative standards, and the detection and resolution of potential conflicts of interest using financial disclosure reports. Underpinning this proactive programme is an effective enforcement system with a range of penalties.

The rights of employees to fair notice of the standards to which they will be held accountable undoubtedly contributes to making the system for managing conflicts appear heavily rule-based in the United States. These rules, however, flow from fundamental principles of public service that embody aspirational goals. It is the task of conveying to employees both the ideals those goals represent and enforceable standards that makes the programme challenging and vibrant.

Introduction

Each of the three branches of the federal government of the United States -- executive, legislative and judicial -- has designed programmes to manage conflicts of interest on the part of the individual officers and employees of that branch. All of those programmes have similar elements, but the executive branch programme is highlighted in this chapter because it is the most extensive. While these ethics programmes focus on individual integrity, they function within a larger framework of systems that are designed to promote institutional integrity.

Key elements designed to support *institutional integrity* include: an independent judiciary; open, public legislative processes following standardised procedures with a written, public record; executive offices charged with conducting effective investigations and prosecutions; open judicial, administrative and contracting processes (again) following public, standardised procedures with written public records; public appropriation and budgeting processes; a generally merit-based civil service with adequate pay, training and standardised processes for imposing disciplinary sanctions or protecting employees from reprisal; public rights of access to government proceedings, documents and information; and checks and balances of power across the three branches. In addition, the government functions under the eye of an engaged civil society and free press.

Building upon those institutional systems, the three branches of the United States Government have developed programmes to prevent, address and manage individual conflicts of interest -- as well as the appearance of those conflicts, as mentioned in the following section. The common elements of these programmes include:

1) A body of *enforceable standards* comprising complementary criminal statutes (applying to both the government official and any private party working in association with the official), civil ethics statutes and administrative codes of conduct based upon core public service concepts.

2) Public and, within the executive branch, confidential *financial disclosure systems* that are designed to identify and then to address potential conflicts of interest defined by the statutes and regulations comprising the standards.

3) Systematic *training and counselling* services available to officers and employees regarding all restrictions; and

4) Effective enforcement mechanisms.

Most of the elements contained in these programmes have evolved over the last thirty years. Experiences during this period have led to fundamental changes in the programmes, and will undoubtedly lead to more.

Building frameworks: shifting the emphasis from prosecution to prevention

Prior to the 1960s the United States addressed conflicts of interest of its federal officers and employees (including judges) almost exclusively through *criminal statutes* and proceedings. As a particular scandal developed, new conflict laws were enacted to address it. Scandals involving officials making unfounded claims against the government treasury or personally profiting during the US. Civil War (1860s) from contracts for goods that never arrived or were defective, gave rise to a series of criminal laws designed to prohibit government officials (and those who colluded with them) from personally profiting by their involvement in government decisions and processes. The same basic prohibitions that arose from those scandals remain in effect today.

In the early 1960s there was renewed interest in public service as a respected profession, generated in part by the election rhetoric of President John F. Kennedy. This brought increased attention to the relationships that should exist between government employees and the public, and resulted in two major changes. First, the individual criminal statutes dealing with conflicts of interest were re-enacted together in one chapter of the criminal code, and standardised terms were used throughout the provisions. Second, the Kennedy Administration embarked on a project to establish an administrative (non-criminal) code of conduct for executive branch officials that addressed not only actual conflicts of interest but also activities that give rise to the *appearance* of such conflicts. This approach was based upon a belief that the public's trust in the government was damaged whenever it appeared that a conflict of interest had occurred. Thus began a shift in focus from simply criminal prohibitions to more preventive and aspirational standards.

In 1965, following President Kennedy's assassination, President Johnson issued Executive Order 11222 which set forth six basic principles of public service and some specific restrictions regarding gifts and other activities. The Civil Service Commission (now called the Office of Personnel Management) developed a model regulation for executive branch agencies to use in developing their own regulatory standards of conduct based on the executive order. Each agency was then responsible for interpreting and enforcing its own standards. While the Civil Service Commission did have a limited role, there really was no centralised authority responsible for ensuring consistency of the programme throughout the branch. Not surprisingly, over the next 15-20 years it became apparent that while the words of each agency's standards were similar, the application by individual agencies differed greatly.

After the Watergate scandal, a number of good governance measures were enacted in an effort to help restore the public's confidence in the government. One such measure, found in the 1978 Ethics in Government Act, was the creation of the *Office of Government Ethics*. OGE is responsible for the overall direction of executive branch policies related to preventing conflicts of interest. A small agency, OGE leveraged its position by building upon the then current responsibilities of each agency head. OGE began by re-enforcing the concept that each head was ultimately responsible for the ethics programme of his or her agency. However, it then required each head to appoint an ethics official and provide sufficient resources so that that official (and any additional necessary staff) could carry out the day-to-day activities of an ethics programme composed of elements specified by OGE. As a part of its oversight responsibilities, OGE periodically reviews agency ethics programmes to ensure that they are carried out within a consistent framework. It is through this network of ethics officials that OGE began working and continues to work to bring some consistency to the programme within the branch.

In 1989, President George H.W. Bush issued Executive Order 12674 setting forth 14 *fundamental principles* of ethical service (see Box below). The order directed OGE to write "a single, comprehensive, and clear set of executive branch standards of conduct that shall be objective, reasonable, and enforceable". In carrying out this directive, OGE made a conscious decision to move from the more limited regulations developed in the 1960s to more extensive, detailed regulatory standards that addressed core subjects much more specifically. The subjects chosen were those that raised the most questions based upon agencies' years of experience with the application and enforcement of the earlier standards and criminal statutes. Each section of the standards was followed by examples of its application.[1]

The change was intended to help make interpretation among the agencies consistent; to provide more actual concrete examples and thus increase awareness among employees subject to the standards; and, importantly, to create *one set of written "government ethics" standards* that, if followed, would prevent an employee from inadvertently violating a criminal conflict of interest or civil ethics statute. In drafting the standards, every attempt was made to ensure that an employee who followed the standards would need not fear that his or her conduct was in violation of a civil or criminal ethics statute. On the other hand, an employee who chose to act in significant violation of the standards would also run the risk of his or her conduct triggering an underlying criminal statute. For example, depending upon the facts, accepting or soliciting a "gift" might actually be viewed as accepting a bribe or engaging in extortion; misusing government resources might actually be criminal conversion of government property.

The standards were drafted, reviewed internally within the executive branch and published for public comment. OGE received over 1 000 comments from interested parties. These comments were addressed in writing in a preamble when the final regulation was published in August 1992. The effective date of the regulation (standards of conduct) was six months beyond publication in order to give agencies time to make their employees aware of the new code and its provisions.

These administrative standards of conduct have now been in effect for nine years. When they were new, agencies properly focused their training resources on the requirements they contained as a minimum level of acceptable conduct. Given the passage of time, employees are now expected to be more comfortable with the standards, and OGE is exploring ways to raise the level of discourse from simple compliance to *aspiring to the highest principles* on which those standards are based.

The administrative standards of conduct are not the only aspect of the ethics programme that has changed since the 1960s. As a part of the 1989 Ethics Reform Act, the criminal statutes were amended to include the options of civil and injunctive authority. Previously, a statutory conflict of interest could only have been charged as a felony or a misdemeanour; now civil actions could be brought and injunctions sought for the same conduct, giving prosecutors a wider range of options to address statutory violations.[2] In addition, Congress enacted some civil ethics restrictions applicable to high-level officials of all three branches that limit outside earned income, compensated and uncompensated service in certain fiduciary positions, and the receipt of honoraria. These restrictions were enacted in conjunction with a significant pay rise to relieve the pressure to accept private compensation in order to meet the expenses of living and working in Washington.[3]

Thus, over the last 40 years the US Federal Government has moved away from purely criminal conflict of interest restrictions as the only standard governing public service. Now there are civil "ethics" restrictions primarily dealing with outside activities that produce compensation; conflict of interest statutes that provide the prosecutor with criminal or civil options for penalties; and, in the executive branch, comprehensive administrative standards of conduct designed to be a single source of guidance to employees with regard to all conflicts and ethics restrictions.

Elements of the executive branch ethics programme

The elements of the executive branch ethics programme include a core of enforceable statutory and regulatory standards; systems for publicly available and confidential financial disclosure reports; systematic training and counselling; and a functioning enforcement system.

Enforceable standards

"Conflict of interest" is not defined as a single term in the laws and regulations that make up the core restrictions and ethics principles applicable to officers and employees of the executive branch. Rather, a variety of circumstances, described by individual statutes and regulations, can create a conflict of interest.

The *criminal conflict of interest prohibitions* (which have their bases in laws over a century old) apply to the following types of conduct:

- The acceptance or demand by and/or the payment to a public official of something of value in exchange for an official act, for or because of an official act, or for certain witness fees (bribery and criminal gratuities restrictions of 18 US.C. § 201).

- The acceptance of and/or payment to an officer or employee of compensation for representations made by the officer or employee in an unofficial capacity or by another to any federal agency or court in a matter in which the United States has an interest (18 US.C. § 203).

- Uncompensated representations by certain officers or employees in an unofficial capacity to any federal agency or court on a matter in which the United States has an interest, and the payment to and acceptance by an officer or employee of compensation for assisting another in a claim against the United States (18 US.C. § 205).

An executive branch employee's taking an official action in a particular matter in which:

- The employee.

- The employee's spouse.

- The employee's minor child.

- The employee's general partner.

- An organisation in which the employee serves as an officer, director, general partner, trustee or employee; or

- An organisation with whom the employee is negotiating or has an arrangement for future employment

has a financial interest (the criminal self-dealing restriction of 18 US.C. § 208).

- The acceptance of and/or payment to an executive branch officer or employee of any salary or salary supplement as compensation for official duties (18 US.C. § 209).

- The representation of others before the government by former executive and legislative branch officers or employees on a variety of matters (the post-employment restrictions of 18 US.C. § 207).

Conduct that violates these restrictions may be prosecuted criminally as a felony or a misdemeanour with possible incarceration and/or monetary fines, or as a civil case with only monetary fines.

The *civil ethics statutes* have a much more recent history. They were enacted in response to concerns for the outside compensated activities of Members of Congress, judges and the most senior non-career executive and legislative branch officers and employees. The most recent version of the restrictions was imposed in conjunction with a substantial pay rise for these senior officials. Restrictions include:

- A limitation on the amount of income that can be "earned" outside of government duties by these senior officials (currently that amount is USD 22 500)(5 US.C. app. § 501).

- A prohibition on the receipt of any compensation for:
    - affiliating or being employed by a firm, partnership, association or other entity that provides professional services involving a fiduciary relationship;
    - permitting one's name to be used (even without compensation) by any such firm, partnership, association, corporation or other entity;
    - practising a profession that involves a fiduciary relationship;
    - serving as an officer or other member of the board of any association, corporation or other entity; or

- teaching without the prior notification and approval of the appropriate government ethics oversight body (5 US.C. app. § 502).

A statutory prohibition on the receipt of honoraria by any government official (enacted at the same time as the two noted above) was held unconstitutional by the Supreme Court, as the law would apply to a certain class of employees. Based upon the written opinion of the Court, the Department of Justice determined that the prohibition was also unenforceable as to employees outside this class. The restriction remains as a rule of the United States House of Representatives and the United States Senate.

The administrative Standards of Conduct for Employees of the Executive Branch are based upon *14 Principles of Ethical Conduct* set forth in Executive Order 12674. These standards replaced those based upon Executive Order 11222 of 1965. A President may issue executive orders concerning conduct based on his authority granted by the Constitution over the officers and employees of the executive branch. The principles from Executive Order 12674 are shown in Box 1:

The standards of conduct derived from those principles are enforced by administrative sanction that can include reprimand, suspension, demotion or dismissal. Employees are also directed to continue to apply the principles in situations that may not clearly be covered by the standards, and the principles are made a part of the standards. The specific subjects covered by the standards of conduct are:

- Gifts from outside sources.

- Gifts between employees.

- Conflicting financial interests.

- Impartiality in performing official duties.

- Seeking other employment.

- Misuse of position, which includes:
    - use of public office for private gain,
    - use of non-public information,
    - use of government property, and
    - use of official time.
- Outside activities.

Box 1. General principles

1. Public service is a public trust, requiring employees to place loyalty to the Constitution, the laws, and ethical principles above private gain.

2. Employees shall not hold financial interests that conflict with the conscientious performance of duty.

3. Employees shall not engage in financial transactions using non-public government information or allow the improper use of such information to further any private interest.

4. An employee shall not, except pursuant to such reasonable exceptions as are provided by [OGE] regulation, solicit or accept any gift or other item of monetary value from any person or entity seeking official action from, doing business with, or conducting activities regulated by the employee's agency, or whose interests may be substantially affected by the performance or non-performance of the employee's duties.

5. Employees shall put forth honest effort in the performance of their duties.

6. Employees shall not knowingly make unauthorised commitments or promises of any kind purporting to bind the government.

7. Employees shall not use public office for private gain.

8. Employees shall act impartially and not give preferential treatment to any private organisation or individual.

9. Employees shall protect and conserve federal property and shall not use it for other than authorised activities.

10. Employees shall not engage in outside employment or activities, including seeking or negotiating for employment, that conflict with official government duties and responsibilities.

11. Employees shall disclose waste, fraud, abuse, and corruption to appropriate authorities.

12. Employees shall satisfy in good faith their obligations as citizens, including all just financial obligations, especially those – such as federal, state, or local taxes – that are imposed by law.

13. Employees shall adhere to all laws and regulations that provide equal opportunity for all Americans regardless of race, colour, religion, sex, national origin, age, or handicap.

14. Employees shall endeavour to avoid any actions creating the appearance that they are violating the law or the ethical standards promulgated pursuant to this order.

The standards of conduct were written with the goal of providing executive branch employees with one source of guidance that, if followed, would help the employee avoid a violation of the criminal and civil statutes listed previously.

In addition to the standards of conduct that are applicable to every executive branch employee, agencies could, with the approval of the Office of Government Ethics, develop more specific restrictions for all or a portion of those employees. The following are examples of *mission-related conduct restrictions* that have been approved:

- *Customs employees* may not be employed by a customs broker, international carrier, bonded warehouse, foreign trade zone, carts man[4] or law firm engaged in the practice of customs law or the importation department of a business, nor be employed in any private capacity related to the importation or exportation of merchandise (5 C.F.R. § 3101.110).

- *Tax officials* of the Internal Revenue Service (IRS):

  - shall not recommend, refer or suggest any attorney or accountant (or firm of either) to any person(s) in connection with any official business which may/involves the IRS, and

  - may not be involved in the following types of outside employment or business activities which are prohibited and shall constitute a conflict with the employee's official duties:

    1. Performance of legal services involving federal, state or local tax matters.

    2. Appearing on behalf of any taxpayer as a representative before any federal, state or local government agency in an action involving a tax matter, except with the written authorisation of the head of the IRS.

    3. Engaging in accounting, or the use, analysis and interpretation of financial records when such activity involves tax matters.

    4. Engaging in bookkeeping, the recording of transactions or the record-making phase of accounting when such activity is directly related to a tax determination.

    5. Engaging in the preparation of tax returns in exchange for compensation, gift or favour. (5 C.F.R. § 3101.106)

- *Prosecutors* and other officers and employees of the Department of Justice may not engage in outside employment that involves:

    1. The practice of law, unless it is uncompensated and in the nature of community service, or unless it is on behalf of himself, spouse, children or parents.

    2. Any criminal or habeas corpus matter, be it federal, state or local.

    3. Litigation, investigations, grants or other matters in which the Department of Justice is or represents a party, witness, litigant, investigator or grant-maker.

The statute and regulations noted above are not the sole sources of restrictions or guidance for the performance of official duties. Quite the contrary, there are a significant number of statutes and regulations directed at ensuring that employees do not engage in activities that will undermine the full and proper exercise of their official duties. They are administered as a part of the complementary systems that support the ethics programme. A selected listing of subjects covered by other prohibitions follows:

- Fraud or false statements in a government matter.

- Acceptance or solicitation of anything of value to obtain appointive public office for another.

- Acting as an agent of a foreign principal.

- Embezzling, stealing, purloining or converting public money, property or records.

- Disclosure of classified, proprietary and other confidential information.

- Lobbying with appropriated money.

- Failing to account for public money.

- Solicitation of political contributions under certain circumstances.

- Misuse of government-paid postage.

- Counterfeiting or forging transportation requests.

- Concealing, mutilating or destroying a public record.

- Unauthorised use of documents relating to claims from or by the government.

- Interference with civil service examinations.

- Maintaining, disclosing or requesting or obtaining certain personal records under certain circumstances.

- Disloyalty and striking (suitability and conduct provisions of the law dealing with government organisation and employees).

- Excessive use of intoxicating beverages (suitability and conduct provisions of the law dealing with government organisation and employees).

- Misuse of appropriated funds or government vehicles (appropriations law).

- Political activities (Hatch Act Reform Amendments).

- Retaliation against whistleblowers (Whistleblower Protection Act).

- Participation in the appointment or promotion of relatives (anti-nepotism statute).

- Arbitrary and capricious withholding of public records (Freedom of Information Act).

While it is critical that government officials have standards of duty owed to the public, the burden of governmental processes free from taint is not borne solely by the government official. Those in the *private sector* who deal with the government must also adhere to certain standards. As noted above, many of the criminal conflict of interest statutes, 18 US.C. §§ 201-209 as well as many others, apply to the conduct of the private sector individual or organisation dealing in association with the government employee. Further, under the Federal Sentencing Guidelines, private sector entities found guilty of illegal conduct may receive reduced sentences if they have an established ethics programme recognised under the federal requirements. Many private sector entities have established these programmes as a consequence. In addition, the Foreign Corrupt Practices Act established in 1977, prohibits US corporations from paying bribes to foreign public officials. The prohibitions contained in that Act provide guidance to the private sector on what kinds of activities are impermissible in their dealings with foreign officials.

Publicly available and confidential financial disclosure reports

Executive Order 11222 of 1965, which established the first administrative standards of conduct, also required high-level executive branch officials to file *confidential financial disclosure reports* with the Civil Service Commission. In addition, the Commission was directed to issue regulations requiring confidential financial disclosure reports from other agency employees in order to help determine potential, actual or apparent conflicts of interest of the officers and employees. Each agency initially collected and reviewed these forms before sending copies of the senior officials' forms to the Commission. And, like the first standards of conduct, agencies managed this programme in differing ways. Some agencies collected the reports and used them constructively to help counsel employees on how to avoid potential conflicts that were disclosed on the reports. Other agencies failed to collect or to properly review the reports, or to use them as a counselling tool.

This experience was one of the considerations of Congress when, as a part of the 1978 Ethics in Government Act, it enacted the statutory requirement that high-level officials of all three branches file *publicly available financial disclosure reports*. The publicly available financial disclosure report was intended and continues to:

- Increase public confidence in government.

- Demonstrate the high level of integrity of the vast majority of government officials.

- Deter conflicts of interest from arising because official activities would be subject to public scrutiny.

- Deter persons whose personal finances would not bear public scrutiny from entering public service.

- Better enable the public to judge the performance of public officials in light of an official's outside financial interests.

The information required to be reported is quite specifically set out by law, and the information requested is directly related to conflict of interest statutes or regulations.[5] In general, however, the information required to be reported, with minimum threshold triggers, is as follows:

- *Sources and amounts of income,* both earned (by exact amount) and investment (by specific categories of amount).

- *Assets* and their values reported by categories of amount.

- *Liabilities,* their terms and the highest amounts owed during the reporting period, reported by categories of amount.

- *Gifts and reimbursements* accepted during government service with their values or amounts.

- *Fiduciary and employment positions* held outside the government with the dates the positions have been held.

- *Agreements and arrangements* regarding future employment, leaves of absence, continuing payments from or participation in a benefits plan of a former employer, with dates and details.

- For first reports only, the names of *major clients* (persons or organisations for whom personal services were performed for compensation in excess of a specified threshold amount).

The filer must also report assets, certain income, liabilities and some gifts of the filer's spouse and dependent children. The publicly available reports are filed upon entry into government service, annually thereafter, and upon termination of government service. There are approximately 20 000 filers of public reports within the executive branch alone.

The public financial disclosure requirement is also used as a *preventive measure* in the confirmation process of the President's nominees to the highest positions in the executive branch. Each of the nominees is required to file a publicly available financial disclosure report no later than five days after nomination. In practice the forms are filed quite early with the White House and are a factor in the President's decision whether to nominate the individual for a particular position. The forms are shared by the White House, OGE and the agency in which the individual would serve. When the individual is nominated, the agency conducts a final review and forwards a copy to OGE, who then certifies the form and sends an opinion letter to the Senate. OGE recognised this as an opportunity to review with the agency and the White House the financial holdings and relationships of a nominee, and to require the nominee to agree to take whatever steps are necessary to avoid potential conflicts before he or she assumes the new position. These steps, explained more fully later, can include divestiture, resignation from outside positions, recusal, waiver or a blind trust.

The critical step OGE took in 1979, one not clearly set forth in the financial disclosure statute, was to work with each of the Senate confirming committees to ensure that OGE could complete this review before the Senate confirmed the individual. Doing so offered two advantages. The first was time; normally, confirmation must occur before appointment. The second was consistency. Historically, each Senate confirming committee had made its own decisions about financial conflicts, and not necessarily based upon applicable laws and regulations. By providing its analysis and opinion to the committees, OGE could shoulder more of this responsibility and the committees could focus on suitability rather than financial conflicts. Thus, OGE's review and opinion have become an integral part of the confirmation/appointment process, and new appointees are now aware before they take office of the conflict of interest requirements to which they must adhere. This process is one of the most important conflict prevention tools for senior-level officials available in the programme.

Public financial reporting helps ensure that every citizen can have confidence in the integrity of the most senior officials of the federal government. However, in order to further guarantee the efficient and honest operation of the government, the executive branch continues to require other, less senior employees whose duties involve the exercise of significant discretion in certain sensitive areas to report, on a confidential basis, their financial interests and outside business activities to their employing agencies. These confidential reports facilitate the agency's review of possible conflicts of interest and provide a vehicle on which to base individualised ethics counselling and training.

Approximately 275 000 individuals file financial disclosure reports on a confidential basis throughout the executive branch.

The declaration of a financial interest or an affiliation does not in itself resolve a conflicting situation. Additional steps must be taken, including:

- *Divestiture:* an official agrees to dispose of a conflicting interest, such as selling an asset or returning a gift. Officials are expected to decline gifts or benefits that either raise or appear to raise conflict of interest issues, or voluntarily return gifts that are problematic.

- *Waiver* of the potential conflict if the government determines in a public, written document that the financial interest is not so substantial as to be deemed likely to affect the services of the individual in a given matter, or that the matter's effect on the employee's financial interest is too remote or too inconsequential.

- *Transfer of duty:* officials can either recuse themselves (non-participation) on an individual matter or can be reassigned to a new position.

- *Resignation:* an official may be requested to resign from a private position in order to continue to act in matters that may affect the organisation; or, in rare instances, an official may decide to refrain from government employment or resign in order to retain a private position.

- *Voluntary blind trust*: placing all financial assets under the trusteeship of a neutral third party pursuant to strict OGE guidelines.

A very important feature of the procedures used to resolve conflict of interest situations is their attempt to ensure the *transparency* and scrutiny of decisions. When the government determines to "waive" a conflict, it is done through a written public document. If an individual agrees to recuse on certain matters and the agreement is put in writing, that document is generally publicly available (as are most documents supporting executive branch decisions). The transparency of the system empowers the public to exercise their rights as citizens and contributes to a culture of accountability and integrity that is integral to democratic governance. Another basic characteristic of the system is that the financial disclosure report is a basis upon which employees may be given personalised training and counselling.

While prevention of conflicts is a significant purpose of collecting and reviewing these disclosure reports, the reports can also be used to help in prosecutions of individuals who have violated conflicts or other statutes. In some instances, the employee will disclose information that, on the face of it, indicates a violation of a statute or regulation. The form is then used as a basis for further investigation and for possible prosecution. In other instances, information will become available about activities and interests of the employee that a subsequent investigation reveals the employee has intentionally failed to report properly. In those cases, the employee can be charged criminally with knowingly filing a false statement on the financial disclosure report. This charge would be in addition to whatever other charges might be involved; it is especially useful when the proof of the underlying illicit act is difficult to obtain or prove in a court proceeding, while the proof of the false statement on the report is not.

Systematic training and counselling

One of the real strengths of the ethics programme of the executive branch is the systematic training of employees with regard to the regulatory standards and the conflict of interest statutes. In the executive branch, agencies are required to provide this training to the highest-level officials once a year. All new employees must be given an opportunity to familiarise themselves with the standards of conduct when entering government service. In addition, every agency has an ethics official or officials available in person, over the telephone, or via email to answer any questions employees might have about application of the statutes or standards. Supervisors and managers are also available to help direct an employee to the designated ethics officials. Employees who in good faith seek advice from these ethics officials and follow that advice (even if the advice turns out to be wrong) will not suffer any penalty for their conduct. This aspect of the programme is intended to encourage employees to ask questions before they engage in conduct about which they are unsure.

In a recent survey of a cross-section of executive branch employees, OGE found that employees who had received ethics training were more aware of the ethics requirements and more apt to seek guidance when questions arose. Not surprisingly, the survey showed that employees judged the ethical culture of their agencies by the actions of their immediate supervisors and their executive leadership.[6] To OGE this was a clear indication that more training resources should be directed to those in supervisory positions.

Experience has also shown that as training increases, so does the use of counselling services; the two go hand in hand. The training sessions are intended to raise the consciousness of employees to the issues that can pose questions of conflict. If the employee subsequently has a question that is not clearly answered to his or her satisfaction by the written standards, the employee is strongly encouraged to seek assistance from an agency ethics counsellor prior to engaging in the conduct that is of concern. Individual employee counselling is provided primarily at the agency level, where there is likely to be a more direct understanding of the employee's responsibilities in the programmes administered by the agency. (OGE's training and counselling, which is more detailed and specific, is primarily provided to agency ethics officials.)

Effective enforcement mechanisms

Each agency has the primary responsibility of determining which measures should be applied to resolve a potential (future) conflict of interest on the part of an employee in that agency. Agencies must also seek an appropriate investigation where a conflicting act on the part of the official has already occurred.

The criminal and civil statutes and the standards of conduct are enforced using *standard procedures* that are not unique to these restrictions and did not have to be designed specifically for them. When confronted with an allegation of abuse, the agency can turn to its independent Inspector General (IG) for investigation or, if the agency is small and without an IG, it can make arrangements to "borrow" an investigator from another agency. An agency can also refer potential criminal conduct to the Department of Justice for investigation. If an official engages in misconduct that violates only the administrative standards of ethical conduct for executive branch employees, the agency is responsible for instituting administrative penalties against the official according to standard procedures. If the misconduct violates a civil or criminal statute, the Department of Justice is responsible for pursuing those matters through the courts. An official may be subject to both administrative and civil or criminal sanctions for the same conduct.

Prior to 1989, only the most serious cases were prosecuted; less serious violations of the criminal conflicts laws were not pursued for reasons related to such things as balancing prosecution resources and jury appeal. With the 1989, addition of civil penalties and injunctive relief, and with the proactive ethics programme having been in existence for ten years, the Department of Justice began to pursue more conflict allegations. Faced with the real possibility that actions would be brought against them, individuals under investigation began offering to settle the cases with a civil monetary payment. The payment was determined with reference to the amount of the fine that could have been imposed upon a finding of guilty. Each settlement concluded with a written public statement containing both the government's and the employee's views of the employee's conduct. These settlements achieved timely disposal of issues that might otherwise have required lengthy and complex investigations. They also have had the salutary affect of indicating to the public and to employees that the statutes are to be taken seriously. Furthermore, they provide an extremely useful tool in educating employees, using specific cases often involving identifiable high-level officials.

There are *reporting systems* among agencies involved in prevention, investigation and prosecution efforts for conflict of interest enforcement. In some instances, this information is made available to the public. The media play an active role in informing the public of the results of investigations into these matters and the prosecutions of officials. Each year OGE also publishes a description of all prosecutions as well as all civil settlements. That document is sent to all ethics officials and posted on OGE's Web site for public review.[7]

The regulatory standards of conduct are enforced administratively by the agency in which the employee serves, using standard procedures that must be followed in order to take any disciplinary action against the employee.[8] It is also possible to impose civil penalties and take measures such as injunctive relief and the cancellation of the affected decision (as determined by various statutes – for example, 18 US.C. § 218). The standards of conduct do not have to include a detailed enforcement mechanism; they simply refer to the existing system for taking disciplinary actions against employees. Enforcement authority has consciously been made the responsibility of the head of each agency as an effective management tool, and as a way of holding the head of the agency accountable for its standards. OGE reviews each agency's ethics programme generally on a four to five year cycle to determine whether it is being carried out properly.

Recent developments: challenges and directions

The widening variety of financial investment instruments and the diverse business lines within individual corporations continue to raise new issues when determining whether a particular financial investment will create a conflict with the duties of the official who might own it. In addition, the desire to downsize the government continues to create tensions with the conflict of interest statutes. Those in the government who might well be in the best position to help it contract or devolve certain of its responsibilities may also be in the best position to carry out those responsibilities in the private sector. This creates an inherent tension: questions of objectivity (when officials whose jobs will be affected are allowed to make the decisions) or competence (when they are not and others step in to make the decisions) can frequently arise.

Conflict of interest policy and guidance has also been affected by litigation. Long-standing statutes and an OGE regulation have been challenged as unconstitutional or as misapplied in a prosecution, and have resulted in court opinions requiring a change in guidance and/or regulation. This includes litigation involving honoraria, criminal gratuities (as opposed to the OGE gift rules, which were not affected), and travel expenses reimbursed to employees for trips to speak unofficially about their areas of official responsibilities.

In 2000, as a part of the Presidential Transition Act, Congress requested that the Office of Government Ethics review the Presidential nominee process. In its report, OGE made specific recommendations regarding changes in the public financial disclosure law that would reduce strictly technical aspects of the public reporting system without diminishing programme effectiveness. The Administration, through OGE, submitted those recommendations as proposed legislation in Summer 2001, and a bill that included a substantial portion of those recommendations was introduced. That bill is still pending in Congress.

Finally, the Office of Government Ethics has also publicly committed to undertake a study of the criminal conflict of interest statutes as they apply to the executive branch to determine if they need to be revised to more accurately reflect the needs of today's government and the public interest. OGE is also studying new ways of measuring the effectiveness of the executive branch ethics programme. In short, that programme -- while maintaining core requirements -- continues to adapt and to change, based upon experience.

NOTES

1. The Standards of Ethical Conduct for Employees of the Executive Branch are found in Part 2635 of Title 5 of the Code of Federal Regulations. These standards together with the examples can be accessed on OGE's Web site *at www.usoge.gov/pages/forms_pubs_otherdocs/forms_pubs_other_pg2.html.*

2. These conflict of interest statutes can be accessed at *www.usoge.gov/pages/laws_regs_fedreg_stats/statutes.html.*

3. 5 US.C. App § 501 et seq.

4 A bonded carrier that is generally licensed by Customs for transporting goods under Custom's authority.

5. The forms currently used in the executive branch for public financial disclosure reports and confidential financial disclosure reports can be accessed on OGE's Web site at *www.usoge.gov/pages/forms_pubs_otherdocs/forms_pubs_other_pg3.htm.*

6. The full results of this survey and a copy of the survey instrument can be found on OGE's Web site at *www.usoge.gov/pages/daeograms/dgr_files/2001/do01007.pdf.*

7. Conflict of Interest Prosecution Surveys can be viewed at *http://www.usoge.gov/pages/laws_regs_fedreg_stats/other_ethics_guidance.html.*

8. Administrative sanctions for a violation of the standards of conduct can include reprimand reassignment, suspension, demotion or dismissal.

CAN NEW TECHNOLGIES BE A SOLUTION?
CONFLICTS OF INTEREST CASES IN ARGENTINA

by

Nicolás R. S. Raigorodsky
Manager for Legal Affairs,
Anti-Corruption Office, Ministry of Justice and Human Rights
Argentina

If policy to prevent conflict of interest is to be effective, it must address two major issues. One has to do with the collection and management of information for case detection, the other with defining adequate rules on conflict of interest and finding suitable ways of enforcing them.

Handling these two issues has been a central objective of Argentina's Anticorruption Office (AO) since its creation in 2000. There are two main divisions within the AO: an Investigations Department that looks into alleged administrative wrongdoings in the public sector, and a Transparency Policies Department whose aim is to prevent the occurrence of irregular situations. The latter is responsible for dealing with both the financial disclosure system and the conflict of interest issue.

This chapter describes the work performed by the AO's Transparency Policies Department in the last two years, the problems encountered, and the solutions implemented. Since the problems concerning information had a direct connection with the financial disclosure system, there is a brief description of the new FDS, the ways in which it differs from the old system, and its impact on Argentina's current policy on conflicts of interests. This is followed by a brief review of the country's experiences with the conflict of interest. The chapter ends with some provisional conclusions that take into account the current challenges.

The financial disclosures system in Argentina before 2000

Before Law 25.188 was passed, public officials were required to complete a short financial disclosure form, once when entering office and again upon leaving. Both forms were held for safekeeping by the *Escribanía General de la Nación* (Argentina's Office of the General Notary). They were confidential; public access to their contents was restricted. Only a judge through formal proceeding could have access to the information enclosed in such forms.

In 1999, Decree 41/99 changed the content of financial disclosure forms and allowed the public to request access to the information contained in them. Although that permission existed legally, public access to the information never became a reality. Among other problems, the new FDS forms were not sufficiently user-friendly for the general public, as shown by the very few requests introduced before the *Oficina Nacional de Etica Pública* (ONEP) (National Office of Public Ethics). Those few requests were never answered or were answered too late to build public trust in the accessibility of the system.

The use of paper forms for the information was another significant problem, both for public officials completing the forms and for those responsible for overseeing them. Filling in the forms was a long and complex process, and directions given to (ostensibly) facilitate that process were vague and misleading. As a result, soon after the system was introduced, there were a great number of rejected forms and the paper traffic produced a jam that clearly indicated the system would be unmanageable and too expensive to operate. No substantial modifications to the content of the disclosure forms were made; the ONEP simply collected the 35 000 forms and kept them in a bank vault. Meanwhile the paperwork required to manage the forms was huge, and the significant number of rejects created extra work with no added value – as well as an administrative cost of about USD 70 per financial disclosure.

Steps towards a new financial disclosure system

According to Roberto De Michele,[1] head of the Transparency Policies Department of the Anticorruption Office, implementation of the new FDS took into account a new set of considerations.

First, financial disclosure systems in less developed countries have traditionally been created following the model of more developed public administrations.[2] Therefore, in transplanting elements of these models, it is important to consider contextual factors that help to explain the success of the original blueprint. When the models are transplanted into different administrative contexts without these factors, the likelihood of under-performance is high. This occurs, for example, when models demand change-resistant bureaucracies or have operators who lack skills to manage technological complexity or are under-motivated to acquire these skills because of low pay.

Second, the system should cope with the problem of highly decentralised agencies, such as the fiscal service, the foreign service and the armed forces. With the paper-based system, it was very difficult for these agencies to comply with the requirements of the law on time.

Third, the proposed system should try to reach a proper balance between two potentially conflicting values underpinning these policies. On the one hand, transparency and access to information are recognised as strong and effective principles to prevent corruption. As a corollary, these principles support full disclosure policies. On the other hand, there is a privacy expectation with regard to the individual's confidential and personal information, whether or not he or she holds public office.

Fourth, the new system should stress the importance of information that could determine the existence of conflicts of interest. The power of this information to serve as a means of preventing wrongdoing has often been overlooked. Prior to the reform, there existed no significant precedents in the Argentine public sector for detecting and preventing conflicts of interest. Normally, such questions were considered within the scope of criminal law, an area also lacking helpful precedents. Besides the capacity of detection and prevention, the system could provide information valuable in identifying cases of public officials holding more than one occupation.[3]

Fifth, the system should enlist civil society and the media as monitoring forces. Specifically, it should attempt to empower every citizen and journalist to act as an "auditor" of public officials. Complying with this ideal requires, at a minimum, equipping citizens with the ability to consult financial disclosure forms, while respecting the privacy expectation of officials and the requirements of law. This element is crucial, since civil society and the media are sometimes a more effective – and always the least expensive – auditing firm. The task also emphasises the responsibility of citizens in a democracy to act as stewards of the republic.[4]

The public's perception of the forms is undoubtedly a critical issue concerning financial disclosure systems. The necessary balance between protection of privacy for the public officials and the citizens' right to information on the finances and private interests of these officials is a delicate topic. An intense debate is under way between those who believe that privacy values should not be sacrificed on behalf of public trust and those who consider public scrutiny the very core of democracy. The United States, for example, has implemented a financial disclosure system where senior officials' forms are accessible to the general public. On the other hand, in Canada financial disclosure forms are strictly confidential. The balance between these two positions varies from one country to the next. Any reasonable analysis of public access to disclosure forms should take into account the particular country situation and its social and political environment.

In Argentina's case, the Congress has established by law that the general public is to have access to the financial disclosure forms of every public official, but it has also established the confidentiality of certain sensitive information contained in these forms, such as bank account numbers, private addresses and credit card numbers.

Another element to consider is that some countries, including Argentina, have criminalised illicit enrichment and that financial disclosure forms are a key tool in detecting such crimes.[5] On the other hand, is also true that in Argentina's case court decisions are questioning the constitutionality of using the forms to that end.

As international awareness of corruption and its prevention grows, the whole topic of public access to information will become a subject of debate around the world. The framework for the negotiations towards a United Nations convention against corruption is going to be one of the arenas for that debate.[6]

Argentina's new electronic FDS has produced positive results in terms of performance, consistency of the information received, and the absence of rejected financial disclosure forms, as shown by the charts included in the following section.

The impact of the new FDS in numbers

The following tables illustrate the preliminary impact of the new system.[7]

Table 1: Levels of Compliance

	Former System	Electronic System
Public officials required	36.000	25.503
Level of compliance	24.198 (67 %)	24.994 (98 %)

Table 2: Number of FDF Requested

	Former System	Electronic System
Through the Internet	Not available	560
By Paper Forms	66	263
Total requests	66	823

Table 3: Estimated cost per FDF

Former System	Electronic System
USD 70 per form	USD 8 per form

Table 4: Profile of Users

	Former System	Electronic System
FDF requested by the press	43	612
FDF requested by citizens	23	211

Table 5: Impact on Cases of Conflicts of Interest

	Former System(1999)	Electronic System(2000 - 2001)
Conflicts of Interests files opened	40	331

Conflicts of interest in Argentina

A democratic system demands that public officials justify their actions and decisions by providing cogent reasons. The notions of fairness and impartiality are the basis for that cogency. In the conflict of interest issue these notions must indeed be sustained, since the decisions that a public official takes will generate economic benefits to certain individuals or corporations, or will affect fundamental rights.[8]

In the conflicts of interest field the demand for justification is certainly, in line with Robert Behn's view, a demand for accountability, especially in terms of fairness and impartiality of the decisions. It must be pointed out that there is debate between accountability for finances and fairness on the one hand versus accountability for performance on the other. This debate can be seen as a little too premature in less developed countries, like Argentina, where we experienced major problems in enforcing the regulations. In these countries, the notion of seeking accountability for performance could seem highly unrealistic. This is an obvious consequence of the profound differences in ethics between developed countries and transitional democracies.[9]

Working on conflict of interest means dealing with the opposition between public and private interests. Under a constitutional democracy, the people might reasonably expect the public interest to prevail above claims and demands from particular citizens, interest groups or economic sectors.

Before Law 25.188 was passed, different statues regulated conflict of interest situations. Some of these focused only on civil servants while others referred to political appointees, such as secretaries or ministers. At the same time, decentralised agencies had their own rules concerning conflict of interest. The overlapping of such systems generated uncertainty, and the absence of effective sanctions for violation of these rules deepened the crisis.

The Argentine Penal Code added yet more confusion with the criminalisation of "unacceptable negotiations with public duty", the meaning of which is quite similar to that of conflicts of interest.[10] It is difficult to find references to "unacceptable negotiations" in criminal jurisprudence, and judges differ radically in their interpretation of the term in the few cases that exist.[11]

When Argentina signed the Inter-American Convention against Corruption, things started to change. Law 25.188 incorporates the ICAC into national legislation and its Chapter V (Articles 13 to 17) creates an entirely new system for regulation of conflict of interest. Article 13 is key, because it is meant to define situations where a public servant is involved in a conflict of interest.

However, Article 13, the key clause in the said Chapter, suffers from a number of flaws. First, the legal concepts it contains are only vaguely defined. Second, it does not provide a reasonable definition of conflict of interest. Third, it fails to establish acceptable distinctions between different professional activities (e.g. different treatment in a conflict of interest situation between a freelance consultant and a person who is on the board of a corporation). Chapter V also refers to previous and subsequent conditions for access to and exercise of public office, and these rules also suffer from various defects. In spite of such problems, however, the AO was able to accomplish its enforcement duties on conflict of interest detection and control. The way it did so is summarised in the following sections.

Management targets on conflict of interest situations

Since the creation of the Anticorruption Office, almost 350 files analysing conflict of interest were opened. These files had their origin in one of the following causes:

1) An unclear situation detected in the routine analysis of the financial disclosure forms; a file is opened in order to gather more information and perform a more detailed analysis.

2) A complaint against a public official lodged with the Office by a citizen or the mass media.

3) A public official initiating an inquiry into his or her own situation.

The implementation of Law 25.188 had a strong effect on public opinion, reflected in both citizens' and the media's increasing demands for government action against corruption. A significant number of accusations were presented before the AO, many of them involving officials in very high positions.

Financial disclosures submitted by public officials are the Anticorruption Office's primary source of information in its investigation of conflicts of interest matters. Given that the compliance level is, as seen above, close to 100%, the Office utilises this vital information in practically every case. After a financial disclosure form is analysed, it is often necessary to seek additional information in order to ensure a thorough evaluation. Citizens, non-governmental organisations and the media have played a vital role in case reviews, furnishing substantial information.

A number of factors, however, have hindered action in conflict of interest matters:

a) Vague definitions of conflict of interest, through the inclusion of complex, "undetermined" legal concepts.[12]

b) Lack of a systematic procedure to analyse financial disclosure forms or collect additional information.

c) Lack of enforcement of the existing statues.[13]

d) Absence of effective sanctions.[14]

Core strategies implemented by the AO in order to resolve those problems were:

a)   The production of a reasonable definition of conflict of interest via a series of administrative decisions. The said definition is aimed to clearly determine the factual conditions in which a public official would be involved in a conflict of interest situation.

b)   The introduction of a standardised procedure based on uniform control of information received, additional data collection, and the different stages of evaluation. All of these are now mandatory steps before a final case decision is issued.

c)   The introduction of general remedies such as divestments, transfers of duties, forced resignations from positions in the private sector, blind trusts, etc.

d)   Finally, the opening of communication channels with civil society and with the administration itself to receive reports and information on potential conflict of interest situations. This particular strategy has been very helpful in Argentina in detecting cases that were not originally reported.

Examination of the decisions taken by the Office reveals that in most cases the solution provided was a preventive one. The primary goal was to avoid the occurrence of possible conflicts of interest by forcing the public officials to abstain from intervening in those matters that collide with their own interests, or matters pertaining to the enterprises for which they previously worked.

This sort of solution is firmly connected to what Behn calls the "deterrent effect" of aggressive holding-people-accountable strategies.[15] The idea behind this type of solution is to establish an acceptable balance between hiring skilled professionals for public positions and safeguarding impartiality in decision-making processes. The AO strongly believes in preventive solutions but is aware that effective enforcement is needed to support such an idea.

Other decisions were focused on requirements for transparency improvement in decision-making procedures in order to avoid a future lack of impartiality. In these cases the Office suggested the implementation of rulemaking-type procedures in order to increase levels of public access to information and, in so doing, to increase levels of fairness, impartiality and accountability. These suggestions proved very effective in cases where those who would be affected by a certain decision had the chance to intervene before that decision was issued.[16]

Finally, in those cases where conflicts of interest had already arisen, the AO decided that the state of affairs should revert to pre-decision status, charging costs to the public official. In any case the remedies established through prior valid regulations were, as already pointed out, quite ineffective.[17]

Some amendments to Chapter V of Law 25.188 were introduced by Decree 862/2001. These mainly deal with conflict of interest situations relating to positions occupied by the appointee before he or she entered the public administration. Although very recent, this new Decree would appear to be inadequate in solving the problems mentioned above.

The impact of the new electronic financial disclosure system on the conflicts of interest policy

What advantages does the new system offer in terms of future work on conflict of interest?

The Anticorruption Office is currently developing new software to improve its capacity to analyse the contents of the financial disclosure forms. It plans to integrate this software into different databases to maximise the use of available information.

The Office expects to enhance its capability to cross-check information from the financial disclosure forms with other sources, such as the local fiscal office or the records of other public agencies – e.g. the *Registro de la Propiedad Inmueble* (which holds information related to the ownership of real estate), the *Registro de la propiedad automotor* (information on cars, ships and boats) and the *Inspección General de Justicia* (information about company incorporation).

Some have expressed concern about the risk of public powers using technology to gain access to citizens' private data, i.e. confidential information that should remain out of the public eye. The AO shares those worries and affirms that the Office itself is not doing anything of that sort. The AO's main goal is simply to improve the links between records that are all already public.

Conclusions

A policy on conflict of interest has, in countries like Argentina, one main goal: to put the public good first. What we now know as a conflict of interest situation was, not long ago, an ordinary situation both in the minds of public officials and in the public eye. Obtaining private benefits was considered "an extra benefit from holding public office".

Effective policy in this area must take into account the complexity of the legal, operational and enforcement components. Rules must precisely define conflicts of interest; the gathering of information should be efficient; and the enforcement agencies must have officials equipped with the skills to properly analyse this type of situation.

An adequate financial disclosure system is a key element in any successful conflict management policy, but its importance must not be overrated – it is but one piece of complex and structured policy. In this sense the AO is supporting the implementation of preventive strategies – such as public hearings, rule-making processes, notice and comments – in different core areas of public administration.

Many transitional democracies require highly qualified experts to enforce the consolidation process. There is an increasing demand from the public to improve government performance, and this should be taken into account in the design of any conflict of interest policy.

Achieving a proper balance between public interest and private rights is a central objective that must never be underestimated.

The work of corruption control agencies must aim to attain reasonable standards. The pursuit of perfection can only lead to dissatisfaction when high expectations collide with reality.

The figures in Section 3 show that the AO has improved its quantitative performance in terms of public officials' compliance with financial disclosure duties and in generation and analysis of conflicts of interest cases. The new challenge is to enhance its qualitative performance in case detection and resolution.

The central challenge is to find a proper balance between hiring officials who can deliver high-quality services that citizens value, and a properly functioning government that operates honestly and above particular interests.

NOTES

1. This section outlines most of the findings by Roberto De Michele in Harnessing Information Technology to Increase Transparency and Control: The Financial Disclosure System in Argentina. This paper was presented by De Michele at the II. Global Forum on Fighting Corruption and Safeguarding Integrity on 28-31 May 2001 in The Hague.

2. The Argentine system follows the pattern of the US legislation. See the Debate in *Parlamentario de la Ley* 25.188. *Imprenta del Congreso*, Argentina.

3. Argentine regulations are not a particularly good example in this domain. A general prohibition is matched by several possibilities of being granted permission in special situations, rendering the system less than reliable. The Anticorruption Office is working on a plan to deregulate this area, setting simple general standards both for conflicts of interest and for the requirements relating to information on the assets of public officials.

4. At the time of writing, the Anti-Corruption Office has been successful in winning all three court cases [against public officials who requested restricting public access to the financial disclosure forms.

5. See the Inter-American Convention against Corruption, Article IX, and Argentina's Penal Code, Article 268.

6. For more on this, compare country documents for the "Informal Preparatory Meeting of the Ad Hoc Committee on the Negotiation of a UN Convention against Corruption" at *http://www.odccp.org/crime_cicp_convention_corruption_prepmtg.html.*

7. Data updated 31 October 2001.

8. See Sunstein, Cass R., "A Republic of Reasons" in The Partial Constitution, Harvard University Press, 1994, Chapter 1.

9. For more on this point see Behn, Robert D., *Rethinking Democratic Accountability*, Brookings Institution Press, Washington, D.C., 2001, Chapters 1 and 2.

10. Argentina's Penal Code Art. 265. - *Será reprimido con reclusión o prisión de uno a seis años e inhabilitación especial perpetua, el funcionario público que, directamente, por persona interpuesta o por acto simulado, se interesare en miras de un beneficio propio o de un tercero, en cualquier contrato u operación en que intervenga en razón de su cargo.* "any public official who directly or through intermediaries or through a simulated act, displays interest in order to gain any private benefit for him- or herself or for a third person, in any contract or operation in which he/she must intervene, shall be punishable by imprisonment from one to six years and lifetime disqualification from holding public office".

11. For an in-depth look into this matter, see Heggelin, Maria Florencia, *La figura de Negociaciones Incompatibles en la Jurisprudencia de la Capital Federal*, Nueva Doctrina Penal, Editores del Puerto, 2000/A, Buenos Aires, Pag. 203/228.

12. For fuller background on this issue, especially on "undetermined legal concepts", see García de Entrerría, Eduardo, La Lucha contra las impunidades del Poder. , Editorial Civitas, Madrid, 1995, p. 33.

13. No formal records indicate the existence of conflict of interest files opened before the AO was created.

14. According to Article 17 of Law 25.188, the only sanction provided was the nullity of the decisions taken by public officials who took those decisions while in a conflict of interest situation.

15. Robert Behn, op. cit., pages 15/16.

16. See Kerwin, Cornelius M., *Rulemaking – How Government Agencies Write Law and Make Policy*, Second Edition, Congressional Quarterly Inc., Washington, D.C., 1999,Chapters 1 and 2.

17. For an in-depth analysis of decisions taken by the AO on conflicts of interest, visit *www.jus.gov.ar - Oficina Anticorrupción – Resoluciones de la Oficina Anticorrupción sobre conflictos de intereses e incompatibilidades en la Administración Pública Nacional. En particular Resolución 38 (Henoch Aguiar) y Resolución 63 (Javier Tizado)*.

BUILDING A CONSENSUS FOR FISCAL REFORM IN CHILE

by

Mario Marcel
Director of the Budget Office, Chile

Marcelo Tokman
Head of the Research Department of the Budget Office, Chile

Introduction

The financial crisis that started in Asia in 1997, brought up a renewed concern over public finances in emerging economies. As most observers failed to detect creeping fiscal disequilibria, large public contingent liabilities, vulnerable asset-liability structures, and time inconsistencies of fiscal policy, international financial institutions committed themselves to promote higher transparency and efficiency in the management of public finances. This has resulted in a stream of transparency codes, guidelines and best practice reports over the last couple of years that intend to prevent such failures in the future.

However, as the world economy enters a new phase of uncertainty and many emerging economies still do not recover from the effects of the crisis, progress towards the new public finance benchmarks is still poor. Fiscal reform appears as the only way to accelerate the pace towards fiscal transparency and efficiency in many emerging economies.

Fiscal reform has indeed been in the agenda of developing countries and international financial institutions for many years, with some success in removing gross distortions, like off-budget deficits from public enterprises or Central Bank lending to governments. Yet many problems remain unsolved while structural changes, like decentralization, have added new pieces to the public finance puzzle.

Fiscal reform, having a medium-term scope, has usually taken a second place to the most acute problems of fiscal adjustment. But the effectiveness of such adjustments to solve long-term problems of public finances might have been limited. Expenditure cuts that concentrate on the discretionary component of budgets, resulting in cuts in salaries, investment programs and social services, may be not only unsustainable but can also put a threat to the effectiveness of public policies. In the case of social programs this may also harm the ability of governments to perform their distributive role.

Modern thinking on public finance is addressing these issues. Macroeconomic theory is paying less attention to the short-term demand effects of fiscal policy than to long-term, portfolio effects. Public sector balance sheets are replacing flow-of-funds charts and medium-term financial sustainability is becoming a central issue in the assessment of fiscal policy measures.

Likewise, budgets are now seen not only as a tool of macroeconomic policy, but also as playing a managerial and political role[1]. To public managers, budgets are a key source of incentives and constraints, as much as markets do so for private companies. In recent years, many governments have been changing financial management rules to enhance accountability and efficiency in public agencies.

Budgets are also a political device: they are prepared by the Executive, as a result of a negotiation between the Ministry of Finance and the spending ministries, and submitted for approval to legislatures and therefore require the support of many actors with different motivations and priorities. Budgets encompass resource allocations for a wide range of activities required for the delivery of public goods and services and usually they result from extensive negotiations and agreements.

The key to successful public finance management is to balance the economic, managerial, and political roles of public finances. It is, therefore, a matter of governance. Fiscal governance is poor when fiscal policy objectives are achieved at the expense of a collapse in public management; fiscal reform has little chance of succeeding when it does not reach the common sense of politicians and the public. Fiscal governance is strong when governments can deliver their fiscal policy in a sustainable way and when public funds do not only comply with macro limits but are also efficiently applied to the provision of public goods and services. Fiscal governance is not reflected in how deep a country can cut into its fiscal deficit, but in how capable it is to prevent it.

This paper describes the initiatives that have been implemented in Chile since the mid-1990s, which amount to a second generation of fiscal reforms aiming at strengthening fiscal governance.

Institutional arrangements and fiscal outcomes

Too frequently, external observers appear to rely on a strong and committed authority to sort out a country's fiscal troubles. But political will is not enough. Fiscal governance largely depends on the quality of institutions that shape public finance management.

Countries differ in their budgetary institutions and in their procedures within the three phases of the budget process: the formulation of the budget proposal within the Executive; the presentation and approval of the budget in the legislature; and the implementation of the budget by the bureaucracy. If such differences determine the influence of diverse interests and economic authorities over budgets, then we should perhaps turn to such differences to seek an explanation of why the fiscal performance of some countries is better than others'. A study of the relationships between these practices might help identify "correct" budgetary institutions that are able to ensure solid fiscal performance.

Milesi-Ferretti (1996) divides studies on the influence of budgetary institutions on fiscal policy into two main categories. On one side there are those that concentrate on fiscal regulations such as constitutional balanced budget amendments, international agreements, like the convergence criteria of the Maastricht Treaty in Europe, Macroeconomic Program Requirements and ceilings on government borrowing imposed by the legislature. Such studies emphasize the usefulness of regulations in eliminating systematic bias in efforts to achieve balanced budgets, and in enhancing the need for budget discussions to focus on achieving the desired fiscal policy outcomes.

On the other side there are studies that focus on budget procedures and on how they give greater initiative and control to actors who represent the interests of the community as a whole *vis a vis* those that advocate particular interests in each of the stages through which a budget must pass. These studies seek to identify at each stage of the process those institutions that assign priority to the economic authority over the various ministries, parliamentarians, pressure groups or government agencies.

Comprehensive analysis of these institutions would reveal whether a country's budget system should be characterized as *hierarchical* or *collegial*. Hierarchical institutions are those that attribute strong prerogatives to the Prime Minister to overrule spending ministers within intra governmental negotiations in the formulation and execution of the budget, and those that limit in a variety of ways the capacity of the legislature to amend the budget proposed by the government. Collegiate institutions emphasize the democratic rule in every stage, like the prerogatives of spending ministries within the government, the prerogatives of the legislature vis a vis the government and the rights of minority opposition in the legislature [see Alesina and Perotti (1999)].

In principle, hierarchical systems should result in better macroeconomic fiscal performance, in terms of capacity to enforce fiscal restraint, avoid large and persistent deficits and implement fiscal adjustments more promptly, than collegiate systems. Statistical evidence across countries confirms such hypothesis. Von Hagen and Harden (1994) find support for this hypothesis using several indices to rank fiscal institutions of all of the countries of the European Community from the most hierarchical to the most collegiate. Alesina, Hausmann, Hommes and Stein (1999) follow a similar procedure for a sample of almost all the Latin American countries and arrive to the same conclusion: more hierarchical procedures are associated with lower primary deficits, after controlling for several economic determinants of the government budget. Figure 1 shows the significant negative correlation between the average index of budget institutions and the average primary deficit for the 1980-1992 period.

Figure 1

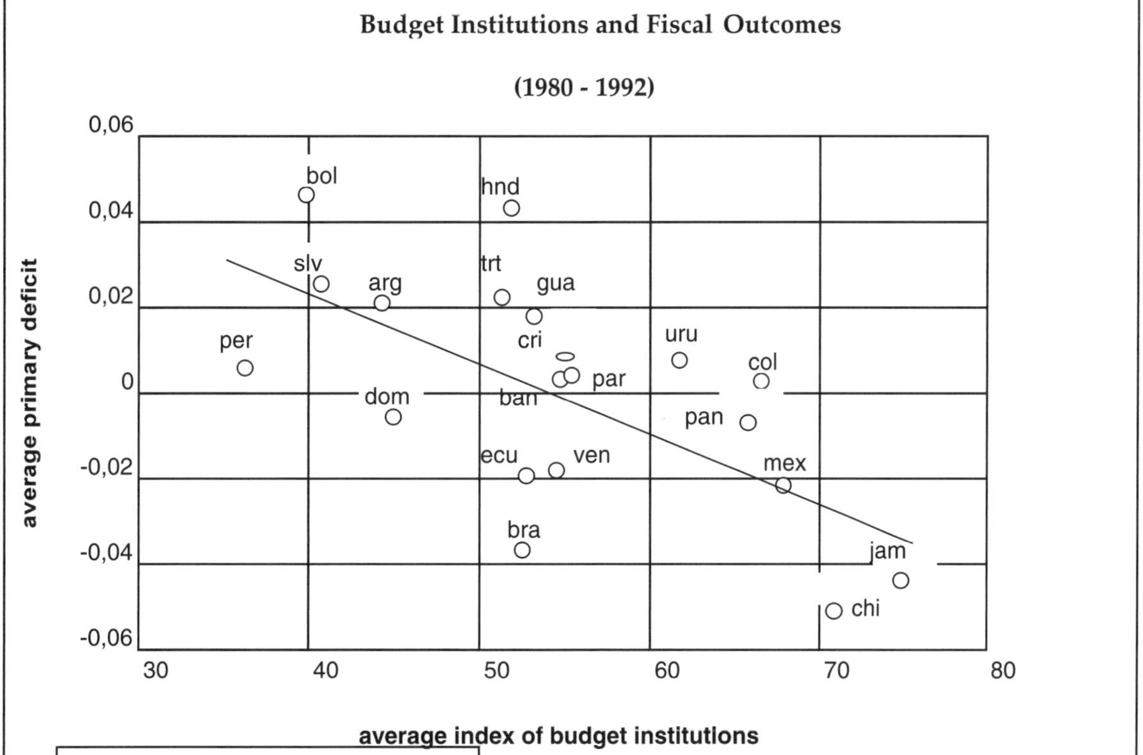

	coef	t-stat
Intercept	0,083	3,33
Index	-0,00151	-3,39

Source: Alessina, Hausmann, Hommes and Stein (1999)

109

Both political science and empirical studies are leading to the conclusion that an efficient fiscal performance does not only require a competent economic authority with the capacity to analyze and define policies, but also adequate institutions to support its role. These institutions must be capable of ensuring the pre-eminence of the Ministry of Finance and the Executive branch during the budget-making process, or otherwise must be able to impose a priori restrictions on that process. Adequate institutions, particularly in terms of transparency and accountability, are important not only to support the job of competent economic authorities, but also to reduce their incentives to be fiscally irresponsible (see Rogoff (1990)). While reforms that reshape budget institutions are not easy, the effort would be worthwhile since the goal is one of the most valued assets in contemporary economies: powerful and stable means for controlling budget deficits.

Chile's budget institutions

Chile has a first hand experience on the social and economic consequences of fiscal imbalances. These imbalances played a major role in determining economic volatility and sustained inflation that characterized the Chilean economy until the mid-1980s. The large share of fiscal revenues generated by copper sales meant that public finances acted as a multiplier of the terms of trade cycle into the domestic economy. Figure 2 shows the strong correlation between the fiscal balance and the price of copper in the 1970-87 period. The graph also shows that this correlation was reduced after 1987, through the creation of the Copper Stabilization Fund, a mechanism which isolates most of the effect of copper price volatility on fiscal revenues.

At various times in the republican era, public finances turned into a political battleground. Such confrontations prompted a civil war at the end of the nineteenth century. Presidents elected under the 1925 Constitution, which usually condemned them to be in a minority in Congress, inevitably complained about the opposition's budget blocking tactics. Even the political crisis during the government of Salvador Allende was reflected in serious conflict over the approval of the budget. For this reason, the Chilean system gradually furnished the Executive branch with greater powers over economic matters and public sector financial management.

Current budget institutions in Chile are determined by provisions of the 1980 Constitution and of the State Financial Administration Act of 1975, which establish that the national budget should be comprehensive, covering the various agencies and ministries of the central government, the judiciary and the legislature.[2] The budget is also comprehensive in terms of the transactions covered, including all fiscal revenues and expenditures.

Figure 2

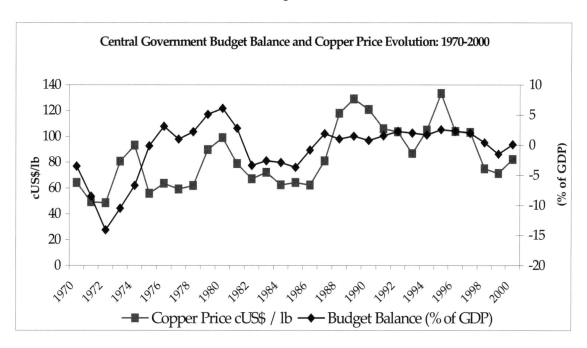

Source: Budget Office, Ministry of Finance, Chile.

The preparation of the Chilean budget is done over a relatively short period of time, with tight deadlines mandated by law. This is accomplished on the basis of a highly centralized financial management system, based in the Ministry of Finance.

Budget discussion in Congress occurs within deadlines mandated by law: the latest date at which the Executive's budget proposal must be sent to Congress is September 30, and the discussion process must be carried out in no more than sixty days. The budgetary powers of Chile's Congress are highly limited. Congress cannot alter revenue estimates, increase expenditures nor reallocate resources between programs. It can only reduce line item expenditures that are not mandated by permanent legislation.

Only the Executive can propose changes to mandatory spending programs and Congress is not allowed to change the contents of the proposal, however they can reject the government's proposals. Once mandatory expenditure programs are approved by Congress, it is not required that they are reviewed on a periodic basis. In the budget discussion, Congress appropriates funds for these programs each year. However, if actual expenditure deviates from the original estimates, the resulting differences are automatically funded. In addition to these restrictions, the Constitution establishes that if the discussion in Congress is not over and the budget law is not passed within the sixty days deadline, the Executive's original budget proposal becomes law.

Budget execution is highly flexible through provisions that allow the Ministry of Finance to adjust item allocations during the year. An important feature of this flexibility is the inclusion in the budget of a central contingency reserve to cover the fiscal costs of legislation passed during the year, as well as contingencies.

The Constitution imposes other constraints on fiscal management: borrowing from the Central Bank and earmarked taxation are strictly forbidden; transfers to state-owned enterprises require specific legal authorization; permanent legislation dealing with taxation, social security, government jobs and financial management can only be considered at the Executive's initiative.

Given these arrangements, the institutional framework responsible for formulating and executing Chile's budget may be categorized as markedly hierarchical. This is confirmed in the study by Alesina et al. (1999) where Chile is included among the two countries whose budgetary institutions enjoy the most clearly established lines of authority and responsibility in Latin America.

Chilean budget institutions to the test

Chile's hierarchical budget institutions, however, were enacted under military rule and thus can hardly provide a test for consensus building for fiscal reform. The real challenge to their sustainability and effectiveness would come only in a democratic environment, as since 1990.

The memory of past fiscal instability made Chilean politicians quite supportive of fiscal restraint. The combination of a governing center-left coalition firmly convinced that its credibility largely depended on its prudent handling of public finances, and a fiscally conservative opposition, generated a favorable climate to apply, build upon and deepen fiscal responsibility during the 1990s.

This is clearly reflected in Chile's fiscal performance during the 1990s. Table 1 shows that central government budgets recorded an overall surplus in every year, except for 1999. Overall surpluses averaged 1.3% of GDP during the 1990's and public savings grew as a share of GDP during most of the 1990s, to reach nearly 6% of GDP in 1996. This allowed a substantial reduction of total public debt (both domestic and foreign) from 47.2% of GDP in 1990 to 14.8% of GDP in 2000.

Table 1: Central Government 1990-2000

(as a % of GDP)

	1990	1991	1992	1993	1994	1995	1996	1997	1998	1999	2000
Overall Surplus	0.8	1.5	2.3	2.0	1.7	2.6	2.3	2.0	0.4	-1.5	0.1
Current Surplus	2.5	3.6	5.0	4.9	4.9	5.4	5.8	5.6	4.1	2.5	3.7
Public Debt	47.2	41.1	34.0	31.6	25.6	19.5	16.7	14.5	13.9	15.0	14.8

Source: Budget Office, Ministry of Finance, Chile.

Prudent handling of public finances during the 1990s contributed to create a virtuous circle that, as shown in Table 2, benefited public funding in return. The cumulative growth rate of Social Expenditure in the 1990's was 101%, and its importance in total public expenditure increased from 65% in 1990 to 70% in 2000. The sectors which exhibited the highest growth rates were health and education, with cumulative growth of 117% and 141%, respectively, during the 1990's. Government investment, that had remained particularly low during the 1980s, grew 172% in the same period. Table 2: Social Expenditure 1990-2000

Real Annual Growth Rate

	1990	1991	1992	1993	1994	1995	1996	1997	1998	1999	2000
Health	-4.5	17.8	16.9	12.1	10.2	4.2	8.6	6.0	8.2	3.1	8.4
Education	-4.4	12.3	15.0	8.6	9.1	11.7	12.9	10.2	11.4	6.9	8.4
Social Expenditure	-0.9	9.2	10.4	9.6	6.1	7.3	9.7	5.6	7.6	7.8	6.1

Source: Budget Office, Ministry of Finance, Chile.

Additional funding for social services and public investments allowed the government to implement many new programs and projects and to strengthen its distributive function during the 1990s. By the end of the decade, government transfers through social programs increased household incomes in the poorest 20% of the population by nearly 85%, while its net impact on the richest 20% was less than 1%. Government spending not only contributed to increase equity, in fact it was the only source of noticeable improvement in income distribution throughout the decade. It also contributed to reduce the poverty rate from 38.6% in 1990, to 20.6% in 2000, and the indigence rate from 12.9% to 5.7% in the same period.

There is no doubt that fiscal institutions supported this performance. While the government felt particularly accountable for its management of fiscal policy, Congress prioritized its role as an overseer of the Executive's handling of public resources. This kept a systematic pressure on fiscal discipline.

But the experience of the 1990s also revealed some shortcomings of Chile's budget institutions. First, Chile's public finance management, despite all its successes, remained fairly conventional, paying more attention to overall financial performance than to the results of the application of public funds, or the true economic cost incurred to obtain such results. In other words, this is a system that may be highly effective in controlling expenditure, but that does not necessarily facilitate or promote efficient management of public institutions.

Second, the hierarchical structure of the public financial system was not completely accepted by the different actors in the budgetary process. Ever since the country's democratic institutions were fully restored members of Congress complained at the limited role assigned to them in the budget approval process, and sought means to apply greater pressure on the Executive than is permitted under those regulations. For their part, line ministries resented the discretion that the Ministry of Finance enjoyed in drawing up the budget and the controls and authorizations required to execute it.

Third, the discretionary powers given to economic authorities did not guarantee that such powers would be consistently applied in the future. The same powers that helped the authorities to balance the budget might be used to unbalance it. The lack of institutional checks and balances generated uncertainty over the future behavior of authorities and prevented the country from fully reaping the benefits of fiscal discipline. In other words, since hierarchical budget institutions were not accompanied with accountability mechanisms over the authorities' management of public finances, the benefits of such arrangements would remain limited.

These problems became apparent by the mid-1990s and prompted a series of initiatives to strengthen public finance management. By 2001, such measures amount to a second generation of fiscal reforms aiming at strengthening fiscal governance in Chile into the 21st century.

Reforming public financial management in Chile: the 1990s

Throughout most of the 1990's, the government and Congress agreed to introduce new regulations and practices into the budget. Most of these measures were formalized as political agreements attached to the budget and, in some cases, written into specific amendments to the Budget Law. These reforms, together with the most recent ones implemented by the government of President Lagos, were designed to address each of the three shortcomings of the Chilean budget institutions identified in the previous section:

- Mechanisms to evaluate performance of programs and institutions were designed and incorporated in decision-making procedures to improve the budget allocation decisions and to make them more transparent.

- New management instruments were introduced to improve performance and to promote efficient management of public institutions.

- To limit the discretionality of the Executive over its command over public resources, several rules were established.

- To increase and strengthen the contributions of Congress to the budget discussion process, relevant background information was generated and distributed to congressmen, and commitments resulting from budget discussion were formalized.

In short, the second generation of fiscal reforms being implemented over the last decade aim to improve the Chilean budget institutions and the quality of fiscal policy by increasing transparency and accountability and by limiting discretionality of the Executive over its command over public resources.

Cash limits

In the early 1990s, Congress charged that budget flexibility provisions allowed the government to increase spending above authorized appropriations in the budget as long as it had the funding. In response to this claim, the Executive and Congress agreed to limit these powers by introducing a specific provision (Article 4) into the annual Budget Law establishing overall cash limits for current and capital expenditures. According to these regulations, government can enjoy flexibility to reallocate resources among line items, but not to increase the overall amount or to transfer resources from capital to current expenditure.

Budget execution reporting

By the early 1990s, the government had no specific obligation to report on budget execution, other than to accountants at the Comptroller's General Office. This meant that both Congress and the public would learn about actual budget execution with a significant delay. The Ministry of Finance has since then agreed and committed to report budget execution on a quarterly basis and to report on the use of the central contingency reserve on a monthly basis. Starting in the year 2000, these reports were made available on-line in the Web page of the Budget Office of the Ministry of Finance (*www.dipres.cl*). The Budget Office also started publishing full provisional financial statements at the end of the year, ahead of the statutory reports of the Comptroller's Office.

Performance indicators

Since 1994, the Budget Office has requested ministries and government agencies to provide quantitative and qualitative information on their performance in terms of the delivery of outputs and services. With this information, a system of performance indicators has been developed and they are included in the background information provided to Congress during the discussion of the annual budget. This system currently includes 537 indicators of effectiveness, efficiency, economy and quality in 109 government units. Despite some questionable attempts at using these indicators to support performance-related pay, the Budget Office has been cautious to avoid building a mechanistic connection between indicators and budget decisions. Instead, it has preferred to view the system as a means to strengthen accountability for results to the general public and to provide information to budget negotiations.

Program evaluation

In 1996, government and Congress acknowledged that indicators could only provide information on the evolution of performance over time but not on the effectiveness of government programs. For that reason, they agreed to further improve performance assessment in the budget process by developing a system of program evaluation. Since 1997, the Government Program Evaluation System has provided independent, ex-post assessments of more than 120 programs. These evaluations are performed by a panel of experts from outside the public sector that can request information from the executing agency and commission specific studies to support their assessments. These evaluations, which are carried out in a period of five months, follow the logical framework methodology to determine the consistency and capacity of the program to achieve its objectives. Conclusions and recommendations are then submitted to the Ministry of Finance, the Presidency and Congress to feed back into the decision-making process.

Starting in the year 2001, the Government Program Evaluation System has been improved by complementing the five-month-long program evaluations with one-year-long in-depth evaluations of programs. The objective of these in-depth evaluations is to generate an integrated assessment of the programs' results -- understood as short, medium and long term benefits of the programs -- the efficiency and economy in the use of resources and features related to the management of internal procedures. The first two in-depth evaluations are currently being performed by the departments of engineering and economics of the *Universidad de Chile*, perhaps the most prestigious university in Chile, and they will be completed in March 2002.

Management improvement programs

Also, in the context of improving the public management in 1998, the government started the implementation of Management Improvement Programs (MIP). MIPs consist in several programs aimed to improve the public management by linking goal attainment to employees' monetary rewards.

After three years of implementation, the MIP system has been reviewed. As a result, during the year 2001, MIPs have been redesigned to focus on the development of key management systems rather than in narrower performance targets, about which MIP can exercise little judgment and/or control. The key management systems have been selected to guarantee a better global performance of the public institutions, mainly in terms of services provided to the citizens, working conditions and valorization of public servants. The management systems translate into a matrix of key management systems and standardizing progress stages. Public agencies identify current and expected progress, and performance is measured in terms of effective progress against these goals.

It is worth mentioning that special attention has been given to the gender perspective. For the year 2002, a new system named Gender Equity has been introduced to the MIP system. Its objective is that public services operate with procedures that promote equal opportunities for men and women in the delivery of outputs.

Recent developments

The reforms of the 1990s, built upon the inherited hierarchical budget institutions, already provided Chile one of the strongest fiscal systems among emerging countries. Yet, by the end of the decade, it became evident that this might be insufficient to sustain fiscal discipline and effectiveness in a more turbulent environment.

In 1997-99, fiscal balances deteriorated by nearly 4% of GDP, moving from a surplus of 2.5% of GDP in 1996 to a 1.5% deficit in 1999. Public saving fell even more sharply, from 5.8% to 2.5% of GDP in the same period. This was mainly a result of the international financial crisis that halted fast growth in Chile and forced a recession in 1999, but it also reflected a more expansionary fiscal stance. Figure 3 shows how structural expenditure has been growing as a percentage of GDP since 1995, at a faster rate than structural revenues which have remained relatively stable. The structural reduction in the central government's surplus and a build-up of medium term financial commitments meant that fiscal aggregates would not necessarily return to their pre-crisis levels in the upswing stage of the cycle.

The political climate also threatened to become less supportive of fiscal discipline. A string of elections stretching from 1999 to 2001 would be more closely contested between the *Concertacion* coalition and its right-wing counterpart and would make consensus building and co-operation on economic matters less likely than in the past.

The Lagos Administration therefore attached great priority to deepening fiscal reform. During the years 2000, and 2001, this has translated into a bold set of new initiatives to improve medium-term fiscal programming, raise allocative efficiency, improve follow-up of budget discussions, and increase transparency and accountability. The results of which can already be observed in the improvement of the fiscal accounts in the year 2000. Indeed, the Central government's overall deficit of 1.5% of GDP in 1999, was reverted to an overall surplus of 0.1% of GDP in 2000, and the current surplus was raised from 2.5% of GDP in 1999 to 3.7% of GDP in 2000. Figures 3 and 4 show that these improvements are due mainly to the improvement of the central government's structural accounts and not to an upturn of the economic cycle.

Figure 3: Structural Revenues and Expenditures 1987-2000

(as a % of GDP)

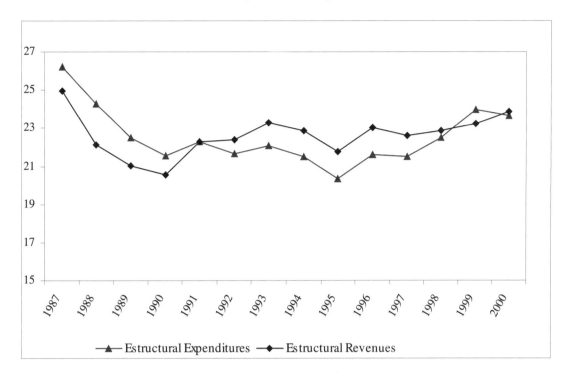

Source: Marcel, Tokman, Valdés and Benavides (2001a).

Improving fiscal policy formulation and medium-term fiscal planning

A fiscal policy rule

After 14 years of continuing budget surpluses in Chile, by the end of the 1990s nothing granted that such performance would continue in the future. As many observers criticized the conduct of fiscal policy in the late 1990s, the behaviour of the new government in exercising its broad discretionary powers over public finances was a major source of uncertainty among economic agents.

The Lagos Administration faced this challenge by committing itself to pursue a strict fiscal policy rule: starting 2001, the government would generate a structural budget surplus equivalent to 1% of GDP (see Marcel, Tokman, Valdés and Benavides (2001b)).

The structural balance measure closely follows a well-established methodology developed by the IMF and the OECD. It aims at assessing the stance of fiscal policy by separating the cyclical variations from the more permanent components of the budget. Such separation does not only provide more transparency into the conduct of fiscal policy, but also provides a sound basis to design and implement it. The fiscal policy rule base on a fixed target for the structural balance allows automatic stabilizers to operate in the short run while keeping a medium-term focus in steering public finances. Indeed, the structural balanced budget rule is an effective instrument to face the politically induced deficit bias [see Alesina and Perotti (1995)] without the limitations of the standard balance budget laws in terms of the counter-cyclical role of fiscal policy and the dynamic optimal taxation theory [see Barro (1979)].

The structural budget balance of the public sector (SBPS), as applied in Chile, reflects the level that revenues and fiscal spending would reach if GDP were at its potential level and if the price of copper were at its medium-term level. Therefore, it excludes the cyclical and random effects of the two most important exogenous factors: economic activity and the price of copper. The SBPS is estimated by (a) making accounting adjustments so that the budget balance becomes a correct proxy of net worth change; (b) estimating potential GDP and the medium-term copper price[3], and (c) re-estimating fiscal revenues on the basis of GDP elasticities.

Applying this methodology to the 1987-2000 period shows that the structural budget balance followed a more consistent path than conventional balances (Figure 4). After a large drop in 1988, it gradually increased until the mid-1990s, when it stabilized around 1.4% of GDP. Between 1997 and 1999 it fell to a minimum of - 0.8% of GDP in 1999, to recover to 0.1% of GDP in 2000. The estimate for 2001 is a structural balance of 0.9% of GDP and the budget for the year 2002 has been structured to achieve the 1% surplus target.

Figure 4: Structural Budget Balance 1987-2000

(as a % of GDP)

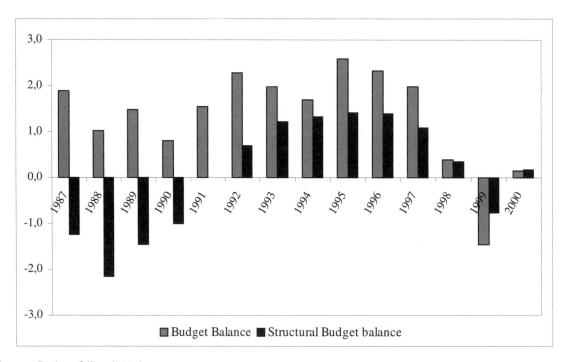

Source: Budget Office (2001).

The 1% SBPS surplus stands out as one of the most strict fiscal policy rules under application in the world. This does not only reflect the commitment of the authorities to strict fiscal discipline, but also some distinct features of the Chilean economy. These features include:

(a) the operational deficit of the Central Bank, originating in the bailing out of financial institutions in the mid-1980s;

(b) substantial contingent liabilities, stemming from guarantees provided under the roads concessions program and state-guaranteed minimum pensions to affiliates of the private capitalization system;

118

(c) the need for the government to contribute to raise domestic saving to fund investment needs without generating large current account imbalances; and

(d) the symbolic nature of fiscal policy as a benchmark to macroeconomic policy in Chile and a cushion against external volatility.

The implementation of the fiscal policy rule is expected to have three major beneficial effects. First, it will reduce uncertainty of economic agents over the conduct of macroeconomic policy and the risk of restrictive monetary policy, reducing long-term interest rates and sovereign spreads in foreign markets. This will stimulate private investment. Second, fiscal policy will play an effective counter-cyclical role by allowing full operation of the automatic stabilizers. And third, it will broaden the programming horizon of public institutions by avoiding the inefficient contraction of spending in recessive periods as well as over-expansions financed under temporary fiscal surpluses (see Ministry of Finance (2001)).

Medium-Term Financial Programming

Building upon a methodology developed in the late 1990s, the Budget Office has started releasing medium-term financial forecasts (MTFF), covering a three-year period. Such estimates are mandatory under the 1975 State Financial Administration Act but they had never been developed or published up until now.

MTFF for the central government are prepared by the Budget Office as a financial projection of existing policies and regulations and therefore do not involve either negotiations or commitments to line ministries and programs. They are therefore presented in aggregate terms as part of the background information to the annual budget.

MTFF has proven to be extremely useful in recent discussions, particularly those related to the Law Against Tax Evasion and the 2001 and 2002 budget discussions. Indeed, MTFF showed that a tax evasion law was required to finance and implement all the proposals contained in President Lagos' government program. These forecasts have also revealed that even after a full recovery of the 1999 crisis, there would be a shortfall of public revenues due to a drastic reduction in transfers from public enterprises, given by the privatization program of the late 1990s. Reverting this phenomenon will require paying special attention at the use of privatization proceeds, increasing pressure on state owned enterprises profitability, widening user charging for public services and raising the profitability of public financial assets, including cash holdings.

Raising allocative efficiency

In order to break away from incrementalistic budgeting, the Ministry of Finance introduced new practices in the preparation of the 2001 and 2002 budgets. Inertial funding was strictly limited and ministries were required to reallocate at least 2% of their inertial expenditures.

Budgetary bids for new or expanded programs are required to compete for a central fund of resources, which is allocated according to the quality of the submitted proposals and their consistency with the government's priorities. Prioritization is based on a logical framework presentation of competing initiatives. This new presentation format emphasizes and encourages a more detailed analysis of the program itself by requiring the statement of the program's general goal as well as the enumeration of specific purpose, components and activities related to the implementation of this program.

The information on the main objectives and goals of public programs provided under the logical framework presentation does not only allow for a better and more efficient allocation of the resources in the budget; it will also feed back into program evaluations in the future.

During the first two years of operation of this fund, US$ 520 millions have been allocated to finance 330 selected proposals. This mechanism has proven to be a transparent and efficient procedure to allocate the budgeted increases in spending.

Raising accountability: closing the budget cycle

Political agreements attached to the approval of the annual budget proved to be an extremely useful tool to foster consensus building for fiscal reform in the 1990s. But such agreements do not only provide a sound political backing to break away from conventional practices and strengthen fiscal discipline; they have also a rationale in themselves.

If the political role of public budgets is due to a large extent to the network of negotiations and commitments that lie beneath them, strengthening and formalizing these commitments may improve the quality of the budget process. Budgeting is indeed a repetitive game, and its outcomes may be improved by feeding back from one fiscal cycle to the next. This can be achieved through formal agreements that address issues that emerged during the discussion of the budget but have no direct effect on the annual appropriations.

On the basis of this rationale, the Lagos Administration paid special attention to the budget agreement that accompanied the approval of its first budget, the 2001 budget. In addition to the agreements covering traditional issues like transparency and evaluation, the government supported two main innovations. First, the budget agreement 2001 included, for the first time, the commitment to develop specific studies on high-profile financial issues, like contingent liabilities, minimum pension guarantees and state owned enterprises profitability. The results of these studies, that were either conducted directly by the Budget Office or prepared by private consultants, were presented to Congress at the beginning of the 2002 budget discussion. Second, it created a new stage in the budget cycle: prior to the discussion of the 2002 budget, the government submitted to Congress the information concerning budget execution, performance indicators, program evaluations and specific studies which allowed Congress to review the government's performance in 2000.

Improving transparency and accountability: the public finance reform program

To strengthen the transparency and efficiency in public management, the Budget Office has designed a program to modernize the financial management of the public sector. This program can be summarized in the following three main elements.

Improving the public sector accounting system

This includes the development of accounting systems that allow measuring, in a more accurate way, the real economic cost of the activities carried out in the public institutions. Moreover, these accounting systems would allow a more effective control of the financial obligations acquired by the public sector. Although currently public sector accounting system is accruals-based, budget formulation and execution operates on a modified cash basis. Transition towards a modified accruals basis will include the development of a commitments control system and capital costs measurement.

Integrated financial management system

In mid 1999, the National Budget Office along with the General Comptroller's Office started a study to produce the Integrated Financial Management System (IFMS). The IFMS would create a single, complete, and uniform information system that would support a more effective and transparent management of the public institutions. Moreover, IFMS would not only facilitate the generation of aggregate information but it also would allow the design of output and performance indicators that will permit a better evaluation of the results. At this moment IFMS is at a design stage and it is being tested, as a pilot scheme in five public institutions. Full implementation of the system is expected for 2004.

Financial assets management

Cash management currently operates in a highly decentralized way. On the basis of an annual cash program, the Treasury transfers monthly cash allotments to ministries and agencies that are then spent according to the existing budget appropriations. Liquid funds, both for the Treasury and government agencies are deposited in non-interest bearing accounts in the Central Bank and the State Development Bank. This system facilitates agencies' management but has a very high opportunity cost. The public finance reform program will device cash management and transfer of funds systems in order to minimize this opportunity cost without compromising financial decentralization.

Final remarks

Regardless of the specific merit of any of the initiatives included in the budget reform program in Chile a valid question remains: Why should such initiatives enhance fiscal governance if the Minister of Finance is already a powerful figure?

The answer rests mostly on political economy grounds. The concentration of power over public finances in the hands of a single authority does not guarantee fiscal governance if: (a) such authority is not accountable for its application of such powers, and (b) if its concerns and priorities are not shared by other influential actors, be them politicians, business or social leaders, or the media. This is particularly true for a coalition government like Chile's.

The limited experience of the Lagos Administration supports this view. The introduction of a fiscal policy rule based on achieving a structural budget surplus of 1% of GDP has already changed the focus of the fiscal policy debate and has been welcomed by both sides of the political spectrum. While fiscal conservatives have seen it as a constraint over public expenditure in the future, spending-prone politicians have valued its capacity to generate a more stable and predictable environment for public policy programming. To the government, the SBPS has shifted attention away from expenditure/GDP ratios and short-term fine-tuning to a medium-term scope in fiscal policy monitoring.

This framework has facilitated the discussions of the 2001, and the 2002 budgets in Congress. Contrasting with recent past experience and with the pessimistic prospects founded on its coincidence with municipal elections in 2000, and with parliamentary elections in 2001, the budget discussions have been quite uneventful and they have been dispatched by Congress weeks before the constitutional deadline. Moreover, political consensus over the budget agreements were easily attained.

Of course, most of the initiatives in the budget reform agenda are yet to be implemented and tested. As it is well documented in the literature, fiscal rules may be easy to draw but more difficult to implement, and their actual effectiveness ultimately depends on their credibility, which is built over long periods of time.

Fortunately, fiscal reform in Chile can rely on the strong basis of the country's past record. As a matter of fact, fiscal reform in Chile now has a good chance of succeeding because it is not a device to overcome a fiscal crisis but to continue preventing it in the future.

NOTES

1. See Marcel (1998) for a description of the different functions of the budget.

2. Although municipalities, the lowest level of government in Chile, are not included in the national budget, the effect of this exclusion in fiscal policy is almost null because they are not allowed to: levy taxes on their own, run deficits nor borrow from the Central Government.

3. To assure transparency and non-discretionality, the medium term price of copper is obtained by consulting a group of experts from the mining, the academic and the financial sectors.

BIBLIOGRAPHY

ALESINA, A., Hausmann, R., Hommes, R. and Stein, E. (1999), "Budget Institutions and Fiscal Performance in Latin America", *Journal of Development Economics*, 59.

ALESINA, A. and Perotti, R. (1999), "Budget Deficits and Budget Institutions" in Fiscal Institutions and Fiscal Performance. Poterba, J. and Hagen, J., eds., The University of Chicago Press.

ALESINA, A. and Perotti, R. (1995), "The Political Economy of Budget Deficits," IMF staff paper, March.

Budget Office (2001), "Aspectos Macroeconómicos del Proyecto de Ley de Presupuestos del Sector Público del Año 2002".

Budget Office (2001), "Estadísticas de las Finanzas Públicas".

BARRO, R. (1979), "On the Determination of Public Debt," *Journal of Political Economy*, 87.

MARCEL, M. (1998), "Los Caminos de la Gobernabilidad Fiscal en América Latina," *Revista Internacional de Presupuesto Público*, 37.

MARCEL, M., Tokman, M., Valdés, R. and Benavides, P. (2001), "Balance Estructural del Gobierno Central Metodología y Estimaciones para Chile: 1987-2000", *Estudios de Finanzas Públicas,* Septiembre.

MARCEL, M., Tokman, M., Valdés, R. and Benavides, P. (2001), "Balance Estructural: La Base de la Nueva Regla de Política Fiscal Chilena", *Economía Chilena*, Diciembre (forthcoming).

MILESI-FERRETTI, G. M. (1996), Fiscal Rules and the Budget Process", IMF Working Paper, 60.

Ministry of Finance (2001), "Exposición sobre el Estado de la Hacienda Pública".

ROGOFF, K. (1990), "Political Budget Cycles," *American Economic Review*, 80.

VON HAGEN, J. and Harden, I. J. (1994), "National Budget Process and Fiscal Performance", unpublished.

PERFORMANCE AND TRANSPARENCY IN AUSTRALIA: ARE "LEADING EDGE" SYSTEMS REALLY WORKING?

by

Tyrone M. Carlin

Lecturer in Management, Macquarie Graduate School of Management, Australia

Introduction

This chapter constructs and explains the content, nature and quality of non-financial disclosures, including those related to performance indicators via a disclosure indicator analysis (DIA) of actual reporting practices in recent Government Budget papers in Victoria. It reports the results of its application to the last three years' budget papers.

The findings highlight the 'turmoil' in the reporting of non-financial performance indicators in the Victorian Budget papers. These results indicate a significant gap between "official" expectations of the type of items required to be reported and actual budgetary reporting practices - some many years after regulation and major financial accountability reforms have taken place.

The public sector in Australia, and in particular, Victoria, in the past few decades has undergone major fiscal, structural, management and financial management transformation (see, Jones, Guthrie, Steane 2001a, b). One area of major transformation has been the changing technologies by which funding, reporting and monitoring for the budget dependent sector are achieved. A recent aspect of this process of reform has been a changing central budgetary regime, and within this a shift towards the presentation of public sector budgeting information on an 'output' basis. This transition began in the mid-1990s and continues to date.

Recent international comparative studies of public sector financial management reforms (Olson *et. al.* 1998, Guthrie *et. al.* 1999) have found a wide diversity of practice in adoption of New Public Financial Management (NFPM) oriented changes, even across multiple international jurisdictions regarded as active reformers. A significant additional finding from this body of literature is the material role of accounting and other financial management techniques in implementation of management-oriented change in government. However, it is interesting to note the degree to which some prior international studies have tended to lack detailed analysis of the practical application of such techniques. The approach taken in this paper, reliant on detailed investigation of actual budget sector disclosures, contrasts with the broader approach taken by some earlier contributors to this body of literature.

Importantly, irrespective of suggestions that NPFM is not a uniform, global movement, some common elements do seem to exist at the "super-technical" level. These may be best understood as the outcome of a 'reforming spirit', intent on instilling private sector financial awareness (e.g., about financial position, accrual accounting, debt or surplus management, capital investment strategy) into public sector decision making. Jones, *et al* (2001), argue that there is no "single answer" and "off-the-shelf" global NPFM solution to cure poor financial management practice despite the official (Guthrie and Carlin, 2000) advocacy in favour of this view from certain change agents, notably in central financial agencies. These studies tend to suggest that there is a considerable risk of the formation of a lacuna between what is promised in relation to the implementation of these techniques, and what is actually delivered, or capable of being delivered. It is this tension between the rhetoric associated with certain technical aspects of NPFM reform, and the underlying reality, which in large part motivates this study. In order to investigate this potential void, we construct and perform a disclosure indicator analysis (DIA), concentrating on the role and effectiveness of performance information disclosures, as part of the overall new public financial management framework.

As indicated, public budgeting in Australia has undergone significant change over the past decade. This change has been manifested in several ways, the most important of which has been the implementation of some form of accrual output based budgeting (AOBB) (Guthrie and Carlin 2000, Carlin and Guthrie 2001). The shift towards output based budgeting has also been closely associated with the employment of accrual methods in public sector budgeting as a replacement for cash based accounting models. A central part of the new budgeting regime has also been the presentation of non-financial performance information. These changes have been justified by their champions on the grounds that they will promote greater efficiency, transparency and accountability by governments (Guthrie *et al* 1999). Yet to accept such claims at face value is to ignore the political and rhetorical aspect of public sector budgeting (Wildavsky, 1974 1992; Jones, 1997). Just as the adoption of accrual accounting by public sector agencies has been critiqued as the reflection of a rhetorical rather than technically neutral process (Guthrie, 1998), changes in budgeting process can be analysed critically. Indeed, it has been suggested that predictions of output budgeting's successes have not been matched in reality, again hinting at a strong rhetorical aspect to public sector budgeting changes in Australia (Guthrie and Carlin, 2000).

Because recent research has identified gaps between the claimed nature and the actual practices of central public sector budgeting, we have undertaken a detailed examination of a set of budget papers to identify and examine the use of performance information within current budget papers.

Background to the changing face of performance disclosures in Victoria

In the past three decades public sectors in various Australian jurisdictions[1] have arguably undergone some of the most significant and far-reaching changes in the country's entire history. These changes have involved transforming the governance, management and accounting technologies (Guthrie and Parker, 1998). A "leader" in these changes during the 1990s was the Victorian government. In Victoria the transformation of the state's institutional rules and public sector administrative practices can be traced to two critical events: the election in 1992, of a conservative government under the premiership of Jeff Kennett, and landmark reports prepared by the Victorian Commission of Audit (VCA, 1993a, 1993b). During the period 1992-99 the government introduced a number of changes based on the VCA recommendations which impacted on the public sector. These include the role of executive government and ministers; the role of departments, and changes to local government including radical financial management reforms. These reforms were underpinned by the use of economic theories to endorse purchaser/provider, policy/operations splits, the funding of outputs to achieve outcomes, and the introduction of contestability into the provision of services (English and Guthrie, 2001; Hughes and O'Neill, 2001). Victoria was not unique it pursuing these types of reforms; what was different in the Victorian case was the depth and speed with which the Victorian government pursued the transformation of the public sector (English, 2001; Shamshullah, 1999). Many of the reforms were borrowed or emulated from previous New Zealand public sector experiments and are largely indistinguishable from the New Zealand model, which has been operating since 1988/9 (Pallot 1998, b).

The main characteristic of the output-management model promoted in Victoria between 1992-99 was the separation of the funder, purchaser and provider roles. The implementation of this model required a number of designated steps, which were supported by well-documented Victorian Department of Treasury and Finance (VDTF) manuals (VDTF, 1997 a, b, c). Key elements of this recent reform program have been the adoption of methodologies such as accrual budgetary accounting, together with outcome and output based budgeting and management systems.

Central to the output management process from a financial management perspective was the conceptualisation of linkages between funding, reporting and monitoring of defined outputs to government strategic priorities and outcomes (VDTF, 1997b, p. 42). In the period under review, English and Guthrie (2001) suggest that these reforms could be depicted as taking place within two main phases, although there is, of course, some overlap between them[2]:

a) *Marketisation phase* (1992-97) typified by the combination of managerialist ideas with economic theories emphasising individualistic self-interest, competitive markets and contracts. Unlike reform attempts undertaken prior to this period, major inroads were made into the financial management of the state and significant changes were made to the machinery of government.

b) *Strategic phase* (since mid 1997) characterised by the emphasis on 'whole-of-government strategies'. The introduction of these reforms resulted in a 'whole-of-government' perspective on strategic planning, management and financial reporting of the state's resources (VDTF 1997a). The changes included adopting accrual accounting for output budgetary purposes and output management and allocation of funds to departments based on outputs delivered in accordance with fully-costed budget targets (VDTF, 1998a, p.2).

In this current model, it is the Government/Cabinet and its advisers (BERC and central agencies) who establish the outcomes and outputs to be funded. The Government as "funder" is responsible for funding service delivery. As "owner" of the State's businesses it also aims to maintain and improve the productivity of the State's asset base, via capital charging and other accounting techniques. This has resulted in a considerable strengthening of the hand of various central agencies, notably, in the Victorian context, the Department of Treasury and Finance.

In the current Victorian public administration model, portfolio Ministers and departmental secretaries act as agents for the government. It is they who purchase the specified services and "manage the purchase relationship in the most efficient and effective manner to meet government outcomes" (VDTF 1997a, p11). The Government, via the Budget Papers, specifies the broad outputs, and responsible Ministers and their secretaries purchase these. Providers of these services can be either internal or external to the public sector, hence the idea of 'contestability'.

At present it is too early to review and evaluate the actual application of OABB and OBM in the Victorian public sector. However, at least one Parliamentary Committee (VPAEC, 1998) has expressed some concern that the current reform direction is ignoring public sector and parliamentary accountability. This is a theme that the VPAEC (1997, p.7) has been expressing for some time:

> *"Accountability is a contract between two parties. In the case of government, the contract is between the public and the government: the public gives government responsibility to govern and manage public resources, and the government is accountable to the public*

through the Parliament for its performance. It is a concept fundamental to our democratic system. It clearly establishes the right of the people both to know what government intends to do, and how well it has met its goals."

That this concern has been raised, despite the growing quantity of financial, non-financial and performance related disclosures provided by a variety of communications mechanisms, speaks volumes. In particular, it raises questions about the quality of disclosures being provided -- quality, rather than quantity, being the dominant hallmark of effective accountability processes.

Performance indicators and budget papers

A central feature of the official position relating to public financial management has been that departmental performance and accountability ought to be viewed in output terms (as expressed in accrual financial statements and performance indicators) rather than in input terms. This shift has in turn privileged the role of accounting, which has moved from a subordinate service role to a dominate, agenda-setting role (Parker and Guthrie, 1993). In particular, these 'new' accounting technologies are said to offer the possibility of according greater decision-making authority and flexibility to managers, while also helping to ensure that management action is in accordance with the broader social and economic objectives of government (VDTF, 1997a, b, c).

Vitally, advocates of these new public financial management techniques argue that they are causally related to subsequent public sector performance improvement. Meaningful performance improvement, it is argued, stems from the adoption of a reflexive output / outcome based approach to management and budgeting, an approach which by its very nature necessitates the production of increased volumes of performance based data. This data is in turn responded to by managers in a circular process of continuous improvement, leading to efficiency and effectiveness improvements.

Consequently, a central feature of the official rhetoric relating to this transformation has been that output performance indicators hold the key to the provision of greater government accountability and better decision making about resource allocation, planning and management practices. Associated with this aspect of the rhetorical NPFM campaign has been a growing emphasis on the production and dissemination of a growing inventory of non-financial and other performance related metrics and information in fora traditionally reserved for narrower, highly financially focused content.

One such forum is the annual budget paper series published in jurisdictions such as Victoria (and most jurisdictions with broadly similar governmental and governance arrangements). Indeed, annual budget papers are generally regarded as a primary vehicle by which budget dependent agencies can communicate accountability information to the parliament and by which they can be held to account in the following year of operations. This accountability process incorporates financial and non-financial as well as performance information.

The suggestion that disclosures relating to performance indicators form a vital component of accountability regimes for a range of entities and entity types is not novel. If a narrow conception of accountability, in which information is disclosed only in order to report (Normanton, 1971) is rejected, then it follows that a part of the role of accountability disclosures is also to explain (Patton, 1992). There seems little reason to believe that the narrow view substantially guides the theoretical underpinnings of accountability regulatory regimes in Australia (MAB, 1993). Rather, if a decision usefulness perspective is applied, the inclusion of data and information surplus to basic financial disclosures can be seen to be of great significance to interested stakeholders. Indeed, it may be that the value of financial disclosures is lessened in the absence of supporting non-financial disclosures (Barton, 1999).

The debate therefore, is not as to whether financial disclosures ought to be accompanied by non-financial disclosures, including those relating to performance indicators, but rather the content, nature and quality of those non-financial disclosures. Empirical studies have highlighted the demand from report users for qualitative and quantitative non-financial information to accompany financial disclosures (Van Daniker and Kwiatkowski, 1986). Of key contextual importance, however, is the recognition that whereas the structure, form and content of financial disclosures is regulated according to a relatively prescriptive model (Micallef, 1997), no such prescription generally exists in relation to non-financial disclosures. These therefore tend to show considerable diversity (Hyndman and Anderson, 1995). Ideally however, in the context of the public sector, performance indicators should assist users of reports in understanding the inputs, outputs, outcomes and policies relating to a particular period of time (Stewart, 1984).

Annual reports issued by public sector agencies have been the focus of considerable attention and research (Cameron and Guthrie, 1993; Guthrie, 1993; McCrae and Aiken, 1994). This reflects the assumed importance of agency annual reports as a component of the overall accountability framework (JCPA, 1989; VPAEC, 1999a). Increasingly, however, the suggestion has arisen in the literature that public sector agency reports are not as widely used or sought after as is conventionally assumed to be the case (Gaffney, 1986; Engstrom, 1988; Hay, 1994; Mack *et al*, 2001). On the other hand, Budget papers are produced with a clear constituency in mind (Carlin and Guthrie, 2001, Guthrie and Carlin 2000), a phenomenon which has continued over an extended period.

Wanna *et al*, (2000, p.1) state that "Budgets are indispensable to executive government; and accountable budgetary processes are a key mechanism of stable, democratic societies." Although the delivery of accountability to parliament has been the key role performed by budget papers, the format of those budget papers has changed significantly in Australia since the mid 1990s. This wave of change was brought about by the introduction of accrual and output based forms of budgeting in Australian jurisdictions.

Previous studies have questioned the introduction of accrual accounting generally, (Guthrie, 1998) and specifically as it relates to the budget process (Carlin and Guthrie, 2001; Guthrie and Carlin, 2000). In attempting to evaluate the various public management initiatives now being implemented across Australia, New Zealand and the globe, in most cases it is too soon to answer the questions "what works, what doesn't, to what extent, in which contexts, and why? (Jones *et al*, 2001). However, in relatively mature examples of NPFM-oriented reform (e.g. several Australia states and New Zealand), adjustments and considerable steering is evident.

It can be said that any significant experimentation with new forms of performance indicators will lead to discontinuities and issues of monitoring. If this is so, it must be asked: When does a system settle down? How long does one have to wait to get it right? Can this aspect of NPFM ever be seen to be able to deliver the claimed benefits? These are all difficult questions to answer. In the Victorian case, is a decade of performance information enough for practice to be 'settled'?

Other jurisdictions are experiencing similar disjunction and problems with these practices. The Victorian experience is therefore instructive, as Victoria has been considered to be a leader in the adoption of Accrual output based budgets and output based management in Australia.

Carlin and Guthrie (2001) examined recent efforts in the Australian and New Zealand public sectors to implement accrual output-based budgeting. While agreeing with the need for public sector accounting reform, the authors used two detailed case studies -- that of Queensland and New Zealand -- to show that the current reforms have not yet achieved the results expected due to weaknesses in implementation. The gap between rhetoric and reality is apparent, for example, in that *de facto* there is little real difference in reporting between cash-based and accrual budgets in these two cases, leading these authors to question the degree to which management practices can change if reporting for decision making is unaltered. We posit that such a rhetoric -- reality gap may also be a systemic feature of the manner in which performance based information is reported in annual budget paper series.

This is a factor of significance, since alongside the change to accrual output based budgeting came calls for the inclusion of greater quantities of performance related information. The function of this information is "officially" to better assist users in determining whether or not claimed efficiencies relating to management improvement programs had been achieved, and to allow more accurate gauging of the efficiency and effectiveness of publicly funded endeavours (VPAEC, 2000; VPAEC, 2001). This has culminated in a situation where, in contemporary budget papers, the quantity of non-financial and performance indicator disclosures outweighs the quantity of financial disclosures. For instance, an indication of this trend is presented in Table 1 below, which documents the growth in the relative level of disclosure of performance indicator data, compared to disclosures of traditional financial data in Victorian budget estimates papers from 1998 to 2001[3].

Table 1: Performance Indicator to Financial Information Ratio

Victorian Budget Estimates, 1998 vs 2001

Department	Performance Indicator to Financial Information page ratio 2001/02	Performance Indicator to Financial Information page ratio 1998/99
Education	3.33:1	2:1
Human Services	5.66:1	2.11:1
Infrastructure	4.57:1	2:1
Justice	5:1	2.87:1
Natural Resources and Environment	5.66:1	3.66:1
Premier and Cabinet	2.5:1	2.25:1
State and Regional Development	3.71:1	3:1

The simple fact that a range of performance indicator data has been disclosed in Budget papers does not mean that the disclosures have resulted in an enhanced comprehension capability on the part of budget paper users. Given the primary parliamentary accountability role fulfilled by the production of annual Budget paper series (VPAEC, 1999), an important research question centers around the degree to which the inclusion of this performance indicator data can be seen as enhancing the quality of accountability discharged as a result of the publication of Budget papers. In this paper, the preferred methodological approach to achieving this task is to concentrate on the primary source data (Broadbent and Guthrie, 1992) within the budget papers (Shaoul, 1997, Edwards and Shaoul, 1996), rather than undertaking analysis of (in this case limited) secondary sources on the matter.

Empirical investigation of performance indicator disclosures in budget papers

Table 1 (above) outlined the changing ratio of disclosure between non-financial performance indicators and traditional financial data. An alternative means of capturing the increase in volume in performance indicator data disclosures is to examine the absolute number of performance indicators disclosed by Departments. Table 2 (Departmental Performance Indicator Counts in Budget Papers) shows this data, and demonstrates that in the case of most departments, there has been significant growth in the quantity of performance indicator disclosure since 1999. The overall growth in performance indicator disclosure over the three year period studied was 32.5%.

Table 2: Departmental Performance Indicator Counts in Budget Papers

Department	1999/00	2000/01	2001/02
Education	131	176	165
Human Services	143	206	258
Infrastructure	158	265	282
Justice	184	207	227
Natural Resources and Environment	268	256	282
Premier and Cabinet	150	192	131
State and Regional Development	225	254	280
Treasury and Finance	147	265	237
Total	1 406	1 821	1 862

Growth rates varied from this average in individual departments, the highest rate of growth being experienced in the Department of Human Services, whose performance indicator count appears to have increased by 80% over the three year data horizon. Over the same period of time, the Department of the Premier and Cabinet actually reduced the number of performance indicators reported on in its budget paper series. This data suggests a prima facie commitment to disclosure quality enhancement by means of increased performance indicator disclosure.

However, despite the material increases in volumes of disclosures, concerns have been raised about the usefulness of these additional disclosures, especially as a result of apparently low survival rates for performance indicators (VPAEC, 2000). Variation in performance indicator disclosure can be measured in several ways. The simplest is to track the rate of change in number of disclosed indicators over time. This provides a basic measure of variation. However, because existing measures may be deleted over time and replaced with new measures, examining the quantity of disclosed measures alone provides insufficient data for a detailed analysis. For this reason, two other phenomena must be studied.

The first of these is the "survival rate". This quantifies the propensity of performance indicators to persist through several reporting cycles. The second is the "novelty rate", which measures the proportion of each year's performance indicators which have been newly introduced relative to the reported set of indicators for a given base year. Together, these three metrics -- number, survival and novelty -- provide a detailed picture of the stability of performance indicator reporting over time, and therefore allow insights into the quality of disclosure and accountability, particularly from an inter-temporal perspective.

In order to develop more detailed insights into performance indicator disclosure characteristics, two of eight Departments were chosen, at random, for examination. These were:

1. Department of Education.

2. Department of Infrastructure.

Within each of these departments, an output group was selected for detailed review. The output groups selected for each of the departments were:

1. Education (School Education).

2. Infrastructure (Metropolitan Transport Services).

All performance indicators for each output within these output groups were then examined on a time series basis[4]. Survival rates stated in the tables are calculated using the 1999/00 disclosures as the base year. Thus, if for a particular output in 1999/00, five performance measures had been reported on, and by 2000/01 only three of the original five continued to be reported on, the stated survival rate for 2000/01 would be 60%. If by 2001/02, only two of the original five indicators set out in the 1999/00 budget papers, the stated 'survival rate' as at 2001/02 would be expressed as 40%.

"Novelty rates" are calculated as follows. If five performance indicators had been specified in 1999/00, and all five continued to be reported on in 2000/01, but an additional five performance indicators were added to the disclosure inventory for that output in that year, then the novelty rate for that output / year would be 50%. If in the following year (2001/02), all of the original ratios continued to survive but an additional five ratios were added, bringing the total disclosed to fifteen, then the novelty rate would be expressed as 67%, because two thirds of the performance indicators reported on for that year would be new, vis a vis the base year (1999/00).

High disclosure instability will therefore be suggested where low survival and high novelty rates are observed. On the other hand, low novelty rates and high survival rates indicate a stable reporting format and content, giving rise to conditions conducive to meaningful reporting and performance analysis, assuming that the reported content is meaningful and representative of the underlying activities of the budget sector entity under review.

Data for each of the detailed reviews is set out in tables 3 to 6 below. The analysis suggests a significant variation in the performance indicator selection and reporting practices of Victorian government departments. Both of the output groups studied (School Education and Metropolitan Transport Services) revealed a surprisingly high rate of performance indicator change, novelty and correspondingly low survival rates over the time series. Note that the performance indicators examined in the tables set out below categorise performance indicators according to three general descriptions -- quantity, quality and timeliness. These categories, used in the budget papers, are also used here for the sake of consistency and interpretability.

Table 3: Department of Education - School Education Output Group

Performance Indicator Count

	1999/00	2000/01	2001/02
Primary P – 6			
Quantity	7	7	11
Quality	4	5	14
Total	11	12	25
Junior Secondary			
Quantity	6	6	10
Quality	4	5	10
Total	10	11	20
Senior Secondary			
Quantity	3	4	5
Quality	4	5	11
Total	7	9	16
Grand Total	28	32	61

Table 4: Department of Education – School Education, Survival and Novelty Analysis

	Survival Base + 1	Survival Base + 2	Novelty Base + 1	Novelty Base + 2
Primary Education				
Quantity	57%	14%	43%	91%
Quality	50%	50%	60%	80%
Junior Secondary				
Quantity	67%	33%	33%	80%
Quality	100%	100%	25%	60%
Senior Secondary				
Quantity	100%	33%	25%	80%
Quality	100%	75%	20%	73%

Table 5: Department of Infrastructure – Metropolitan Transport Services

Performance Indicator Count

	1999/00	2000/01	2001/02
Metropolitan Train Services			
Quantity	1	2	2
Quality	1	4	4
Timeliness	2	0	0
Total	4	6	6
Metropolitan Tram Services			
Quantity	1	3	2
Quality	1	5	6
Timeliness	1	0	0
Total	3	8	8
Metropolitan Bus Services			
Quantity	1	1	2
Quality	3	4	3
Timeliness	1	1	1
Total	5	6	6
Grand Total	12	20	20

Table 6: Department of Infrastructure -- Public Transport Services,

Survival and Novelty Analysis

	Survival Base + 1	Survival Base + 2	Novelty Base + 1	Novelty Base + 2
Metropolitan Train Services				
Quantity	0%	0%	100%	100%
Quality	100%	100%	75%	75%
Timeliness	0%	0%	0%	0%
Metropolitan Tram Services				
Quantity	0%	0%	100%	100%
Quality	100%	100%	25%	60%
Timeliness	0%	0%		
Metropolitan Bus Services				
Quantity	100%	100%	25%	80%
Quality	100%	50%		
Timeliness	100%	100%	20%	73%

Note the combined volatility of the underlying performance disclosure inventories, as captured by the three dimensions, number, survival and novelty. This tends to reinforce concerns set out above, in relation to the potential gap between indicator quantity and indicator quality.

The quality of performance indicator disclosures

There is no necessary nexus between the fact of disclosure and the quality of the information transmitted within the disclosure. The data reported in this paper suggests a growth in the quantity of performance related disclosures over the period studied, both in absolute and relative terms. However, this paper has raised concerns about the ability of that data to effectively articulate useful perspectives on agency performance, due to high turnover, high novelty and low survival rates. From a quantitative analytical perspective, the measurement of change in numbers of reported indicators, survival and novelty rates captures a vital dimension of performance indicator quality. However, in order to be more comprehensive, a six component quality assessment methodology which rates quality in terms of six key factors is proposed. It is posited that performance indicator data captured and reported by agencies should be:

- *Correlative:* The suite of indicators selected by an agency should correlate closely with its key operational imperatives and activities. Indicators whose content relates to matters which are largely peripheral or cosmetic should be excluded. If this dimension of quality is satisfied, then performance indicator disclosures assist the accountability process in two interrelated ways. First, the indicators, because they correlate closely with the underlying activities of the agency, provide an additional descriptive framework to assist report users in developing comprehension of the scope and nature of the activities undertaken by the agency. Secondly, and derivatively, they assist report users in assessing the effectiveness and efficiency of the agency's operations. A detailed review of reported performance indicators for a sample of Victorian budget sector agencies suggests that a significant degree of compliance with this quality dimension is currently being achieved.

- *Controllable:* In order to facilitate meaningful analysis of the degree to which an agency's changing performance profile has been driven by endogenous rather than exogenous factors, it is preferable that performance information published by agencies relate to factors which are largely within their control. This dimension is far less satisfactorily satisfied in the budget paper disclosures we reviewed. While comprehensively cataloguing the nature of observed deviations from this objective is outside the scope of this paper, a number of common stylistic errors were observed during the conduct of the empirical research. For example, many agencies report extensive data on the number of projects they have initiated or completed during a particular period of time (for example "number of road safety campaigns conducted"). It is suggested however, that whether a program is run or not is largely due to the influence of external funding decisions, rather than factors internal to the agency. A better approach to shaping data in relation to programs undertaken would be to concentrate on the internal value added dimension – for example, level of participation in road safety programs, changed level of awareness as a result of road safety programs, and so on. A similar problem exists when agencies report on indicators such as "households receiving mains electricity concessions". Again, it is observed that whether or not households are able to receive such concessions is the result of a non agency based policy decision. What would be more useful from an agency focused performance analysis and reporting perspective would be to report data such as "percentage of eligible households receiving mains electricity concessions" and so on. In that way, the operational effectiveness of the implementing agency would be highlighted, rather than the impact of a high level policy decision to offer concessions to a segment of the population.

- *Comprehensible:* In order to be useful, report readers must be able to understand reported indicators. A starting point is to ensure that a relevant unit of measure is provided for each reported indicator. There were almost no observed exceptions to this requirement in the Victorian budget papers we reviewed. In addition to clear specification of appropriate unit measures, performance indicators ought to be able to be described succinctly and pointedly. Again, a detailed review suggests that this is generally the case.

- *Contemporaneous:* In order to maximise usefulness, reported indicators should relate as closely as possible to the present. Unfortunately, this is a dimension that is systematically breached in budget paper reporting of performance data. In the 2001 / 02 Victorian budget papers, the latest year for which actual data is reported on any performance indicator is 1999. This means that data is largely out of date by the time that it is reported in the budget paper series, a phenomenon which arises from the production of budget estimates before the completion of the prior period, necessitating a two period delay for the disclosure of actual data.

- *Consistent:* it is argued that consistency across time is a key dimension of quality in performance reporting. Since earlier sections of this paper have included detailed data on the degree to which a sample of agencies' reported indicators satisfy this criterion (they did not), no further comment is made here other than to reinforce that this quality dimension has been systematically breached in Victorian budget paper disclosures.

- *Constrained:* it is argued that the selection of a suite of performance indicators for reporting purposes must be the result of a disciplined, focused process. Reported indicators should be constrained to that set necessary to convey a clear and accurate picture of the operations of a reporting agency, rather than expanded to include measures of potentially little interest or use. An empirical review suggests, on the basis of an observed increase in the population of reported performance measures, that this quality dimension may not be receiving adequate attention at present.

Performance information and audit in Victoria

The above-mentioned suggested means of improving the quality of performance information and therefore public accountability and confidence in these "new" types of reporting and to ensure transparency of information and accountability of performance information in Budget Papers and departmental annual reports, is to subject this information to scrutiny by an independent body. That is, there is a potential need for independent review and evaluation of the performance information in Budget papers and annual reports.

For at least the last 6 years the VPAEC has raised the issue of reliability and consistency in the reporting of performance indicators in annual reports and budget papers. An example of this is the call made by the Victorian Public Accounts and Estimates Committee in its review of the 1999/2000 Victorian Budget Estimates (VPAEC, 2000), in which recommendation 1.3 suggests: "The outputs, performance measures, targets and actual figures reported in the Budget Papers and annual reports should be independently audited or evaluated."

In 1999, the Victorian Parliament amended the *Audit Act* to provide the authority for the Auditor-General to audit performance measures and to express an opinion as to whether they are:

- Relevant to the stated objectives of the department.

- Appropriate for the assessment of actual performance; and

- Fairly represent actual performance.

However, the Victorian Auditor General's Office has not, for a variety of reasons, taken up this legislative challenge even though in his most recent report on Ministerial Portfolios it was found that (VAG, 2001):

- "Considerable progress has been made by the Government in implementing a new performance management and reporting framework for the budget sector. The framework is not yet sufficiently developed for audit opinions to be issued regarding the relevance, appropriateness and fair presentation of performance information."

- "The output measures incorporated in the Government's Budget Papers may not be the most appropriate indicators of departmental performance."

The key Victorian accountability requirements under the *Financial Management Act* 1994, and the Management Reform Program that followed, have been for all departments and public bodies to:

- Establish a corporate and business planning process.

- Define measures relating to quantity, quality, timeliness and cost measures for various output groups, as part of the annual budget process.

- Prepare audited annual financial statements and a report of operations; and

- Table the financial statements and report of operations in Parliament, through their relevant Minister.

In the past decade a number of Victorian performance audits have examined and reported on the quality of performance information reported by departments. As indicated above, the audit legislation was amended in December 1999 to provide the Auditor-General with a further mandate. The legislation specifically provides for the following:

"The Auditor-General may audit any report of the operations of an authority under section 45 of the Financial Management Act 1994 to determine whether any performance indicators in the report of operations:

(a) are relevant to any stated objectives of the authority; and

(b) are appropriate for the assessment of the authority's actual performance; and

(c) fairly represent the authority's actual performance."

These provisions are clearly directed at providing the Auditor-General with discretion to issue audit opinions on performance information reported publicly by departments and public bodies, including in Budget papers and annual reports.

However, the current VAG has not taken up this legislative challenge as

> *"4.1.19... We have formed the view that it has not yet been sufficiently developed to enable audit opinions to be issued regarding the relevance, appropriateness and fair presentation of performance indicators (emphasis in original). We have also identified a number of areas relating to the framework which need to be addressed, to achieve a sound public reporting regime."*

This concern with budget papers and performance information is not confined to Victoria. Recently the Commonwealth Joint Committee of Public Accounts and Audit announced a major public hearing as part of its review of the effectiveness, and options for enhancing the format and content of, the current budget documentation. In announcing the public hearing the Chairman, Mr Bob Charles MP (JCPA, 2001), said:

"The Committee has had an ongoing interest in accrual accounting. In 1995 it recommended to government that it consider the merits of requiring budgets to be prepared and appropriations to be made on an accrual basis. However the Committee has become concerned about the possibility that the benefits of the accrual approach are not being realised. Of fundamental importance to the democratic system is the ability of the Parliament to undertake effective scrutiny of the Executive. The Committee notes the following concerns raised in submissions: information about expenditure on particular Government activities is being obscured by the way in which it is reported; the inability for observers to track the expenditure on particular programs from year to year; and performance measures being used by agencies are not meaningful."

Further evidence of significant interest in these issues by various jurisdictions can be found in the report from the 2001 Australasian Council of Public Accounts Committees 6th Biennial Conference held in Canberra (ACPAC 2001). While we note that there is currently high interest in the potential need for audit of performance related disclosures, we conclude that in Australia at least, for the present, this quality control is not being systematically applied.

Summary and conclusions

The empirical review of performance indicator disclosure in recent Victorian budget papers over three budget cycles reveals considerable turmoil in indicator disclosure. This runs contrary to the goal of enhancing the quality of disclosures in budget papers, because users are often, by reason of high turnover, unable to observe time series results. Furthermore, when new indicators are added to budget papers, it will often be the case that no data relating to actual outcomes with respect to that indicator will be available for up to two years after the indicator is first reported. Given the low survival rates noted in our empirical analysis, this means that in many cases, no actual data is ever reported in respect of performance indicators. Instead, during the (often brief) period of their survival, the only reported data is in the form of targets. An inability to compare actual outcomes with targeted outcomes is a fundamental flaw in any system of accountability. Likewise, the inability to construct consistent performance time series represents a serious weakness in the current budget accountability regime in Victoria.

These difficulties should be viewed in light of the technical characteristics of the reform process and model outlined above. Specifically, recall that a key claim made in relation to the operation of the accrual output based budgeting and management model is that it is a causal trigger for enhanced agency and sector performance. That causal link, however, rests on the structure provided by reflexive performance feedback generated with respect to the linkages between inputs, outputs and subsequent outcomes. The empirical analysis conducted within this paper suggests, however, that the information performance bridge necessary for the sustenance of the reflexive improvement process, discussed above, is consistently and systematically broken, as a result of performance disclosure inconsistency.

This paper has not speculated about the causes of the apparently high turnover, low survival and high novelty rates of performance indicator disclosures in Victoria over the period under consideration. A hypothesis proposed elsewhere in relation to annual report disclosures suggests that disclosure variability may be related to a desire on the part of report preparers to obfuscate (Courtis 1998). Explanations of variation in the budget papers we examined tended to suggest that changes were based on a desire to improve the extant performance indicator inventory, to provide an enhanced view of the underlying operations, efficiency and effectiveness of Victorian government agencies. At present there appears no reason to prefer either explanation, and this may offer an opportunity for further research in the future. However, irrespective of the inability to reach conclusions as to the cause of the high performance indicator turnover we observed, there is no difficulty in concluding that at least at present, the quality of disclosure has suffered as a result of the observed lack of disclosure stability, as well perhaps as a result of the lack of a systematic audit quality control framework in Australian jurisdictions. Resolving this problem represents a significant challenge for policy makers and practitioners.

NOTES

1. Australia is a federation and includes three levels of government: federal, state and local. Victoria is one of six states and has its own parliament and executive government. Each state plays a major role in service delivery in areas such as education, health care, police and security, and social services.

2. The scheme adopted here is similar to what Pallot (1998b) reports for New Zealand. The earlier phases are:

    Traditional phase (prior to 1982), typified by cash accounting and controls over inputs and reliance on the established budgetary, executive and Westminster parliamentary systems.

    Managerialist phase (1982-1992), characterised by attempts to introduce private sector management techniques and accrual accounting for external reporting and management purposes into the Victorian public sector. This phase also involved a reliance on setting objectives, performance indicators, performance evaluations and parliamentary oversight of performance.

3. The ratios within the tables are calculated on the basis of page counts.

BIBLIOGRAPHY

ACPAC, 2001, Report of the 6th Biennial Conference, February, Canberra.

BARTON A., (1999), "Public and Private Sector Accounting – The Non Identical Twins", *Australian Accounting Review,* 9, 2, 22 – 31.

BROADBENT, J., and J. Guthrie, (1992), "Change in the Public Sector: a Review of Recent Alternative Accounting Research", *Accounting, Auditing and Accountability Journal,* 5, 2, 3-31.

CAMERON J., and J. Guthrie, (1993), "External Annual Reporting by an Australian University: Changing Patterns", *Financial Accountability and Management,* 9, 1, 1– 15.

CARLIN, T. and J. Guthrie, (2000), "Central Public Sector Budgetary Integrity: an evaluation model", ANZAM Conference 2000, MGSM, Sydney, December 3-6 2000, 1-6.

CARLIN, T., and J. Guthrie, (2001), "Lessons from Australian and New Zealand Experiences with Accrual Output Based Budgeting", in Jones, Guthrie and Steane, eds, *Research in Public Policy Analysis and Management* , 11, A, 89 – 100.

COURTIS, J., (1998), "Annual Report Readability Variability: Tests of the Obfuscation Hypothesis", *Accounting, Auditing and Accountability Journal,* 11, 4, 459 – 471.

EDWARDS, P. and J. Shaoul, (1996), *Reporting Accounting,* Working Paper (Manchester University, Manchester).

ENGLISH, L., (2001) (forthcoming), "Emasculating Accountability in the name of competition: reform of State Audit in Victoria", *Critical Perspectives,* Special Issue Government Accountability and the Role of the Auditor General.

ENGLISH, L., and J. Guthrie, (2001), "Public Sector Management in the State of Victoria 1992-1999: Genesis of the Transformation", in L. R. Jones, J. Guthrie, and P. Steane, eds, *Learning From International Public Management Reform* (London Elsevier-Oxford,) 45-59.

ENGSTROM, J., (1988), *Information Needs of College and University Decision Makers* (Stamford: Governmental Accounting Standards Board).

GAFFNEY, M. A., (1986), "Consolidated versus Fund Type Financial Statements: The Perspectives of Constituents", *Journal of Accounting and Public Policy,* 5, 3, 167 – 190.

GUTHRIE, J., (1993), "Australian Public Business Enterprises: Analysis of Changing Accounting, Auditing and Accountability Regimes", *Financial Accountability and Management,* 9, 2, 101 – 114.

GUTHRIE, J., and T. Carlin, (2000), "Australian Experiences with Output Based Budgeting: when theory and practice don't meet", The 1999 ASCPA Annual Research Lecture in Government Accounting, ASCPA Research Monograph, Melbourne.

GUTHRIE, J. and L. Parker, (1998b), 'Managerial' and 'Marketisation' in Financial Management Change in Australia', in Olson, O. *et al.* (Eds), pp. 49-75.

GUTHRIE, J., C. Humphrey, and O. Olson, (1997), "Public Financial Management Changes in OECD Nations", *Advances in International Comparative Management*, Supplement 3, pp.255-269.

GUTHRIE, J., O. Olson, and C. Humphrey, (1999), "Debating developments in new public financial management: the limits of global theorising and some new ways forward", *Financial Accountability and Management*, 15, 3 & 4, 209-228.

HAY D., (1994), "Who Uses Public Sector External Reports? An Exploration", *Accounting Forum*, March, 47 – 65.

HYNDMAN, N. S., and R. Anderson, (1995), "The Use of Performance Information in External Reporting: An Empirical Study of UK Executive Agencies", *Financial Accountability and Management* 11,1, February 1995, 1 – 17.

JCPA, 2001, *Hearing Into Accrual Ouput Based Budgeting,* press release, June 2001, Canberra.

Joint Committee of Public Accounts (JCPA), (1989), *Guidelines for Departmental Annual Reports*, Report 304, Parliament of Australia, AGPS, Canberra.

JONES, L., (1997), "Changing How we Budget: Arron Wildavsky's Perspective", *Journal of Public Budgeting, Accounting and Financial Management*, 9, 1, 46-71.

JONES, L. R., J. Guthrie, and P. Steane, (2001), "Learning from International Public Management Reform Experience", in Jones, L. R., J. Guthrie, and P. Steane, eds, *Learning From International Public Management Reform* (London: Elsevier-Oxford, 2001), 1-26.

JONES, L. R., J. Guthrie, and P. Steane, (eds), (2001 a, b), Learning From International Public Management Reform (London: Elsevier-Oxford, 2001).

MACK J., C. Ryan, and K. Dunstan, (2001), *Local Government Annual Reports: Australian Empirical Evidence on Recipients,* APIRA 2001 Conference, Adelaide.

Management Advisory Board (MAB), (1993), *Accountability in the Commonwealth Public Sector*, June 1993.

MCCRAE, M. and M. Aiken, (1994), "AAS 29 and Public Sector Reporting: Unresolved Issues", *Australian Accounting Review,* 4, 2, 65 – 72.

MICALLEF, F. (1997), "Financial Reporting by Governments: The Big Picture", *Charter*, 68 1, 50-51.

NORMANTON, E. L., (1971), "Public Accountability and Audit: A Reconnaissance", in Smith, B., and D. C. Hague, eds, *The Dilemma of Accountability in Modern Government: Independence Versus Control* (St Martin's Press).

NORMANTON, E. L., (1966), *The Accountability and Audit of Governments A Comparative Study* (Manchester: Manchester University Press,).

OLSON, O., J. Guthrie, and C. Humphrey, eds, (1998), *Global Warning: Debating International Developments in New Public Financial Management*, (Bergen, Norway: Cappelen Akademisk Forlag).

PALLOT, J., (1998a), "New Public Management Reform in New Zealand: The Collective Strategy Phase", *International Public Management Journal*, Vol. 1. Issue 1. 1-18.

PALLOT, J., (1998b), "The New Zealand Revolution", in Olson *et al.,* eds, *Global Warning: Debating International Developments in New Public Financial Management*, (Bergen, Norway: Cappelen Akademisk Forlag), 156-184.

PATTON J. M., (1992), "Accountability and Governmental Financial Reporting", *Financial Accountability and Management* 8, 3, Autumn, 165 – 180.

Victorian Report of the Victorian Commission of Audit (VCA) Vol. 1, (1993a) Melbourne: The Graphic Print Centre, May.

Victorian Report of the Victorian Commission of Audit (VCA), Vol. 2, (1993b) Melbourne: The Graphic Print Centre, May.

VPAEC, (1999), *Report on the Inquiry into Annual Reporting in the Victorian Public Sector* (Government Printer of the State of Victoria, Melbourne).

VPAEC, (2000), *Report 33 - The Budget Estimates* (Government Printer of the State of Victoria, Melbourne).

VPAEC, (2001), *Report 38 – The Budget Estimates* (Government Printer of the State of Victoria, Melbourne).

VPAEC, (1997a), *Nineteenth Report to Parliament Report on the 1996-97Budget Estimates and 1995-96 Budget Outcomes* (Government Printer for the State of Victoria, April).

VPAEC, (1997b), *Twenty-Third Report to Parliament Report on the 1997-98 Budget*

VPAEC, (1998), *Twenty-Seventh Report to Parliament Report on the 1998-99 Budget Estimates* (Government Printer for the State of Victoria, November).

VPAEC, (1999a), *Report No 28 Annual Reporting in the Victorian Public Sector* (Government Printer for the State of Victoria, May).

VPAEC, (1999b), *Thirty-Third Report to Parliament Report on the 1999-2000 Budget Estimates* (Government Printer for the State of Victoria).

VPAEC, (2000), *Thirty-Eighth Report to Parliament Report on the 2000-20001 Budget Estimates* (Government Printer for the State of Victoria November).

SHAMSHULLAH, A., (1999), "The Policy of Confidence: Politics in Victoria 1992-1998" in Costar, B. and N. Economou (eds), 1999, *The Kennett Revolution Victorian Politics in the 1990s*, (Sydney: UNSW Press Ltd).

SHAOUL, J, (1997), "The Power of Accounting: Reflecting on Water Privatisation?", *Accounting, Auditing and Accountability Journal*, 10, 3, 382 – 405.

Victorian Auditor-Generals (VAG), (2001), *Report on Ministerial Portfolios*, June 3, (2001), Victorian Auditor-Generals Office, Melbourne.

VAN DANIKER, R., and V. Kwiatkowski, (1986), "Infrastructure Assets: An Assessment of User Needs and Recommendations for Financial Reporting", research report, GASB.

VDTF (1997a), *Output Costing Guide* (The Department, Melbourne).

VDTF (1997b), *Output Specification and Performance Measurement* (The Department, Melbourne).

VDTF (1997c), *Reform of the Budget Sector Victoria: elements of financial management* (The Department, Melbourne).

VDTF (1998), *A Guide to the Budget Papers, DTF* (The Department, Melbourne).

WANNA, J., J. Kelly, and J. Forster, (2000), *Managing Public Expenditure in Australia*, (Allen and Unwin, Sydney).

WILDAVSKY, A., (1974), *The Politics of the Budgetary Process*, (Little, Brown, Boston).

WILDAVSKY, A., (1992), *The New Politics of the Budgetary Process*, 2nd 3d, (New York: HarperCollins).

ACCESS TO INFORMATION – A LONG WAY TO GO

by

Cláudio Weber Abramo
General Secretary of Transparência Brasil
Member of the Board, Transparency International

The right of access to information generated within or held by the public sector has become one of the touchstones of the struggle to enhance public scrutiny of the state and to reinforce public officials' accountability. In many countries, freedom of information acts have been promulgated or are under discussion. In a few others – Canada, for example – freedom of information as provided by law is being continuously improved. These cases offer other countries a wealth of examples and policies actually in operation.

Of course, powerful forces are at work against widespread access to information in many of the countries that most need such access. These forces can be inert or dynamic. The former category includes a prevalence of inherently opaque administrative practices and attitudes, general inaptitude, and a real lack of sufficient human and material resources. Among the dynamic forces are a multitude of agents that resist openness, ranging from vested private interests to semi-institutional schemes to protect incompetence and systematic corruption from public scrutiny. In a country like Brazil, where many state structures cannot allege the almost complete lack of resources that affects other countries, often the only explanation for the absence of organised means to provide information is deliberate inaction.

Other areas in which information is clearly lacking are the judiciary, including data on administration and procedures; actual expenditures based on a previously approved budget, especially at state and municipal levels; follow-up to annual federal executive and legislative negotiations on budget amendments, also at state and municipal levels; and social security. Many other examples could be given of spheres where a lack of organised information feeds notoriously corrupt schemes.

Resistance can also come from unexpected sources. Multilateral financing agencies acting in concert are one such source. Following a recommendation contained in a "Master Bidding Document for Procurement" approved by all international financing agencies, the World Bank, the Inter-American Development Bank and financing agencies in all continents stipulate that, in procurements made with their money, the decision phase must observe a confidentiality clause that states:[1]

> *Information relating to the examination, clarification, evaluation, and comparison of bids, and recommendations for the award of a contract, shall not be disclosed to bidders or any other persons not officially concerned with such process until the award to the successful bidder has been announced. Any effort by a bidder to influence the Employer's processing of bids or award decisions may result in the rejection of the bidder's bid.*

The rationale behind the clause is expressed in the last sentence, but in practice the effect produced is often the opposite. Dishonest officials use the clause to withhold any information whatsoever about why and how they reach decisions, rejecting or accepting proposals on the basis of a given requirement. Meanwhile the same set of rules states that either the administration or the participants may initiate the swapping of "clarifying" information on a private basis, and this can be kept from the others by the confidentiality clause. Corruption is thus encouraged, rather than the contrary.

Such confidentiality has been turned down in Brazilian courts of law. (One case involved the World Bank-financed construction of Salvador's subway.) But because these decisions are not binding when applied to other spheres, officials repeat attempts to invoke the confidentiality clause. This forces interested parties to keep returning to the courts -- and not always successfully, due to the inconsistent behaviour of the Brazilian judiciary.

The picture is not entirely bleak, however: a handful of valuable measures have been initiated at the Brazilian federal level. Recently, procurement of standard goods and services by the federal government has been centralised in ComprasNet, thus allowing for instant price comparisons in public offices throughout the country. Some states, São Paulo among them, are also making efforts in that direction. Voluntary federal transfers (i.e. politically motivated programmes that transfer money from the federal treasury to municipalities to assist poor populations) have until recently brought about huge losses due to "friction" corruption. They have now been streamlined[2] following the relatively simple measures of:

1. Providing information through the Internet on the amounts of and schedules for municipalities' entitlements.

2. Installing automated auditing instruments.

This is not unlike what happened in Uganda,[3] where the simple measure of publishing the amount each school was entitled to receive from the government permitted the reversal of a situation in which 85% of the money disappeared along the way. In 2000, two years after the new system was inaugurated, only 5% of the money was lost -- 95% actually found its way to the schools.

Brazil's federal government programme entitled "Brasil Transparente" (lead by BNDES)[4] provides guidance and financing of state and municipal initiatives for the development of other programmes and tools to enhance transparency in the management of public affairs.

In other words, the capability seems to be there, and a few government sectors are showing real commitment to the task of enforcing access to information. Spreading this commitment not only to the rest of the executive structures but also to the legislative and to the judiciary is of course no easy task, but it is nevertheless a task that should be embraced by all concerned.

An appropriate legal framework is clearly needed as a condition for transparency but equally clearly, it will not be sufficient. A wide array of intervening factors must be in place to ensure that legal provisions are in fact implemented. Among them are:

- The existence of appropriate regulation, extending to all public agencies, establishing not only responsibilities but also the consequences of non-compliance.

- Training of public managers for transparency.

- The existence of organised demand, expressed by knowledgeable groups of stakeholders.

- Devising sensible systems and allocating human and material resources to actually put in place mechanisms of data organisation and retrieval.

The remainder of this chapter will briefly address the last of these factors.

Cutting through the bramble

Even when proper legislation is in place, if the right measures are not taken, providing access to information can very well take the form of stacking documents in (virtual) warehouses and leaving interested parties to find their way among a bewildering array of atomic bits of data. Thus, assuming the commitment is genuine, the main task is to open paths through the bramble.

This journey into the wilderness must be guided by one overall principle: in order to be valuable, information should be structured -- otherwise it is useless. The same set of primary data can be structured in many ways, and each of those ways is associated with a certain type of recovery. The state generates many kinds of information and those interested in gaining access to this information vary, as does the type of aggregation needed. Consequently, the elaboration of managerial procedures and design of technical tools for filing, searching and retrieving data are crucial.

Automated information recovery

Access to information is all about citizens easily getting hold of data. In the majority of countries, such access cannot be based on direct telematic solutions because the penetration of the Internet among the poorer categories of the population is almost nil. On the other hand, it would be absurd to base data retrieval systems on the physical manipulation of paper documents. Thus, the natural answer is to conceive interfaces that would be operated by front-line officials -- themselves perhaps barely computer-literate -- who would in turn would interact with interested citizens. This is a delicate task, since the less computer-literate the user is, the harder it is to design the systems they will operate.

One particular pitfall that can affect this type of initiative is the confusion between enforcing the right to information and bridging the so-called digital gap. While the latter has merits of its own, its aims, mechanisms and scope are not the same. Bridging the digital gap is not a necessary condition for widening access to information, because this can be facilitated by intermediation (provided by the state itself, by NGOs, by professional, business and community associations, etc.).

Centralisation vs. decentralisation

The enormous variety of data to be provided, the high variability affecting each family of data, and the need to provide for the most swift updating possible all strongly argue against centralised solutions. It is simply not possible to direct all information to a mammoth clearing house and proceed from there. On the contrary, each information node should be responsible for gathering, processing and making available data.

Decentralisation, however, comes with its own problems, chaos the first among them. In order to avoid chaos proper models should be developed, but models sufficiently flexible to allow for a certain degree of adaptation. If searching is to be efficient, mechanisms for cross-referencing and indexing should be built in at the very beginning. These mechanisms should be defined by users and not government alone.

Structuring information

One inexplicable cultural trend now encountered in organisations is that every time information is mentioned, the person from the IT department is called upon to advance suggestions, do the planning, and ultimately implement the solution. Alas, structuring information has no substantial relation to computer technology. Faced with the problem of deciding what to say during a negotiation held by teleconference, no one would contemplate seeking the answer from the person responsible for the phone switchboard. The situation here is no less absurd. The main piece of software required to structure information resides in the human brain; information technology is only the means to structure data according to an intellectual conception.

The key to an efficient information-processing facility is dedicating time and effort to intelligently considering which information should be related to which other information; which aggregations are useful to which ends; and, most importantly, how information is to be presented in order to be of the greatest value to which public. This consideration requires ample and constant consultation among stakeholders, including civil society organisations and professional and business associations. And it is a job requiring the collaboration of communications professionals. (Communication, by the way, is not advertising, public relations, or press relations; those three elements are aspects of it but do not constitute the whole.)

The overall objective -- providing useful information to the public -- must be constantly kept in mind. Many government Internet sites seem to forget that ultimate goal, and as a result many of these sites fall short of delivering their promises. One example is the São Paulo state procurement Web site, managed by Imprensa Oficial do Estado, the state's printing/publishing facility.[5] The search engine provided there does not allow for searches based on the nature of the thing procured, nor does the database seem to be keyword-indexed. There are only three fields: office, city and something mysterious called "various". This of course prevents finding procurement pertaining to specific economic activities and thus frustrates the main objective of having a procurement Web site, which is to broaden participation in order to lower prices.[6]

A second example is the federal government's site on organisational information,[7] under the responsibility of the Planning Ministry (Ministério do Planejamento, Orçamento e Gestão). The site provides information on the structure and upper-echelon personnel of all federal executive offices up to the presidency -- encompassing more than 25 500 officials responsible for more than 46 000 offices. At first sight it is a near-excellent site -- the "near-" arising from the fact that information on people's earnings is presented implicitly in the form of their functional codes, and not explicitly as their salaries. The person wanting to understand what "DAS 101.6" means in terms of money must embark on a frustrating search. Of course it is possible to phone a friend in the federal government and ask for directions, but that is not an option for most ordinary people. To this day, the author does not know how much money a DAS 101.6 person earns, as the Secretary of Administration does not appear to maintain a Web site. Obviously, the organisational site should link the salary code to the respective amount, a task that does not require hiring a Bill Gates.

NOTES

1. The "Master" currently refers only to goods, but the principles contained are being applied to all types of procurement. A history of this document can be found at the Asian Development Bank Web site: *http://www.adb.org/Documents/Periodicals/ERO/2000/procurement.asp.*

2. By the Federal Secretary of Internal Finance Control, Ministry of Finance. A number of Brazilian states replicated this policy.

3. With help from the United Nations Development Program.

4. Banco Nacional de Desenvolvimento Econômico e Social, the Brazilian official development agency.

5. *http://www.imprensaoficial.sp.gov.br.*

6. It is perhaps worth mentioning that the *Imprensa Oficial* home page registers almost 9 million visitors since 1997, while the procurement page registers only 707 (30 October 2001). There must be something to be learned from that.

7. *Sistema de Informações Organizacionais do Governo Federal, http://www.siorg.redegoverno.gov.br.*

PUBLIC SCRUTINY AND ACCESS TO INFORMATION IN FINLAND

by

Katju Holkeri
Counsellor, Ministry of Finance, Finland

Introduction

In Finland, openness is an underlying value in the public administration. It is also, along with access to information, an issue to which constant attention is paid in public management development work. Openness is not only about laws and regulations -- it is also very much about attitude and commitment.

In Finland there are three key issues to be emphasised in this respect:

- A strong legislative base.

- Continuous development.

- The use of information and communication technology and new tools to enhance openness and citizen participation.

General context

Although the issue has perhaps been discussed more frequently in recent years than previously, the participation and consultation of citizens and their access to information have always been high on the Finnish Government's agenda. The degree to which the administration values openness is reflected, for instance, in:

- The structure of the Finnish administration, the strong self-government of municipalities, and the fact that decision-making power is close to citizens.

- Participation that has a strong basis in legislation (the Constitution, the Local Government Act).

- The strong role of citizen organisations. There are about 110 000 of these in Finland, of which 63 000 are active.

The current government states in its programme that it aims to create a constantly developing society that will guarantee everyone the opportunity to participate actively.

The government wants to ensure the democratic development of its policy of governance and real possibilities for citizens to influence matters on all administrative levels. It is also keen to increase the administration's openness and transparency. This aim will promote the role of the state and municipalities, as well as that of civic organisations, in attending to common issues. The state will also strive to remove obstacles from the activities of citizens and their organisations.

Reforming central government 2000–01

In May 2000, the Finnish Government decided that it would initiate a new reform of central government. A group of ministers was formed to head the project, supported by another group of civil servants which had one representative from each ministry. In September 2000, 13 projects were launched to carry forward the reform.

One of the reform's goals was to strengthen the trust citizens and personnel placed in their administration. Consequently, a subproject has been to increase the participation possibilities for citizens and NGOs in the preparation of socio-political programmes. The reform has also included a study on citizens' trust in ministries.

Strong legal framework

Government decision on principles of external information and communication

The guiding principles of Finland's information and communication policy are stated in a Government Decision (1994). These guidelines are also drawn from the Administrative Procedure Act and the Act on the Openness of Government Activities. One principle relates to the fair use of languages (Finnish and Swedish are both official languages in Finland). The policy aims to inform citizens about government administration and, in so doing, enhance democracy and the functioning of government. The climate of government openness in which policy is carried out allows citizens to exercise their rights and perform their duties. Government informs and communicates both directly and through the media. Each civil servant is well versed in the information relating to his/her own expert area. To ensure the success of information campaigns, an information officer has a right to participate in all relevant groups when important projects are in preparation.

The Government Decision (1994) states that a positive attitude towards information and communication and the new related challenges is needed throughout government. General principles include monitoring the effectiveness of internal communication, because it in turn underpins good external communication. Openness, correctness, reliability and swiftness are key factors. The decision also states that it is important to use language that is sufficiently clear and to try to present complicated matters in a way that is easy to understand. Communication is a two-way process. Information officers have to react if they see that the demand for knowledge is growing.

Administrative Procedure Act of 1982

The principles and rules established by this Act concern, *inter alia,* the publicising of proceedings, the initiation of matters, the hearing of parties concerned, basic information on and notification of a decision, and the correction of a procedure.

The Administrative Procedure Act regulates the participation of interested parties in a given matter. The Act prescribes that before a decision is made, the party shall be given an opportunity to respond to the claims put forward by others, and to present any evidence that may affect the decision. If the decision is likely to have substantial impact over a wider area or on the circumstances of several people, the public shall be informed of the matter pending.

Other laws such as the Water Act and the Act on Environmental Impact Assessment establish specific hearings for interested parties in the case of construction projects that have an effect on the environment or on water systems (e.g. the construction of roads, factories, energy plants or water projects).

The New Local Government Act of 1995

This Act emphasises the importance of members of the community and service users being able to participate in and directly influence democratic processes. Transparency and right of access are among the basic principles of local government.

Act on openness of government activities

At the beginning of December 1999, legislative reform pertaining to the secrecy of and access to information on government activities came into force, replacing a law dating from 1951. The new Act on the Openness of Government Activities implemented the right of access to information contained in official documents in the public domain. The right was extended to all those exercising public authority irrespective of the type of organisation involved. The new Act also codifies the most central provisions on secrecy.

The goals of the reform

The reform aims to increase the openness of government activities, to enhance the implementation of the openness principle, to improve the possibilities of participating in public debate and to influence the management of common issues. The Act applies to state and municipal enterprises as well as administrative authorities and the courts. It also applies to private-law organisations and private individuals performing functions involving the exercise of public authority or commissioned by an authority.

The new Act applies to all documents in the possession of the authorities irrespective of their manner of storage (paper, electronic). Access to information pertaining to issues of general importance is a prerequisite for the social debate that precedes decision-making. Access to preparatory documents allows people the possibility of ascertaining the grounds on which authorities make their decisions.

Before the new Act, access to internal accounts prepared by an authority and other preparatory documents required the permission of the authority in question. The new Act changed this main rule: with the exception of secret documents, all preparatory documents relating to decision making enter the public domain, at the very latest when the decision has been made. The reform thus enhances the openness of decision making.

Under the new Act, certain documents also enter the public domain earlier than they had before. Various studies, statistics and comparable accounts relating to the preparation of a project of general importance normally enter the public domain as soon as they have been finalised. The reform will also permit earlier access to the ministries' budget propositions.

One totally new aspect is that the authorities are now responsible for making available information on legislation being drafted and on other pending projects of general importance by means of (*inter alia*) a project register. All this facilitates the monitoring of matters that are pending and their preparation.

The reform also repeals a provision of the Penal Code under which it was a punishable act to disclose information in a document whose access was at the discretion of an authority. These documents usually related to matters that were pending. Amending the Penal Code created possibilities for the authorities to participate in public debate in their areas.

Promoting access to information

The right of access to information contained in documents in the authorities' possession is a basic right. Since under the Finnish Constitution public power has to promote the practical implementation of basic rights, the authorities are obliged to promote this access.

The authorities have to ensure that documents central to their activity are easily available. Indexes will have to be maintained of material in the public domain. The authorities have themselves actively produced information on their activities and social conditions. This information includes publications describing the activities of the authority, statistics, and a register of decisions. The Act also requires that the authorities ensure that this information is available in libraries and data networks.

Also new is the obligation laid down for all those exercising public authority to inform citizens of their activities. This obligation has long been part of the legislation on municipalities.

Access to a document in the public domain has to be granted as soon as possible, and in any event within one month (from the beginning of the year 2003, within two weeks) from the time the request is received.

The basis for interpretation: the openness principle

Access to a document is the main rule; secrecy is the exception. Therefore, restrictions on access to information will have to be interpreted narrowly. Otherwise, the authority will have to take the general principles of governance into account. Access to information may not be restricted any more than is necessary to protect the interests in question. On the practical level, if a document is only partly secret, access will be provided to those parts of the document that are in the public domain.

Principles for customer service

Under the new act, the authorities are required to ensure that their customer service functions well. Persons requesting information should be served quickly and efficiently. Where necessary, they will also be assisted in locating the information they want. All persons requesting information will be treated on an equal basis.

Planning and Building Act: dissemination of information and consultation with residents

Since the 1990s the general trend has been to disseminate information more effectively and increase public participation. In 1990, the Building Act was amended so that consultation that had focused mainly on landowners was shifted to broader consultation with the general public. In 1994, regulations came into effect on environmental impact assessment in land use planning. In recent years many local authorities have adopted more advanced forms of co-operative consultation based on genuine interaction with the people, instead of issuing the traditional "public announcements".

In the new Land Use and Building Act, people are given even better opportunities for involvement than before, particularly in the early stages of planning. The Act calls for a special participation and assessment scheme to be drawn up when land use planning work begins. Participation is organised separately plan by plan in consultation with all interested parties -- i.e. not only landowners, but also those whose living and working conditions and other circumstances are likely to be affected by the plan. Interested parties also include all authorities and organisations whose sphere of operations is concerned by the plan.

Environmental Impact Assessment Procedure Act

In an assessment procedure the environmental impacts of the project are established and assessed, and authorities and those whose circumstances or interests may be affected by the project are heard. If the project is likely to have a substantial impact over a wide area or on the circumstances of several people, those parties will be informed of the procedure by the co-ordination authority, unless they have already been adequately informed through other means. The information can also be provided by another authority, as provided (in greater detail) by the Act.

The co-ordination authority shall see to the assessment report's publication in the project's probable area of impact following public announcement. It shall also ensure that the public is invited to comment on the report, and given the opportunity to express views on the adequacy of the investigations and the environmental impact of the alternatives studied.

Environmental Permit Procedure Act

The permit authority shall ensure that those whose rights or interests may be affected by the matter have an opportunity to lodge objections to the application in writing. The same opportunity shall be extended, within the same fixed period, to persons other than the interested parties and bodies not representing the interested parties.

Land Extraction Act

Notice of a pending application for a land extraction permit shall be posted on the municipal notice board, and the owners and holders of property within or adjacent to the property containing the quarry shall be given an opportunity to state their case. If the project under application is likely to have significant impact on a wide area or on the interests of a large number of people, notice shall also be posted in at least one newspaper that is widely distributed within the locality affected.

Nature Conservation Act

During the drafting of the programme, any party whose interests or rights are affected shall be given an opportunity to state their case. When the programme is in the early stages of being drafted, the Ministry of the Environment shall inform the public in such way as to provide an opportunity for public debate.

New tools

Despite the strong legislative basis, there are democratic problems relating to citizens' participation and (thus) their opportunities to have an influence. This can be seen in the reduced interest in representative democracy, reflected in a decrease in voting activity. This is why it has been seen that also the development of new tools to enhance participation is also necessary. This view has been strengthened by the fact that the respect for public institutions -- the Parliament, municipal administration and public officials -- has diminished lately. Institutions the citizen values highly include the police, the education system, the Salvation Army, the legislative system, the church and the trade union. Those they least value are the political parties, the European Union, the municipal administration and the government.

The register on projects and legal preparatory documents of the Finnish Government (www.hare.vn.fi)

The government's register on projects and legal preparatory documents is both a tool for the authorities and a public information service for citizens. It includes all public projects launched by the government, the Parliament or the ministries. The register makes it easier to obtain information on, monitor and evaluate these projects.

Meanwhile, the Internet version of the register contains all public documents. The most frequent users of this major information system are the ministries; closely followed by the rest of the state administration and students. The register was designed to increase the openness of government while serving as a useful tool for the work done in the ministries. It gives citizens the opportunity to know what kind of projects are going on in the different ministries and their aims, as well as the people behind the projects or working groups. Data include news on how a given project is progressing, relevant publications, and how it relates to the government's programme and both Finnish and EU legislation. When a project ends, its documents are transferred automatically to government archives and the register itself produces a final report that is also archived.

The service providers for the Internet register are the ministries and Parliament. Projects go onto the sight as soon as they are launched. The register includes data on preparatory legal documents and reports to the Parliament, committees, boards of the state enterprises and agencies, and on study projects. The information provided is all public, and shown in the same format to both the information providers and the viewers. Citizens can use the register free of charge; no access codes or user names are needed.

From Citizen's Guide on the Web: Towards a national portal (www.Suomi.fi)

The Citizen's Guide was first published as a paperback book in 1992. With the development of information technology a decision was taken to cease publication on paper and to offer the content on the Internet. The idea behind Citizen's Guide Web pages (*www.opas.fi*) was to increase the availability of up-to-date information on all sorts of issues. The Guide, free of charge and available everywhere there is an Internet connection, is also a tool for companies, communities and organisations. Apart from the Finnish-language guide there is a guide in Swedish, for Finnish persons whose mother tongue is Swedish. An English version is under construction.

The Citizen's Guide has a link that enables people to use electronic forms for some services; new forms will be added later this year. The guide also has a directory of municipalities, each with its own linked Web page.

The information offered by the guide is grouped according to different life situations (childhood, adolescence, work life, the elderly, family, etc.). Subjects range from work, income, education and health services to culture, traffic, and opportunities for participation. The content is furnished by over a hundred different authorities and information providers. There are short texts on each subject, as well as links to the Web pages of these authorities where more specific information is available. Each authority is responsible for ensuring that the information furnished is both correct and up to date; this responsibility had been centralised when the guide was published in book form.

Finland has built its national portal of public sector information and services. The portal has just become operational in Spring 2002. In 2000, the Ministry of Finance initiated a project to establish the portal's objectives and plan its content and functions. A pilot portal was built first in order to encourage discussion and collect feedback from users. The most important target user group is citizens; other groups include corporations and public sector organisations themselves. Several aspects were established from the project's conception:

- Development of services directly from the citizens' needs.

- Usability and accessibility of the content.

- Synergistic benefits among the public sector organisations in conjunction with the Web services.

- Development of public sector know-how in Web-services.

- Empowering citizens with interactive services.

- Promotion of the openness, quality and image of the public sector.

Feedback on the pilot portal was positive. A questionnaire survey was conducted among over 100 users, including both citizens and civil servants. They listed the services they most desired from the portal:

- Information about public sector organisations and their services.

- The electronic transaction services of the organisations.

- Contact information of the organisations.

In addition, citizens wanted answers to their questions from government organisations via the portal.

In April 2001, construction began on the actual portal, based on the experiences of the pilot. The current content of the *www.suomi.fi* is based on the Citizen's Guide, which operated as a Web service for the Finnish public sector from 1997 until the opening of the present Web site.

The editorial team of the portal is based in the Government Information Management Unit in the Ministry of Finance. The team is responsible for ensuring that the text and links are kept up to date. Each of the authorities, organizations and bodies producing material for the site is responsible for the accuracy of its own information. The purposes of the portal are:

- To increase the openness and visibility of the public sector and to strengthen its unity.

- To improve the accessibility and quality of public sector services to meet the needs of citizens.

- To make it easier to find public sector information.

- To promote interactivity between citizens and authorities.

- To minimise overlapping work among authorities.

- To help citizens find the right authority for their special needs.

- To obtain sufficient resources for the portal in order to ensure the its development after the first version.

At this first stage the portal contains:

- A Citizen's Guide.

- Access to public sector organisations – their services and contact information.

- Access to municipalities.

- Access to a common electronic form service (provided by the Ministry of the Interior).

- A discussion forum, which has been provided for a year by the Ministry of Finance.

- News of the ministries.

- A public e-mail and contact directory service of civil servants.

The portal, *www.suomi.fi*, is in Finnish and Swedish, with portions in English as well (at both this address and at *www.publicservices.finland.fi*).

The Parliament's Web pages

The Parliament of Finland has been on the net since 1994. The legislative process and debates are now more transparent and subject to closer public scrutiny. The members of Parliament have a homepage and e-mail address -- new ways to meet and keep in touch with their voters.

There has been live Web debates. One example was discussion of a motion by the Committee for the Future. The text was (of course) available on the net, along with comments of 15 Committee members on video. In addition to live video transmission, the Internet offers the possibility of viewing the interventions of members of parliament afterwards, whenever it suits the interested citizen, who in turn may feed back comments and opinions. Now more than ever, the words and acts of members of Parliament are in the public eye.

Databank of laws and regulations

The state has a databank of laws and regulations (FINLEX) on a dedicated Web site: *http:\\finlex.om.fi*. It is free of charge and includes Finnish legislation as well as a number of precedent cases. The Supreme Courts have their own Web pages, as do some other courts.

State budget on the net

One of the concrete acts of transparency is the publishing of the budget proposal on the Internet. Instead of seeing only the final version (normally in September), citizens have a chance to examine the ministries' initial proposals as early as July. The Web site is (SMGL-) structured so that different kinds of search are possible. There are also links to, *e.g.* the FINLEX site.

JULHA -- a register of contact addresses

There exists a register containing the contact addresses of public administration civil servants on the Web. The directory, still under development, does not yet include all the different administrative sectors. Gradually, however, more ministries are being added.

The Hear the Citizens project

The Hear the Citizens project was launched as part of a major central government reform to increase consultation and participation in central government. The project took a number of approaches to this issue. The first was to examine the current situation. A national survey posed questions such as: What kind of existing consultation and participation forums are there in the Finnish ministries? What kind of new ideas, experiments or pilots are there in the ministries to hear citizens and citizen organisations? What kind of experiences do the different parties have of these experiments? What kind of possibilities and threats are there? Civil servants from the ministries as well as 130 citizen organisations were consulted. Not surprisingly, the administration judged the current situation to be better than did the citizen organisations, which perceived the need for new forms of participation and consultation. Both groups recognised the importance of the Internet with respect to consultation, and both were concerned about the fact that not all citizens have access to it.

This study was the basis for the project work. Many OECD countries have devoted much effort lately to issues of strengthening citizen-government connections. Looking at new international innovations in this area -- such as the People's Panel in the United Kingdom -- was an important part of the project.

Most important, however, was the co-operation with the citizen organisations. The project organised two meetings and invited all 130 of these organisations. The idea behind the meetings was to bring to the discussion ideas, models, viewpoints and international experiences related to increasing the participation opportunities for citizens and citizen organisations. These meetings were very important in deciding what ideas to carry forward as proposals of the project.

One proposal was that all ministries should have a specific strategy for working with citizen organisations. This would involve, *inter alia,* organising events and regularly sending the organisations an advance survey of coming issues in the ministry's field. The strategy should ensure that whenever a new project or drafting of legislation starts, top priority is given to consultation and participation.

The project underlined the need for ministries to have information strategies that truly take into account citizens and citizen organisations, and that place emphasis on interaction. Training members of the civil service in participation is also needed, to ensure that the strengthening of citizen-government connections is really a concern of every civil servant.

The project also proposed that consultation should be open to everyone through the Internet -- that is to say, every citizen should be able to submit an opinion on questions taken up by the ministries.

The Participation Project

This is a development project initiated by the Ministry of the Interior in February 1997. It is centred around the programme of the government, and its objective is to widen citizens' possibilities of participating in and influencing common affairs. It also aims at increasing the openness and transparency of the administration.

The Participation Project arose out of serious anxiety about the credibility of the democratic system. The low voting rate in the previous municipal elections in particular speaks clearly about the citizens' declining interest in representative democracy; it dropped from 70.9% in the municipal elections of 1992 to 61% in 1996 and 55.9% in 2000.The citizens do not respect public institutions the way they did formerly. Surveys taken from the beginning of the 1980s show that in the eyes of the citizens, the trustworthiness of government officials, Parliament, the trade union, the judicial system and the church has diminished. While in 1983, almost 70% of Finns had either "quite a lot of" or "a lot of" confidence in the Parliament, in 1993, the same confidence figure was only 20%. In the same way, interest in being involved in municipal politics either as a candidate or as a member of one of the boards of a municipality has, has diminished markedly.

Changes in the social environment have fuelled discussions about civil society. The European unification process has brought with it concepts like "democracy deficit" and "subsidiarity principle". When making decisions about social development, it is necessary to define the changed roles of the state, municipality and region, and above all the meaning of citizenship in "internationalising" and supranational decision making.

Tasks

The core of the Participation Project is the municipality, which is a central actor in civil society and its social responsibility. The most important task of the project is to strengthen citizens' participation and influence in common affairs and to strengthen the preconditions for realising the project's aims.

Heading the operation is a Project Manager, who is supported by a steering group, an evaluation group, a legislative group, a personnel group and a project secretary. The Association of Finnish Local and Regional Authorities and the ministries provide the project with expert help in legislative affairs.

Altogether, 50 municipalities were involved in the first phase with 70 local projects. The most promising projects of 17 municipalities then took part in the second, extended phase of the project. The projects have been implemented by the municipalities independently in co-operation with different citizen's organisations, village committees and companies.

Share Your Views with Us

Share Your Views with Us (*www.otakantaa.fi*) is a discussion forum through which ministries can consult citizens. It was originally intended to be a one-year pilot project for discussion on public management reform. The forum was launched by a project called "New technology and citizen's possibilities to influence", which aimed at finding new ways of consultation and participation through new technology.

In March 2001, one year after its launch, the forum was changed to cover the entire state administration. This year brought another change: each of the twelve ministries is in charge of hosting the forum for one month at a time. Later on the forum may have a joint editor-in-chief with the ministries working more closely together. But it was seen that it is good practice for each ministry to get to know the running of the forum for one month before going into a more horizontal model of operation. The more horizontal model will of course serve citizens even better than the current model, and it is therefore the next step.

The basic principles of the forum have been the same from the outset. It is considered important that the forum be open to all citizens, so no registration is needed. It is thus possible to write to the forum anonymously. There are issues that people may want to touch upon in the discussions that concern, for instance, their own family, their workplace or some other topic they would hesitate to bring up if they had to register. In the time the forum has been operating the number of inappropriate comments requiring deletion has been almost zero.

The other fundamental principle of the forum is that the questions discussed should be limited to areas where preparatory work is going on in the government. It should not be discussion for discussion's sake. The idea, rather, is that the comments and views received really will be used in preparing the issues -- the connection is essential. That of course does not mean that all ideas will become decisions, but it *does* mean that the discussions will be read through carefully and used in the preparatory work. It is also important that the preparatory work be at an early stage, so that there is a real possibility for the discussions to have an influence. They are not just issues to say yes or no to.

There is also background material on the *otakantaa* Web pages, as well as links. The idea is to acquaint citizens with the issues under discussion. The background material of course varies with the issue; in fact, both the civil servants responsible for running the forum and citizens have brought in further background information and additional links in their comments on the discussion. These additional elements have proved most welcome from the citizens' point of view.

One aspect of the forum that citizens writing in clearly value is the involvement of politicians and civil servants. The forum is always moderated by civil servants, and those in the hosting ministry take part in the discussions. Each month the Cabinet minister(s) of the hosting ministry participates in a one-hour online session. To ensure that as many people as possible take part, comments or questions to the minister may be sent in beforehand through the Web pages. These questions will be answered during the session. In addition to ministers, high-level civil servants and committees of the Finnish Parliament have appeared on these online sessions.

Immediately after online discussions are concluded, they can be viewed from the pages of the *otakantaa* forum. All earlier online sessions and all other forum discussions are available on the Web site, both in their entirety and in résumé form.

THE RIGHT OF ACCESS TO INFORMATION AND PUBLIC SCRUTINY: TRANSPARENCY AS A DEMOCRATIC CONTROL INSTRUMENT

by

Alfredo Chirino Sánchez
Director of the Judicial Training Center, Costa Rica

Public scrutiny of state affairs and access to information are key phrases in the current debate on the development of democracy -- and not by chance, since they offer a real guarantee of transparent government. The two concepts are interdependent, since one cannot play its part under the rule of law without the other. There can be no public scrutiny without access to information. Moreover, such access is an indispensable precondition for the exercise by the citizen of other constitutional rights -- such as, for example, the right to vote and freedom of expression -- and, in general, for the free development of the individual.

These constitutional rights increasingly require broad access to every kind of information, public and private. It is even possible to conclude, along with several modern authors, that the level of democracy attained by a country should now be measured in terms of the volume and quality of the information in circulation. The value of information as a guarantee of democracy seems indisputable. In the context of the fight against corruption, this assertion is steadily gaining in importance: it is increasingly understood that the scourge of corruption can only be eradicated by nurturing a culture of scrutiny, transparency and accountability -- an information culture.

In English-speaking countries the debate has been conducted under the heading "freedom of information", a term that covers most of the topics dealt with in legislation that has been prepared to meet citizens' expectations of public participation and responsibility.

The purpose of this chapter is to describe the characteristics of the legislation in Central America designed to fulfil the democratic aspiration of freedom of information. A second objective is to explore the relationship between freedom of information and the anti-corruption campaign.

Like many countries in Latin America, those in Central America do not have special legislation ensuring access to information. There are only a few constitutional provisions that guarantee citizens' access to government offices for the purpose of seeking information and obtaining certain services. Of course, these constitutional provisions require ordinary legislation to enable the principle of access to be widely applied, laws that have so far been lacking. In addition, there are a number of administrative practices that prevent the public from obtaining access to a great deal of information. These include the simple expedient of classifying the data in the files as state secrets -- a deplorable practice that has become a real obstacle to the development of a culture of transparency and accountability in the countries of Central America.

Freedom of information legislation has developed in what are called "proactive countries", which attach special importance to transparent government and the assumption of responsibility by their citizens. It is estimated that over 20 countries around the world have legislation of this type,[1] in keeping with long traditions of openness and respect for civil rights.

Freedom of information laws offer a guarantee of broad access to most government departments. The few exceptions usually relate to the genuine protection of certain sensitive aspects of state management or the protection of privacy. An important aspect of these laws is that the right is exercised directly by the citizen, without the intervention of intermediaries. The need to be told by others what the government is holding in its files and archives has been obviated by information tools and communications technology. The modern concept of virtual government offices is another step along the path to genuine participatory democracy.

Clearly, freedom of information legislation seeks to do more than merely provide access to information or limit the data processing that civil servants must carry out in order to perform their tasks. Most importantly, it seeks to establish a balance between the aims of the state and private interests in a practical spirit of agreement that widens the horizons of citizen participation, both in monitoring the actions of the authorities and in taking decisions on issues of national importance. Freedom of information not only leads to greater transparency in the functioning of institutions, but also makes it easier for citizens to exercise their political rights. However, it is necessary to bear in mind that the goal of achieving transparency cannot justify sacrificing a citizen's ability to protect their personal affairs from the abusive scrutiny of the state or private individuals. Modern societies are thus confronted with a very complicated and difficult dilemma. How can they balance their need for information and the new configuration of international economic relations on the one hand, and the interests of individuals -- keeping them better informed in every branch of knowledge and culture and protecting them from misuse of personal data -- on the other?

In protecting his or her own privacy, the citizen is not only exercising a right of defence against the government but also asserting rights relating to freedom of communication and action under the rule of law. There are valid concerns that, because of the complexity of the subject matter, incorporating numerous provisions relating to the traditional right of data protection in a freedom of information bill could overload the process of legislative approval. Nevertheless, the aim should be to achieve an appropriate balance between the two rights and break through old watertight compartments that led to the artificial split between public and private, the individual and the collective, the particular and the general. The door would then be open to debate on the social spaces in which citizens can interact to achieve common objectives, using newly developed means of communication to exploit new aspects of freedom.

This modern dimension of privacy quickly manifested itself in the legal developments of the 1970s and 80s, which took place within the framework of the right to "informational self-determination". This right is deeply rooted in principles such as human dignity, personal freedom, self-determination and democracy, all of which took on a new aspect under the rule of law. Initially, in the early days of what we now know as the "information society", the main function of this "dual right" was to preserve an ideal of the human being that was steadily becoming more unreal in the face of the extraordinary advances in technology. The ideal related to the desire to have an effective influence on one's social environment in the face of the unlimited power in the hands of those in authority -- some of whom may hold sensitive personal information as well as the power to use it as they think fit. Another objective, closely related to the first, was to protect the "material worth" of the human being. That worth was becoming increasingly relative, not only because of the mobility of the individual's role within society but also because of the depersonalising to which every technocratic form of organisation is susceptible.

Any freedom of information legislation should include the following:

164

1. A right of access to the archives and files maintained by the authorities, manually or in electronic form, whether the archives have been compiled by them or are based on information from third parties.

2. The creation of a freedom of information culture, which would involve obliging all government services, central and decentralised, national and devolved, to publish information on the kind of archives and data they hold, on the methods of access, and on the possibilities of obtaining additional information of interest to the citizen.

3. The establishment of mechanisms for keeping the public informed at all times. The legislation should oblige administrations to make use of the available technology for facilitating access, notably the Internet.

4. The fixing of reasonable time limits within which information requested must be made available to the citizen.

5. Dealing with access costs as is usual, in accordance with the principle of free provision of services. However, if documents have to be copied for the person requesting them, the payment of a specific fee may be authorised. Likewise, there may be reasonable service charges when, to obtain the data requested, it is necessary to perform a series of searches in the archives that could take a great deal of time and call for significant material and human resources.

6. A list of exceptional circumstances in which information requested will not be made available to the public -- for example, when the data might harm private interests (e.g. disclosure of trade secrets or privileged information, national security, a criminal prosecution or the right to privacy).

7. Special emphasis on facilitating access and keeping the procedures simple, so that members of the public can obtain the data they need. Legislation should also provide for certain remedies where information is not made available in time and lay down administrative and criminal penalties for civil servants who are negligent in the performance of the relevant duties.

8. Provisions relating to special conditions of access deserve to be taken into consideration for the benefit of the mass media, which in this respect play an important role in modern societies by reporting the facts that people need in order to take a responsible position.

9. The Model Freedom of Information Law, prepared under the auspices of the Organisation of American States, places special emphasis on the inclusion of provisions protecting the right of citizens to "informational self-determination", i.e. the power to determine who will have access to personal information and when and where that access will be granted. The aim is to stimulate debate in the countries of Central America on the need to deal with problems that may arise in connection with the delicate balance between the right to privacy and the need for freedom of information in order to ensure transparency and fight corruption.

In general, freedom of information legislation is usually a complex mix of guarantees and functional provisions. These depend not only on the clarity of the rules but also on the existing institutional culture, as well as the resources available for their effective implementation.

In conclusion, it should now be clear that it is not possible to fight corruption in the absence of a culture of transparency. Building such a culture can begin with a legislative commitment to the public that breaks with the many years of concealment and the persecution of those who take an interest in public affairs. Failure to set out along this path would involve a serious risk for the democracies of the region.

Legislation of this type must overcome the huge temptation to control access to information as a means of maintaining the conditions under which an authoritarian state can achieve its objectives. It must also overcome a culture of blatant isolation, behind which administrations have long sheltered in an effort to avoid "undesirable" interference in their affairs.

he obstacles described are merely additional reasons for introducing legislation of this kind. The accumulated experience of the countries that have such laws -- such as the United States, Denmark, Sweden and Australia -- shows that it is possible to break away from these patterns of behaviour by restoring the public's trust in its representatives, and convincing people that they need to take an interest in issues which, sooner or later, are going to affect them.

NOTE

1.   See the survey conducted by "Privacy International", available on the Internet at *http://www.privacyinternational.org/issues/foia/foia-survey.html.*

THE MEXICAN MUNICIPAL TRANSPARENCY EVALUATION SYSTEM – "SETRAMUN"

by

Bernardo Avalos
Head, Co-ordination of Citizens's Alliance, Office of the President, Mexico

Introduction

In discussing transparency, we need to begin by defining, however briefly, what we want to combat: corruption. Nye's[1] characterisation will suit the purposes of this chapter: corruption is behaviour that deviates from lawful public function in the interests of gaining private economic or bureaucratic benefits; or, the violation of rules of conduct to the benefit of private interests.

However, it should be remembered that although corruption is viewed negatively, it may reflect actual behavioural patterns. Thus its explanation and (therefore) its solution may necessarily extend beyond an understanding of individual interests.

Given the problem's seriousness, it must be made clear to the citizenry that corruption runs contrary to shared values and, above all, that it is necessary to produce new norms consistent with those shared values. Governments must take action to build a truly transparent system with real citizen participation and free access to public information without interference from the authorities.

Establishing transparency within governments that are susceptible to corruption is vital for building a better social environment that translates into the well being of people. A government makes itself accountable to its citizens when it

1) Informs clearly and pertinently of its actions.

2) Involves society in its work through open communication; and

3) Defines jointly with society the means to satisfy citizen's needs.

Transparency is thus invaluable in the pursuit of a just and modern society. It is also the only way to gain trust and support for government actions.

In its desire to actively participate in building and developing the environment required to reach a better quality of life, civil society in Mexico has in recent years pressed for the opening up of municipal, state and federal governments. In response, the Secretaría de Contraloría y Desarrollo Administrativo (SECODAM, the Ministry of the Comptrollership and Administrative Development) has begun to develop a Municipal Transparency Evaluation System, referred to as SETRAMUN.

Objectives

The point of departure for SETRAMUN's evaluations will be the *municipio*, the smallest administrative unit of Mexico's Federation. (There are several *municipios* in each state.) The system will try to identify those municipal programmes that are susceptible to corruption, and generate what may be called "spaces" of citizen participation to oversee and evaluate those programmes. Administrative procedures will be rated, but the focus is on measuring the transparency level of local authorities rather than the corruption level. The idea is to encourage those *municipios* with good transparency ratings to continue their efforts, and to stimulate other *municipios* to emulate them by incorporating practices that will build citizens' trust. Publicising good municipal practices – bringing them to the attention of the media, academic institutions, civil organisations and the citizenry in general – will in turn reinforce those practices. There is thus created a virtuous circle to foster disclosure by the authorities of what they are doing, why they are doing it, and how they involve citizens in determining it.

Ultimately the remit of the Municipal Transparency Evaluation System will extend beyond the *municipio* level, and SETRAMUN will try to measure activities and problems faced by higher levels of government. The transparency indexes will be specific to the programmes, projects and plans in question, and classified according to the level of government involvement. There are seven categories: 1) federal; 2) state; 3) municipal; 4) federal-state-municipal; 5) federal-state; 6) federal-municipal; and 7) state-municipal.

Methodology

The criteria to be used for SETRAMUN evaluation are the following:

1) Government must inform about actions and decisions.

2) Government must establish spaces for interaction and communication with the community, e.g. councils, committees, neighbourhood meetings.

3) Government must listen to society – that is, receive and consider complaints, proposals, advice, petitions, etc.

Based on these criteria, three fields where transparency plays an important role in municipal development were identified:

a) *Information to the citizens:* relevance and content quality of the information supplied by the government to its citizens.

b) *Communication spaces:* levels of representation, quality of the rules governing procedures and the overall proper functioning of spaces for communication between government and society.

c) *Attention to citizen demands:* quality of services rendered, quality of the attention paid to the demands of society and the means for attending to these demands.

Table 1: **Objectives, goals and indexes of municipal action transparency**

1. Citizen information	2. Spaces of government-society communication
Overall objective: To evaluate the level of specificity of information and the process that generates that information, in order to reach a wide citizen base and achieve a true and clear accountability.	Overall objective: To evaluate the spaces for citizen discussion, communication and decision making between government and citizens – specifically, their composition, rules and functioning – so as to reinforce and promote them as key mechanisms for transparency.

<table>
<tr><td align="center">Specific goals:</td><td align="center">Specific goals:</td></tr>
<tr><td>● To evaluate the accessibility of information about municipal providers.</td><td>● To review the make-up and representation levels of, inter alia, the Municipal Development Council, citizen committees, and councils of municipal services.</td></tr>
<tr><td>● To evaluate the accessibility of information about municipal finances and whether this information is made public.</td><td>● To evaluate the functioning of the councils and their rules of operation.</td></tr>
<tr><td>● To evaluate the accessibility of information about both existing and planned infrastructure works within the municipio and whether this information is made public.</td><td>● To evaluate whether local authority sessions and the formation of commissions to follow up measures decided in these sessions are open to the public.</td></tr>
<tr><td>● To evaluate the accessibility of information rules and laws that apply to the municipio and whether this information is made public.</td><td>● To evaluate actions designed to foster citizens' participation in activities to improve their residential area.</td></tr>
<tr><td>● To judge whether the manual of co-responsibility between government and citizens is sufficiently publicised.</td><td></td></tr>
<tr><td>● To evaluate the accessibility of information about the processes of acquisitions and the adjudication of contracts, leases and services to citizens, establishing whether this information is made public.</td><td></td></tr>
</table>

3. Attention to citizens

Overall objective

To evaluate the systems and procedures to process complaints, proposals, advice and petitions, and to evaluate the service manuals as well as the extent to which they are publicised, in order for citizens to be aware of the means at their disposal to satisfy their needs.

Specific goals

● To make public the existence of user manuals of services provided by the *municipio*.

● To make public the means (the Internet, single window portal services, telephone systems) through which citizens are heard.

NOTE

1   Nye, J. "Corruption and Political Development: A Cost Benefit Analysis", American Political Science Review, 1967, vol. 61, núm. 3, pp. 417- 427.

FRAMEWORK FOR ACTION: MEASURES FOR FOLLOW-UP

by

Marilyn Yakowitz,
Head, South America and Brazil Programmes
Organisation for Economic Co-operation and Development (OECD) Centre for Co-operation with
Non-Members

Latin American and OECD: importance of co-operation and policy dialogue

The OECD/OAS Forum on Ensuring Accountability and Transparency in the Public Sector (Brasilia, December 2001)[1] created an opportunity to work with policy makers, NGOs and other stakeholders in the Latin America, launching a process of continuing co-operation. Co-operation with Non-Members is a priority for the OECD. This is not a recent phenomenon. The founding Convention of the OECD [1961] mandates the Organisation to work to increase sustainable economic growth worldwide in Member and Non-Member countries.

More recently, in the framework of the OECD Centre for Co-operation with Non-Members, the aim of this co-operation is to deepen and extend relations with non-OECD countries. OECD outreach builds on the methods and policy analysis conducted with Members countries. It brings Members and non-Members together -- to the table to discuss policy alternatives and "best practices". The intention is to foster open and inclusive dialogue in the many fields where OECD has a particular comparative advantage, and where there is demand and mutual benefit for Member and non-Members countries. OECD is also interested in exchange of information, broadening and deepening the knowledge of the OECD about the economies and societies of non-Members. This work involves an extensive programme of activities in some thirty-five different policy areas, for example, in economics, statistics, finance, fiscal affairs, trade, social and labour policy, environment, agriculture, and public management.

In addition, co-operation includes formal arrangements to work with OECD bodies and instruments. Examples of OECD instruments, which are open to non-Member countries are the OECD Anti-Bribery Convention or the Declaration on International Investment and Multinational Enterprises.

While OECD is an intergovernmental organisation, it recognises the need to involve NGOs, civil society, and the private sector. It has permanent advisor committees from business and industry and trade unions.

The strong commitment of the OECD to work with Non-Members spans borders, extending to Central and Eastern European, to South America and Asia, and very recently in an exploratory way to Africa and the Middle East. For the past several years, OECD has been building and reinforcing its work with Latin America, through its South American Regional Programme, which focuses on emerging economies in Latin America and a country programme with Brazil. As part of this effort, OECD has been pleased to launch, in partnership with the OAS and Brazil, co-operation on public sector governance-transparency and accountability in Latin America.

The output of the forum and what the OECD will do next

This first OECD/OAS regional Forum on Accountability and Transparency has aimed at working out policy guidelines to help the implementation of the Inter-American Convention Against Corruption. Conventions risk remaining beautiful words on paper, without the hard work of implementation, to put the measures into practice.

What do administrations need to do to translate the policy objectives of the OAS Convention into actual reform? Operationally, the Forum participant worked to respond to several questions: How do you go from the Convention to implementation? What to administrations need to do? How can the international community help? The role of the participants in the Forum sessions was to put meat, in an operational sense, on the bones to translate the objectives of the Convention into an operational reality.

It is important to now encourage the parties to take up the reforms and to express support of the dynamics of the OAS mechanism. How can we do this in reality, how to keep the ball rolling and gain momentum?

Next steps have been put into place

The review process that will occur is an opportunity for countries to evaluate the status of the Convention. This process will determine whether there has been progress on the policy measures. The OAS Convention is very broad. It cannot be reviewed all at once. Therefore, there will be review rounds, wherein several issues at a time will be grouped for assessment.

What will the OECD do?

In January 2002, in Washington DC, the OAS, working with the support of the OECD, agreed on a set of key policy issues to be included the first round. In this respect, the donor community needs information about how to help individual countries in the implementation of their efforts. It should be useful for countries to sketch their existing situations, and on the basis of these, which can function as a road map, determine the measures to be accomplished. These road maps can also be used to provide the input for requests for assistance to help take these measures. There is no interest in imposing programmes on countries, rather it is important that initiatives be homegrown, home-driven and have buy-in in the individual countries, if the measures are to work.

The OECD will provide a list of the Member country contacts in the 3 areas of the Forum.[2]

- Promoting sound ethics management system.

- Ensuring fiscal transparency. and

- Strengthening access to information and public participation.

The OECD will also provide information on concrete measures -- on the substance of the issues -- conducting a sort of hot line. This will be connected to the OECD Web site.

The OECD will provide a database on reform experience and make it accessible and visible. Links to other applicable databases will be made, including those of governments, and other stakeholders. Country reviews will be included. There will be an effort to obtain translation of information into third languages – Portuguese, working with the Brazilian administration. For translation into Spanish, a partner(s) is being sought.

Measure to be taken by the OECD South American Programme in Governance

In the context of this Latin American governance outreach initiative, A *Workshop on practical implementation and follow-up mechanisms* was held on 14 January 2002, in Washington DC. It launched the follow-up on the OAS Convention and the OAS and OECD organised the meeting.

It was held back-to-back with *the First Committee of Experts*. This was a technical workshop to share OECD experience and that of the Group of States against Corruption (GRECO) on follow-up mechanisms in practice. Extensive experience was shared, for example, on anti-corruption instruments, such as the OECD Anti-Bribery Convention and the Financial Action Task Force on Money Laundering. Experts from the OECD Bribery Convention, the Financial Action Task Force (FAFT) and country delegations discussed what OECD does through its legal instruments. This was particularly important for conveying information on experience concerning the practical aspects, which is often not recorded in writing.

Later, in September 2002, in Mexico, in collaboration with the Mexican Government, there will be a meeting to reach out to the private sector in Latin America to further involve them in the OAS and OECD Conventions. The focus will be:

- A broad information exercise on the OAS and the OECD Conventions; and

- Two policy areas of importance to the private sector: accounting standards and public procurement.

The support provided by the Government of Brazil made possible the OECD/OAS Forum on Ensuring Accountability and Transparency. The Ministry of Planning, Budget and Management, Brazil, helped motivate the taking of concrete measures on the Conference follow-up.

On the OECD side, the Public Management Directorate and the Financial, Fiscal and Enterprise Affairs Directorate are driving the substantive follow-up of the Conference, as outline in the Programme of Activities 2002 of the OECD Centre for Co-operation with Non-Members, and in co-operation with the OAS and other partners,

NOTES

1. The partner organisations included: the Brazilian Ministry of Planning, Budget and Management; the Public Ethics Commission; the Office of the President of Brazil; the United Nations; and the World Bank Group. The Associate Partners included: UNDP: Transparency Brazil and the Inter-American Development Bank (IADB).

2. This aspect is being organised by Mr. János Bertók, Principal Administrator, Public Management Directorate, OECD.

THE ORGANISATION OF AMERICAN STATES AND THE FIGHT AGAINST CORRUPTION

by

Jorge Garcia-Gonzalez
Director, Department of Legal Co-operation and Information
OAS General Secretariat

Corruption has been identified as one of the most serious obstacles and threats for the consolidation of democracy and economic and social development in a number of countries in the Americas. The growing conscience on the severity of this problem, lead the countries of this region, within the framework of the Organization of American States (OAS), on being the first to commit themselves not only from a political point of view, but also a legal one, in order to strengthen co-operation among them to prevent and prosecute corruption.

The essay's purpose is to present the main developments that the countries of the Americas have made, within the OAS framework, for consolidating co-operation among them for combating corruption. In order to put this issue into context, we will first, refer, in a concise manner to the OAS and some of the characteristics of its Member States. Second, we will mention some of the reasons that have lead inter-American co-operation in this subject to strengthen. Finally, we will expand on the specific developments made in this field up until the present.

The OAS: A community of principles and a variety of realities

The Organization of American States (OAS) is an international organisation that brings all of the Nations from the American hemisphere together. It is comprised of 35 Member States, including the Caribbean nations (the government of Cuba was excluded from participation in 1962). It is, without a doubt, an organisation of a political and juridical nature instead of a financial or economic one. It constitutes the only regional setting in which all the countries of the Americas can come together and debate issues of common interest and reach an accord on them. Many of which conclude in legal instruments like Conventions or Resolutions agreed upon by the OAS General Assembly.

The OAS charter was signed in 1948, in Bogota, Colombia, and entered into force in 1951, having been amended on several occasions. The unity of the countries within the OAS framework primarily resides in a series of shared principles and values like those that guarantee continental peace and security; preserve, promote and strengthen democracy and the rule of law, and promote respect and defend human rights.

After the Cold War, the OAS garnered high importance and received mandates for strengthening the hemispherical dialogue and action in all the relevant issues on the international agenda (i.e. democracy, human rights, transnational organised crime, sustainable development, and trade).

Although these shared values and community of interest related to the aforementioned issues, the Member States of the OAS have very different characteristics among them (geography, population, language, legal systems, social and economic development, and the different levels or grades of their political institutions). This variety of characteristics enrich the political and legal debate in the OAS and, with frequency, it concludes being expressed in one way or another, in legal instruments that are negotiated and adopted, just like those related to the fight against corruption.

Three reasons to fight against corruption in the Americas

During the last few years international interest and concern has risen in regards to the corruption phenomenon. The causes that have incorporated this issue on the international agenda are multiple. Notwithstanding, at its origin are the huge transformations that have shaken the world during the past years: end of the Cold War, the demise of the central controlled planned economies, the rise of new values and realities, technology and communication advancement, and changes in the States' role and the role of civil society institutions in issues of common interest.

Assuming the before mentioned is true, it is convenient to emphasise three reasons for which the fight against corruption is perceived as a collective priority, particularly, in Latin America and the Caribbean.

The first reason relates to the impact corruption has on trade, economic growth and sustained development. Numerous studies have empirically proven that when corruption is high in a country, investment and economic growth will decrease. The Economic and Social Progress Report on Latin America of the Inter-American Development Bank (IDB) in 2000 reiterates the point. Accordingly the report states that more than half the differences in the levels of income between developed countries and the Latin American countries are linked to the deficiencies in the institutions of the latter. And in those cases that have to do with the enforceability of the law and the control of corruption, Latin America finds itself in a lowest category among other groups of countries, except for Africa. It is evident that this is a great challenge to the region.

The second reason has to do with the need of preserving and strengthening of democracy. The IDB report highlights that only 35% of Latin Americans are satisfied with democracy; that between 85% and 93% consider corruption is getting worse instead of getting better or at least maintaining stable, and many of them consider it the most serious national problem.

Fortunately, the study also reveals that the "low satisfaction rating" with democracy does not necessarily imply a weak backing to democratic principles. On the contrary, it demonstrates that Latin Americans prefer democracy to any other alternative form of government. In any case, those low levels of satisfaction and confidence in political institutions, without a doubt, are of high alert.

The third and final reason is intimately linked to the enormous social costs brought on by this problem. In Latin America poverty not only has risen in absolute terms but it has constituted itself in the region with high levels of disproportion between the wealthy and poor. Accordingly, studies have also proven that the principal victims of corruption are the poor and that in countries where poverty flourishes there are immeasurable and growing acts of corruption. In this sense the fight against corruption is seen as social justice cause.

Developments within the OAS framework

Background

The fight against corruption has been a constant concern of the Organization of American States. The OAS charter itself states that "representative democracy is an indispensable condition for the stability, peace and development of the region" and Member States have recognised corruption constitutes one of the most serious threat to democracy.

That is why, among other instruments, in the "Santiago Commitment to Democracy and the Renewal of the Inter-American System" and in General Assembly Resolution 1159 in 1992, on "Corrupt International Trade Practices"; the Declaration of Managua for the Promotion of Democracy and Development; the San Jose Declaration on Human Rights of 1993, and the Belen do Para Declaration of 1994, the Organization has reiterated its commitment in fighting corruption and modernising public institutions.

Yet, without a doubt, the Summit process of the Heads of States and of Governments of the Americas introduced with great vigour the treatment of this issue on a hemispherical level. In fact, the first Summit, held in Miami in December of 1994, targeted the issue for the first time. On this occasion, the Heads of States and of Governments acknowledged that this problem was of a multilateral nature and, aware of that, they committed themselves to negotiate within the OAS framework, a hemispherical accord. As a result of this decision and after a process of broad analysis and deliberations, the Nations of the Americas adopted in March 1996 the Inter-American Convention against Corruption.

The Inter-American Convention against Corruption: a road map for collective action

The Inter-American Convention against Corruption is, without a doubt, the most important step that has been taken on a hemispherical level in combating this phenomenon. Ultimately, it is regarded as a road map for collective action in the Americas on this subject.

The itinerary designed by the OAS General Assembly for negotiating the Convention, resulted in a process based on participation that lead to an enriched content and concluded in an integral conception on the way corruption must be combated.

First, as such, the two major purposes of the Convention express the before mentioned sentiment, as follows: to promote and strengthen the development by each of the States Parties of the mechanisms needed to prevent, detect, punish and eradicate corruption; and to promote, facilitate and regulate co-operation among the States Parties to ensure the effectiveness of measures and actions to prevent, detect, punish and eradicate corruption in the performance of public functions and acts of corruption specifically related to such performance.

Second, the Convention expressly recognises, in its preamble and in various articles that this problem cannot be solved with repressive or punishing actions once the evil has emerged. On the contrary, precise decisions of a preventive nature are to be taken also. These are directly linked to the modernisation of institutions and the elimination of its causes or the conditions that facilitate or instigate its use.

Third, the Convention conceives the fight against corruption as a process and not as a simple result of pointed actions, isolated and without any connection or co-ordination. On the contrary, a permanent effort is inferred, upon its reading, begun by the countries, which leads to the Convention and continues -- in a process of "progressive development" -- through the negotiation and adoption of additional protocols contributing to the achievement of the above cited purposes.

Lastly, the Convention, without setting aside state responsibility in eradicating corruption, reveals the importance of action taken by all the actors involved. Especially, it recognises the need of strengthening the participation of civil society in preventing and combating corruption and it expresses that states will extend to each other broad technical co-operation, exchange experiences and give special attention to the ways and forms citizens participate.

Furthermore, it is worth noting that the Convention constitutes the most important inter-American legal instrument for extraditing those who commit crimes of corruption; in co-operation and assistance among the States in obtaining evidence and facilitating necessary procedural acts regarding the investigation or trials of corruption; and for the identification, search, immobilisation, confiscation, and seizure of goods obtained or derived from the commission of the crime of corruption. In regards to investigating or obtaining information by way of banking or financial institutions, the Convention represents an important step towards avoiding that bank secrecy could be used in aiding and abetting those who commit corruption.

In relations to the issue of asylum, the Convention strikes an equal balance between the values that are protected by asylum and those that combat corruption. During the deliberation process of the project it was attested that the reason for and the essence of asylum couldn't be weakened, but it may not serve as way of eluding or facilitating the avoidance of legal action against those who commit acts of corruption.

Within this context, the content of article XVII of the Convention is very important stating the following: the fact that the property obtained or derived from an act of corruption was intended for political purposes, or that it is alleged that an act of corruption was committed for political motives or purposes, shall not suffice in and of itself to qualify the act as a political offence or as a common offence related to a political offence.

Finally, another issue that is touched upon by the Convention and worth mentioning has to do with the fight against transnational bribery. Article VIII of the Convention not only marked a huge step, but it also placed the American hemisphere at the forefront of this issue since regulation and the commitment of punishing this illicit practice was established in an obligatory instrument from a legal point of view like a Convention. This in complete contrast to the timid steps that had been taken up until then within the frameworks of other international organisations.

Developments after the adoption of the Convention

Once the Inter-American Convention against Corruption was adopted, the states realised that this treaty was not the final destination, but, to the contrary, the first major step to address this problem collectively. That is why, the OAS General Assembly adopted in 1997, an Inter-American Program of Co-operation in Combating Corruption. And the Heads of States and of Governments during the Santiago de Chile Summit held in 1998, committed themselves in providing, in the OAS, an adequate follow-up to the progress made in said Convention.

In development of these mandates, the OAS has continued working in this field. Within the framework of the Working Group on Probity and Public Ethics, the states have made great progress. They have taken the recommendations that were adopted in a Symposium held in Santiago de Chile in 1998, the results of a special session held by this Group with government representatives, international organisations and private sector and civil society representatives. Also, a questionnaire on the adjustments made to national legislations in regards to the Convention, whose response permitted a thorough diagnostic on the areas that still require progress in the American countries. The States have also begun to consider an important issue: corporate social responsibility in fighting corruption. On this issue, a hemispherical meeting will take place in 2002, hoping that guidelines and specific plans of action will emerge.

The OAS General Secretariat from it's part, in developing the mandates of both the Summit of the Americas and the OAS General Assembly, has been supporting the process of ratification of the Convention, as well as implementing decisions contained in it or related to it. As a part of this process, in conjunction with the IDB, support has been given to a number of countries in the region in defining the necessary measures for adjusting their criminal legislation to that expressed in the Convention. Following this same line, a "pilot" program was started in Central America, with the finality of assisting the countries in the region, in adjusting their legal systems to the preventive measures expressed by the Convention.

Additionally, an information system on the Internet and a network of inter-American institutions and experts against corruption has been created. Likewise, it is working with the Inter-Parliamentary Forum of the Americas, among others, in all that has to do with the role that corresponds to the legislative bodies in political control matters, as well as in the ethical norms of their members. It has also been participating in an initiative that emerged from the last Ministers of Justice meeting and backed by the Government of Canada, in creating a mutual legal assistance network.

Finally, in conjunction with the Trust of the Americas and other institutions, it has co-sponsored a training initiative for investigative reporting. As a result of this process, the American States have acknowledged the importance of this Convention as a road map for their collective action against corruption. An example of this is that, comparatively, this treaty was one of the fastest instruments to be signed and ratified. Today we have 29 states who have signed the Convention and 23 have ratified it. The General Secretariat has begun a project to assist those states who have not done so yet, in ratifying and implementing the Convention. With all the progress made until now, it is possible to imagine that in the near future, this Convention shall be enforceable throughout the entire hemisphere.

The follow-up mechanism for the implementation of the Convention

The Inter-American Convention against Corruption had its lead role. In 1996, when it was adopted, many states were still discussing if this was an issue that should be considered within an international treaty. In fact, in the United Nations and the OECD, attempts to negotiate conventions on this issue failed. If the viability of international treaties in this field were disputable during this time, the possibility of creating monitoring mechanisms or instruments for evaluating compliance of the treaties by the states was practically unthinkable. In fact, no state or non-governmental organisation introduced a formal or informal proposal during the negotiations of the Inter-American Convention, on the creation of some sort of follow-up mechanism, evaluation or monitoring of compliance of the measures that were to be adopted. The idea simply did not exist nor was it introduced at the time.

Although a short time has passed between the adoption of the Convention and the present time, the circumstances have changed considerably. Ultimately and for different circumstances, the OECD Convention adopted a "monitoring mechanism" for the signatory states. Also, The Group of States against Corruption (GRECO) of the Council of Europe also adopted a monitoring mechanism regarding its commitment to this field. The aforementioned lead to the suggestion of creating a follow-up mechanism for the implementation of the Inter-American Convention against Corruption by the States Parties to it.

The issue itself of monitoring international accords is not something new or strange to the OAS Member States. Many countries are part of monitoring mechanisms, for example, in combating money laundering, some of them participate in the OECD process of evaluation. Within the OAS framework, States have adopted monitoring instruments in areas of collective interests. It would be enough to cite the activities of the Multilateral Evaluation Mechanism (MEM) in regards to drug abuse and to the activities of the Consultative Committee foreseen in the Inter-American Convention against the Manufacturing of and Trafficking in Firearms, Ammunition, Explosives, and other related Materials.

Taking into account these new circumstances. The OAS General Assembly in June of 2000, requested of the Permanent Council[1] that they analyse the existing mechanisms and develop a recommendation on an appropriate model that could be used by the States Parties. The Permanent Council, thanks to the efficient and opportune work of the Working Group on Probity and Public Ethics, of a meeting of experts in this field and of the Conference of States Parties held in Buenos Aires, Argentina, in May of 2001, completed it's task. As a result, within the framework of the ordinary session of the General Assembly held in San Jose, Costa Rica, on June 4, 2001, the States Parties, through a declaration, approved the "Follow-up Mechanism for the Implementation of the Inter-American Convention against Corruption". Of the approved text, it is worth mentioning the following:

- First, the objectives that have been defined for the follow-up mechanism, which strike an adequate balance between the necessity of following-up the progress made by the States and facilitating co-operation among them as to assure compliance, implementation and application of the Convention.

- Second, the fact that the mechanism was developed within the objectives and principles established in the OAS Charter, for example principles like sovereignty, non-intervention and legal equality of States.

- Third, the characteristics defined for the mechanism like impartiality and objectivity in its operation and conclusions, as well as the absence of sanctions.

- Fourth, the search for an adequate balance between confidentiality and transparency in its activities is very important through the publication of the rules and procedures of the Committee of Experts, the selection of issues and methodology, the selection of countries and the final report.

- Fifth, although the mechanism is of an inter-governmental in nature, it has foreseen the acceptance of opinions given by civil society and that the Committee, in its procedural rules, will regulate their participation.

- Finally, the follow-up mechanism incorporates its content within those of the OAS charter and the guidelines for the participation of civil society in the activities of the Organization, as well as establish headquarters for the Committee of Experts and that the functions of Secretariat will be offered by the OAS General Secretariat.

The starting of this follow-up mechanism, without a doubt, marks an important moment at a hemispherical level as to insure the effectiveness of the measures that will be adopted in strengthening inter-American co-operation in combating corruption.

This is, in general terms, the road taken so far within the OAS framework in strengthening co-operation among the Nations of the Americas in their fight against corruption. It is clear that the road taken is not complete but, in fact, the road taken is a permanent one, one that starts but never ends and, above all, a road with no return.

The Heads of States and of Governments of the Americas reiterated in their last Summit meeting, held in Quebec, Canada in April of 2001, when they stated their commitment in combating corruption, "acknowledging that corruption undermines core democratic values, challenges political stability and economic growth and thus threatens vital interests in our Hemisphere, we pledge to reinvigorate our fight against corruption. We also recognise the need to improve the conditions for human security in the Hemisphere."

NOTE

1.   Body integrated by the Permanent Representatives before the OAS of the Member States.

PRINCIPLES FOR MANAGING ETHICS IN THE PUBLIC SERVICE

"Although governments have different cultural, political and administrative environments, they often confront similar ethical challenges, and the responses in their ethics management show common characteristics... ...Member countries need to have a point of reference when combining the elements of an effective ethics management system in line with their own political, administrative and cultural circumstances..."

Preamble to the OECD Recommendation

The OECD Council adopted a Recommendation on Improving Ethical Conduct in the Public Service on 23 April 1998. The Recommendation is based on a set of Principles for Managing Ethics in the Public Service agreed in the Public Management Committee, to help Member countries to review their ethics management systems.

Challenges for managing ethics

High standards of conduct in the public service have become a critical issue for governments in OECD Member countries. Public management reforms involving greater devolution of responsibility and discretion for public servants, budgetary pressures and new forms of delivery of public services have challenged traditional values in the public service. Globalisation and the further development of international economic relations, including trade and investment, demand high recognisable standards of conduct in the public service. Preventing misconduct is as complex as the phenomenon of misconduct itself, and a range of integrated mechanisms are needed for success, including sound ethics management systems.

Reviewing the ethics management system

Increased concern about decline of confidence in government and corruption has prompted governments to review their approaches to ethical conduct. In response to these challenges, the Public Management Committee agreed to a set of Principles for Managing Ethics in the Public Service to help countries review the institutions, systems and mechanisms they have for promoting public service ethics. These principles identify the functions of guidance, management or control against which public ethics management systems can be checked. They draw on the experience of OECD countries, and reflect shared views of sound ethics management.

The Principles have broad practical application

The principles may be used by management across national and sub-national levels of government. Political leaders may use them to review ethics management regimes and evaluate the extent to which ethics is operationalised throughout government. The principles are intended to be an instrument for countries to adapt to national conditions, and to find their own ways of balancing the various aspirational and compliance elements to arrive at an effective framework to suit their own circumstances. They are not sufficient in themselves – they should be seen as a way of integrating ethics management with the broader public management environment.

Principles for Managing Ethics in the Public Service

Ethical standards for public service should be clear.

Public servants need to know the basic principles and standards they are expected to apply to their work and where the boundaries of acceptable behaviour lie. A concise, well-publicised statement of core ethical standards and principles that guide public service, for example in the form of a code of conduct, can accomplish this by creating a shared understanding across government and within the broader community.

Ethical standards should be reflected in the legal framework.

The legal framework is the basis for communicating the minimum obligatory standards and principles of behaviour for every public servant. Laws and regulations could state the fundamental values of public service and should provide the framework for guidance, investigation, disciplinary action and prosecution.

Ethical guidance should be available to public servants.

Professional socialisation should contribute to the development of the necessary judgement and skills enabling public servants to apply ethical principles in concrete circumstances. Training facilitates ethics awareness and can develop essential skills for ethical analysis and moral reasoning. Impartial advice can help create an environment in which public servants are more willing to confront and resolve ethical tensions and problems. Guidance and internal consultation mechanisms should be made available to help public servants apply basic ethical standards in the workplace.

Public servants should know their rights and obligations when exposing wrongdoing.

Public servants need to know what their rights and obligations are in terms of exposing actual or suspected wrongdoing within the public service. These should include clear rules and procedures for officials to follow, and a formal chain of responsibility. Public servants also need to know what protection will be available to them in cases of exposing wrongdoing.

Political commitment to ethics should reinforce the ethical conduct of public servants.

Political leaders are responsible for maintaining a high standard of propriety in the discharge of their official duties. Their commitment is demonstrated by example and by taking action that is only available at the political level, for instance by creating legislative and institutional arrangements that reinforce ethical behaviour and create sanctions against wrongdoing, by providing adequate support and resources for ethics-related activities throughout government and by avoiding the exploitation of ethics rules and laws for political purposes.

The decision-making process should be transparent and open to scrutiny.

The public has a right to know how public institutions apply the power and resources entrusted to them. Public scrutiny should be facilitated by transparent and democratic processes, oversight by the legislature and access to public information. Transparency should be further enhanced by measures such as disclosure systems and recognition of the role of an active and independent media.

There should be clear guidelines for interaction between the public and private sectors.

Clear rules defining ethical standards should guide the behaviour of public servants in dealing with the private sector, for example regarding public procurement, outsourcing or public employment conditions. Increasing interaction between the public and private sectors demands that more attention should be placed on public service values and requiring external partners to respect those same values.

Managers should demonstrate and promote ethical conduct.

An organisational environment where high standards of conduct are encouraged by providing appropriate incentives for ethical behaviour, such as adequate working conditions and effective performance assessment, has a direct impact on the daily practice of public service values and ethical standards. Managers have an important role in this regard by providing consistent leadership and serving as role models in terms of ethics and conduct in their professional relationship with political leaders, other public servants and citizens.

Management policies, procedures and practices should promote ethical conduct.

Management policies and practices should demonstrate an organisation's commitment to ethical standards. It is not sufficient for governments to have only rule-based or compliance-based structures. Compliance systems alone can inadvertently encourage some public servants simply to function on the edge of misconduct, arguing that if they are not violating the law they are acting ethically. Government policy should not only delineate the minimal standards below which a government official's actions will not be tolerated, but also clearly articulate a set of public service values that employees should aspire to.

Public service conditions and management of human resources should promote ethical conduct.

Public service employment conditions, such as career prospects, personal development, adequate remuneration and human resource management policies should create an environment conducive to ethical behaviour. Using basic principles, such as merit, consistently in the daily process of recruitment and promotion helps operationalise integrity in the public service.

Adequate accountability mechanisms should be in place within the public service.

Public servants should be accountable for their actions to their superiors and, more broadly, to the public. Accountability should focus both on compliance with rules and ethical principles and on achievement of results. Accountability mechanisms can be internal to an agency as well as government-wide, or can be provided by civil society. Mechanisms promoting accountability can be designed to provide adequate controls while allowing for appropriately flexible management.

Appropriate procedures and sanctions should exist to deal with misconduct.

Mechanisms for the detection and independent investigation of wrongdoing such as corruption are a necessary part of an ethics infrastructure. It is necessary to have reliable procedures and resources for monitoring, reporting and investigating breaches of public service rules as well as commensurate administrative or disciplinary sanctions to discourage misconduct. Managers should exercise appropriate judgement in using these mechanisms when actions need to be taken.

OECD Recommendation on Improving Ethical Conduct in the Public Service

On the proposal of the Public Management Committee the OECD Council recommends that

Member countries take action to ensure well-functioning institutions and systems for promoting ethical conduct in the public service. This can be achieved by:

- Developing and regularly reviewing policies, procedures, practices and institutions influencing ethical conduct in the public service.

- Promoting government action to maintain high standards of conduct and counter corruption in the public sector.

- Incorporating the ethical dimension into management frameworks to ensure that management practices are consistent with the values and principles of public service.

- Combining judiciously those aspects of ethics management systems based on ideals with those based on the respect of rules.

- Assessing the effects of public management reforms on public service ethical conduct.

- Using as a reference the Principles for Managing Ethics in the Public Service to ensure high standards of ethical conduct.

The OECD Council instructs the Public Management Committee to

- Analyse information provided by Member countries on how they apply these principles in their respective national contexts. The purpose of the analysis is to provide information on a comparative basis to support Member country actions to maintain well-functioning institutions and systems for promoting ethics;

- Provide support to Member countries to improve conduct in the public service by, inter alia, facilitating the process of information-sharing and disseminating promising practices in Member countries;

- Present a report in two years' time analysing the experiences, actions and practices in the Member countries that have proved effective in a particular national context.

The Principles were developed with the help of a Reference Group, discussed at the Public Management Committee of the OECD and reviewed at a Symposium held on 4-5 November 1997 in Paris. After a final review by the Committee in March 1998, the OECD Council approved them and issued a Recommendation on 23 April 1998. At their annual meeting of 27-28 April 1998, OECD Ministers welcomed the Recommendation and asked to receive a report on this issue in 2000.

OECD PUBLIC MANAGEMENT POLICY BRIEF ON
BUILDING PUBLIC TRUST: ETHICS MEASURES IN OECD COUNTRIES

Public service is a public trust. Citizens expect public servants to serve the public interest with fairness and to manage public resources properly on a daily basis. Fair and reliable public services inspire public trust and create a favourable environment for businesses, thus contributing to well-functioning markets and economic growth.

Public service ethics are a prerequisite to, and underpin, public trust, and are a keystone of good governance. But, what is needed to build public trust today?

Based on the experience of all 29 OECD countries, this annex describes what makes an effective and comprehensive ethics management policy. It also suggests policy directions to build further trust in public institutions.

Core values underpin public service

Identifying core values is the first step to creating a common understanding within society of the expected behaviour of public office holders. All OECD countries publish a set of core values for guiding their public service in daily operations, and they draw these values from the same substantial sources, namely social norms, democratic principles and professional ethos.

The changing public sector environment requires that core values be articulated. Over one-third of OECD countries have already updated their core public service values in the last five years, and further reviews are still being undertaken. In the course of the revisions, countries have re-emphasised "traditional" values while giving them a modern content and adding "new" values to reflect an increasingly results-based public service culture. For example, impartiality is the most commonly identified core value; it implies equal access to public services, as well as equal standing before the law.

Table 1: The 8 most frequently stated core public service values in OECD countries
(number of countries stating each value)

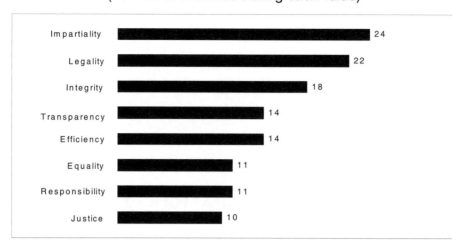

Standards of behaviour set boundaries for conduct

Legislating standards of behaviour has become the primary way to elaborate on stated core values. Almost all OECD countries have developed a more detailed description of the standards expected of all public servants in potential conflict-of-interest situations, particularly in relation to:

- The use of official information and public resources.

- Receiving gifts or benefits; and

- Work outside the public service.

In addition to the general standards applicable to all public servants, OECD countries employ *supplementary guidelines* for specific groups or professions working in sensitive areas or where there is a high risk of conflict of interest, such as law enforcement, tax and custom administrations. Some countries have also elaborated codes for ministers for conducting government business.

Criminal laws penalise specific forms of corruption as well as breaches of core values. While almost all OECD countries criminalise active and passive forms of corruption committed by public officials, more and more countries are also criminalising other forms of corruption, such as indirect and attempted corruption. Furthermore, the OECD Anti-Bribery Convention requires all OECD countries as well as five non-members to make bribery of foreign public officials punishable by effective, proportionate and dissuasive criminal penalties . A growing number of countries are also seeking to punish breaches of core public service values and principles (such as impartiality in decision-making) and the use of public office for private gain.

Putting values into effect starts with communication

Almost all OECD countries use *training* to raise awareness of public servants on ethical issues. However, there is a growing emphasis on developing the necessary skills for handling ethical dilemmas. Over half of the countries focus on new recruits by providing information on values when they join the public service, and in one-third of the countries a statement of values is also part of the employment contract. Some OECD countries also provide regular on-the-job training.

In addition, public servants can seek *advice* from their superiors when faced with ethical dilemmas in the workplace. Some countries also provide access to specialised external bodies to ensure the neutrality of advice.

Involving staff -- directly and/or through trade unions or professional associations – in the revision of values and standards establishes mutual understanding among public servants and leads to smoother implementation. One-third of OECD countries have consulted with defined groups within the public service or beyond; and some have even sought public comment. A growing number of countries are using *new technology*, especially the Internet and interactive CD-ROMs, to provide information on values and expected standards as well as to train public servants on ethics issues.

Ensuring integrity in daily management

The following management measures are essential *for creating a working environment that ensures transparency and reinforces integrity:*

- Setting standards for timeliness.

- Requesting reasons for decisions.

- Providing redress against decisions.

- Requiring the identification of conflict of interest.

OECD countries almost unanimously base recruitment and promotion on merit in their public service. The vast majority of countries secure the openness of their selection processes by publishing both the recruitment rules and vacant positions, and over half of the countries also take ethical considerations into account in recruitment and performance appraisal.

Paying special attention to officials in positions that are particularly susceptible to corruption is a rising concern for OECD countries. The vast majority of these countries require the identification and reporting of conflict of interest. Two-thirds of the countries have developed specific anti-corruption measures in sensitive areas, such as public procurement, and employ supplementary measures such as:

- Specific regulations and guidelines.

- Stricter control.

- Regular redeployment.

Disclosure of private interests makes decision-making more transparent by minimising the possibility of conflicts arising between public duties and private interests. With few exceptions, OECD countries require disclosure of personal financial interests, while half of the countries also oblige officials to disclose outside positions and gifts.

The higher the position, the more transparency is called for. Typically, disclosure is required from elected officials and senior public servants; a few countries require it from public servants in general.

Certain sensitive sectors, such as tax and custom administrations, also demand more stringent disclosure.

Monitoring compliance

Sound ethics management not only sets standards of behaviour but also monitors compliance with these standards. *Internal control is widely used to detect individual irregularities and systemic failures in OECD countries.* They have either strengthened existing legal measures or established a legal framework for internal control. Internal control reviews, generally carried out annually or when the need arises, recommend measures for improving management and, in some cases, directly inform the political level or the general public.

Internal control is accompanied by independent scrutiny. This scrutiny keeps public servants accountable for their actions, ultimately, to the public. In virtually all countries, the legislative branch undertakes reviews of public service activities. Other common types of scrutiny range from external independent investigation by the Ombudsman or the Inspector General to specific judicial or ethics reviews. Empowering an independent Ombudsman to scrutinise mismanagement has become a popular instrument in over half of OECD countries, and more and more countries are appointing a specialised independent unit to oversee the behaviour of public servants..

Reporting misconduct by public servants is either required by law and/or facilitated by organisational rules in two-thirds of OECD countries. A growing need to provide protection for whistleblowers in the public service is also visible across OECD countries. Almost half of these countries offer general protection mainly in their public service framework, where the most commonly provided safeguards are legal protection and anonymity. In two-thirds of OECD countries citizens have access to services, such as complaint procedures, an Ombudsman or Inspector General, and help desks or telephone lines, enabling them to expose wrongdoing by public servants.

Taking action against wrongdoing

Taking action against violations of standards is the shared responsibility of managers and external investigative bodies. OECD countries recognise that disciplinary actions against a breach of public service standards should be taken within the organisation where the breach occurred. All governments have developed a general framework for disciplinary procedures that both allows managers to impose timely and just sanctions and guarantees a fair process for the public servants. OECD countries employ very *similar disciplinary sanctions,* ranging from warning and reprimand through material penalty to temporary or final dismissal, which is the most severe disciplinary consequence in all countries.

Although public sector managers have the primary responsibility for initiating disciplinary measures in their agencies in a timely manner, they may also receive assistance from specific external institutions. These external institutions are the primary instruments for *investigating and prosecuting misconduct* in the public service. These bodies have the power to bring suspected cases of corruption directly to court in all OECD countries. Moreover, two-thirds of countries have procedures and mechanisms to enable the public to signal wrongdoing to bodies exercising independent scrutiny on public service activities.

Citizens trust public institutions if they know that public offices are used for the public good

Lessons from the OECD survey suggest the following steps for building trust in public institutions:

- Defining a clear mission for the public service.

Adapting the mission of the public service to current needs and ensuring that its core values and standards meet changing public expectations is a key challenge for governments in a rapidly changing world.

- Safeguarding values while adapting to change.

The changing socio-economic environment, especially the growing demand for transparency, requires that governments review and adjust mechanisms to ensure that public servants' behaviour corresponds to expected standards.

- Empowering both public servants and citizens to report misconduct.

Clear and known procedures that facilitate the reporting of wrongdoing and provide protection for whistleblowers assist the detection of individual cases. *Integrating integrity measures into overall management*

Integrity measures *are not* a distinct activity, but rather an integral part of all management systems in which integrity measures provide complementary support for the overall management environment.

- Co-ordinating integrity measures: a precondition for success.

Successful integrity measures consist of a combination of actions that are consistent and take into account the wider public service environment. Assessing the effectiveness of measures provides feedback to policy-makers on their implementation and also lays the groundwork for future policies.

- Shifting emphasis from enforcement to prevention.

Sound ethics management policy adequately combines enforcement and prevention measures. However, there is a growing recognition that increased attention to prevention reduces the need for enforcement. Prevention is a less expensive investment in the long term, with a more positive impact on the public service culture and on the relationship between the public service and civil society.

- *Anticipating problems.*

By anticipating situations that might weaken adherence to public service values and standards of behaviour, governments can prepare suitable responses to prevent adverse effects. For example, how can governments meet increasing public demands for more information on private interests that affect public decisions?

- Taking advantage of new technology.

Exploring ways to harness new technologies can help governments find new ways to internalise integrity and inform citizens on standards expected of officials serving the public.

About this Policy Brief...

This Policy Brief outlines the main findings of the OECD ethics survey carried out in 1999-2000 at the request of OECD Ministers at their annual meeting. It is designed to facilitate mutual learning and to support policymakers in constructing modern ethics strategies in both OECD and non-member countries. In other words, this survey was dedicated to building public trust.

Common trends show that the following steps are needed to build a consistent system of supportive mechanisms, namely the Ethics Infrastructure:

- Communicate and inculcate core values and ethical standards for public servants in order to provide clear guidance and advice to help solve ethical dilemmas.

- Promote ethical standards by preventing situations prone to conflict of interest and rewarding high standards of conduct through career development.

- Monitor compliance and report, detect and discipline wrongdoing.

This Policy Brief is based on a survey on managing ethics in the public service which reviewed the implementation in countries of the 1998 OECD Recommendation on Improving Ethical Conduct in the Public Service. The survey was based on self-assessment by all 29 OECD countries: central governments provided information on their systems in place and how they work.

OECD promotes good governance

The rapidly changing socio-economic environment, and especially the growing demand for transparency, requires that governments review and adjust mechanisms to ensure high standards of conduct in public office. OECD supports its Member countries in their actions to promote good governance in both the public and private spheres. Recent initiatives which address both the "demand" and "supply" side of corruption include the work on public ethics as well as the implementation of the 1997 OECD Convention Against Bribery of Foreign Public Officials and the OECD Principles of Corporate Governance.

More information ...

On the survey is available in the OECD publication entitled *Trust in Government: Ethics Measures in OECD Countries*. This publication constitutes a unique source of comparative information on ethics management measures taken in all 29 OECD countries, including overall trends, promising practices and innovative solutions. The database presented in this report aims to assist efforts by countries to evaluate their systems in the context of practices and trends across OECD countries.

For further information on OECD work on public ethics please contact
Email: *janos.bertok@oecd.org*
Fax: +33-1-45.24.17.06 / 89.76
Web site: *http:/www.oecd.org/puma/*

ANNEX 3

OECD BEST PRACTICES FOR BUDGET TRANSPARENCY

Introduction

The relationship between good governance and better economic and social outcomes is increasingly acknowledged. Transparency – openness about policy intentions, formulation and implementation – is a key element of good governance. The budget is the single most important policy document of governments, where policy objectives are reconciled and implemented in concrete terms. Budget transparency is defined as the full disclosure of all relevant fiscal information in a timely and systematic manner.

OECD Member countries are at the forefront of budget transparency practices. At its 1999 annual meeting, the OECD Working Party of Senior Budget Officials asked the Secretariat to draw together a set of Best Practices in this area based on Member countries' experiences.

The Best Practices are in three parts. Part I lists the principal budget reports that governments should produce and their general content. Part II describes specific disclosures to be contained in the reports. This includes both financial and non-financial performance information. Part III highlights practices for ensuring the quality and integrity of the reports.

The Best Practices are designed as a reference tool for Member and non-member countries to use in order to increase the degree of budget transparency in their respective countries. The Best Practices are organised around specific reports for presentational reasons only. It is recognised that different countries will have different reporting regimes and may have different areas of emphasis for transparency. The Best Practices are based on different Member countries' experiences in each area. It should be stressed that the Best Practices are not meant to constitute a formal "standard" for budget transparency.

The Best Practices define "government" in line with the System of National Accounts (SNA). This definition encompasses the non-commercial activities of government. Specifically, the activities of state-owned enterprises are excluded from this definition. Although the SNA definition focuses on general government, *i.e.* consolidating all levels of government, these Best Practices should be seen to apply to the national government.

I. Budget Reports

I.1 *The Budget*

- The budget is the government's key policy document. It should be comprehensive, encompassing all government revenue and expenditure, so that the necessary trade-offs between different policy options can be assessed.

- The government's draft budget should be submitted to parliament far enough in advance to allow Parliament to review it properly. In no case should this be less than 3 months prior to the start of the fiscal year. The budget should be approved by Parliament prior to the start of the fiscal year.

- The budget, or related documents, should include a detailed commentary on each revenue and expenditure programme.

- Non-financial performance data, including performance targets, should be presented for expenditure programmes where practicable.

- The budget should include a medium-term perspective illustrating how revenue and expenditure will develop during, at least, the two years beyond the next fiscal year. Similarly, the current budget proposal should be reconciled with forecasts contained in earlier fiscal reports for the same period; all significant deviations should be explained.

- Comparative information on actual revenue and expenditure during the past year and an updated forecast for the current year should be provided for each programme. Similar comparative information should be shown for any non-financial performance data.

- If revenue and expenditures are authorised in permanent legislation, the amounts of such revenue and expenditures should nonetheless be shown in the budget for information purposes along with other revenue and expenditure.

- Expenditures should be presented in gross terms. Ear-marked revenue and user charges should be clearly accounted for separately. This should be done regardless of whether particular incentive and control systems provide for the retention of some or all of the receipts by the collecting agency.

- Expenditures should be classified by administrative unit (*e.g.*, ministry, agency). Supplementary information classifying expenditure by economic and functional categories should also be presented.

- The economic assumptions underlying the report should be made in accordance with Best Practice 2.1 (below).

- The budget should include a discussion of tax expenditures in accordance with Best Practice 2.2 (below).

- The budget should contain a comprehensive discussion of the government's financial assets and liabilities, non-financial assets, employee pension obligations and contingent liabilities in accordance with Best Practice 2.3-2.6 (below).

I.2   Pre-Budget Report

- A pre-budget report serves to encourage debate on the budget aggregates and how they interact with the economy. As such, it also serves to create appropriate expectations for the budget itself. It should be released no later than one month prior to the introduction of the budget proposal.

- The report should state explicitly the government's long-term economic and fiscal policy objectives and the government's economic and fiscal policy intentions for the forthcoming budget and, at least, the following two fiscal years. It should highlight the total level of revenue, expenditure, deficit or surplus, and debt.

- The economic assumptions underlying the report should be made in accordance with Best Practice 2.1 (see below).

I.3   Monthly Reports

- Monthly reports show progress in implementing the budget. They should be released within four weeks of the end of each month.

- They should contain the amount of revenue and expenditure in each month and year-to-date. A comparison should be made with the forecast amounts of monthly revenue and expenditure for the same period. Any in-year adjustments to the original forecast should be shown separately.

- A brief commentary should accompany the numerical data. If a significant divergence between actual and forecast amounts occurs, an explanation should be made.

- Expenditures should be classified by major administrative units (e.g., ministry, agency). Supplementary information classifying expenditure by economic and functional categories should also be presented.

- The reports, or related documents, should also contain information on the government's borrowing activity (see Best Practice 2.3 below).

I.4   Mid-Year Report

- The mid-year report provides a comprehensive update on the implementation of the budget, including an updated forecast of the budget outcome for the current fiscal year and, at least, the following two fiscal years. The report should be released within six weeks of the end of the mid-year period.

- The economic assumptions underlying the budget should be reviewed and the impact of any changes on the budget disclosed (see Best Practice 2.1).

- The mid-year should contain a comprehensive discussion of the government's financial assets and liabilities, non-financial assets, employee pension obligations and contingent liabilities in accordance with Best Practices 2.3-2.6 (below).

- The impact of any other government decisions, or other circumstances, that may have a material effect on the budget should be disclosed.

I.5   Year-End Report

- The year-end report is the government's key accountability document. It should be audited by the Supreme Audit Institution, in accordance with Best Practice 3.3 (below) and be released within six months of the end of the fiscal year.

- The year-end report shows compliance with the level of revenue and expenditures authorised by Parliament in the budget. Any in-year adjustments to the original budget should be shown separately. The presentation format of the year-end report should mirror the presentation format of the budget.

- The year-end report, or related documents, should include non-financial performance information, including a comparison of performance targets and actual results achieved where practicable.

- Comparative information on the level of revenue and expenditure during the preceding year should also be provided. Similar comparative information should be shown for any non-financial performance data.

- Expenditure should be presented in gross terms. Ear-marked revenue and user charges should be clearly accounted for separately.

- Expenditure should be classified by administrative unit (e.g., ministry, agency). Supplementary information classifying expenditure by economic and functional categories should also be presented.

- The year-end report should contain a comprehensive discussion of the government's financial assets and financial liabilities, non-financial assets, employee pension obligations and contingent liabilities in accordance with Best Practices 2.3-2.6 (below).

I.6   Pre-Election Report

- A pre-election report serves to illuminate the general state of government finances immediately before an election. This fosters a more informed electorate and serves to stimulate public debate.

- The feasibility of producing this report may depend on constitutional provisions and electoral practices. Optimally, it should be released no later than two weeks prior to elections.

- The report should contain the same information as the mid-year report.

- Special care needs to be taken to assure the integrity of such reports, in accordance with Best Practice 3.2 (below).

1.7   *Long-Term Report*

- The long-term report assesses the long-term sustainability of current government policies. It should be released at least every five years, or when major changes are made in substantive revenue or expenditure programmes.

- The report should assess the budgetary implications of demographic change, such as population ageing and other potential developments over the long term (10-40 years).

- All key assumptions underlying the projections contained in the report should be made explicit and a range of plausible scenarios presented.

2.   Specific Disclosures

2.1   *Economic Assumptions*

- Deviations from the forecast of the key economic assumptions underlying the budget are the government's key fiscal risk.

- All key economic assumptions should be disclosed explicitly. This includes the forecast for GDP growth, the composition of GDP growth, the rate of employment and unemployment, the current account, inflation and interest rates (monetary policy).

- A sensitivity analysis should be made of what impact changes in the key economic assumptions would have on the budget.

2.2   *Tax Expenditures*

- Tax expenditures are the estimated costs to the tax revenue of preferential treatment for specific activities.

- The estimated cost of key tax expenditures should be disclosed as supplementary information in the budget. To the extent practicable, a discussion of tax expenditures for specific functional areas should be incorporated into the discussion of general expenditures for those areas in order to inform budgetary choices.

2.3   *Financial Liabilities and Financial Assets*

- All financial liabilities and financial assets should be disclosed in the budget, the mid-year report, and the year-end report. Monthly borrowing activity should be disclosed in the monthly reports, or related documents.

- Borrowings should be classified by the currency denomination of the debt, the maturity profile of the debt, whether the debt carries a fixed or variable rate of interest, and whether it is callable.

- Financial assets should be classified by major type, including cash, marketable securities, investments in enterprises and loans advanced to other entities. Investments in enterprises should be listed individually. Loans advanced to other entities should be listed by major category reflecting their nature; historical information on defaults for each category should be disclosed where available. Financial assets should be valued at market value.

- Debt management instruments, such as forward contracts and swaps, should be disclosed.

- In the budget, a sensitivity analysis should be made showing what impact changes in interest rates and foreign exchange rates would have on financing costs.

2.4   *Non-Financial Assets*

- Non-financial assets, including real property and equipment, should be disclosed.

- Non-financial assets will be recognised under full accrual based accounting and budgeting. This will require the valuation of such assets and the selection of appropriate depreciation schedules. The valuation and depreciation methods should be fully disclosed.

- Where full accrual basis is not adopted, a register of assets should be maintained and summary information from this register provided in the budget, the mid-year report and the year-end report.

2.5   *Employee Pension Obligations*

- Employee pension obligations should be disclosed in the budget, the mid-year report and the year-end report. Employee pension obligations are the difference between accrued benefits arising from past service and the contributions that the government has made towards those benefits.

- Key actuarial assumptions underlying the calculation of employee pension obligations should be disclosed. Any assets belonging to employee pension plans should be valued at market value.

2.6   *Contingent Liabilities*

- Contingent liabilities are liabilities whose budgetary impact is dependent on future events which may or may not occur. Common examples include government loan guarantees, government insurance programmes, and legal claims against the government.

- All significant contingent liabilities should be disclosed in the budget, the mid-year report and the annual financial statements.

- Where feasible, the total amount of contingent liabilities should be disclosed and classified by major category reflecting their nature; historical information on defaults for each category should be disclosed where available. In cases where contingent liabilities cannot be quantified, they should be listed and described.

3. Integrity, Control and Accountability

3.1 Accounting Policies

- A summary of relevant accounting policies should accompany all reports. These should describe the basis of accounting applied (e.g., cash, accrual) in preparing the reports and disclose any deviations from generally accepted accounting practices.

- The same accounting policies should be used for all fiscal reports.

- If a change in accounting policies is required, then the nature of the change and the reasons for the change should be fully disclosed. Information for previous reporting periods should be adjusted, as practicable, to allow comparisons to be made between reporting periods.

3.2 Systems and Responsibility

- A dynamic system of internal financial controls, including internal audit, should be in place to assure the integrity of information provided in the reports.

- Each report should contain a statement of responsibility by the finance minister and the senior official responsible for producing the report. The minister certifies that all government decisions with a fiscal impact have been included in the report. The senior official certifies that the finance ministry has used its best professional judgement in producing the report.

3.3 Audit

- The year-end report should be audited by the Supreme Audit Institution in accordance with generally accepted auditing practices.

- Audit reports prepared by the Supreme Audit Institution should be scrutinised by Parliament.

3.4 Public and Parliamentary Scrutiny

- Parliament should have the opportunity and the resources to effectively examine any fiscal report that it deems necessary.

- All fiscal reports referred to in these Best Practices should be made publicly available. This includes the availability of all reports free of charge on the Internet.

- The finance ministry should actively promote an understanding of the budget process by individual citizens and non-governmental organisations

OECD PUBLIC MANAGEMENT POLICY BRIEF ON
ENGAGING CITIZENS IN POLICY-MAKING:
INFORMATION, CONSULTATION AND PUBLIC PARTICIPATION

Reaping the benefits...

Strengthening relations with citizens is a sound investment in better policy-making and a core element of good governance. It allows government to tap new sources of policy relevant-ideas, information and resources when making decisions. Equally important, it contributes to building public trust in government, raising the quality of democracy and strengthening civic capacity. Such efforts help strengthen representative democracy, in which parliaments play a central role.

...by taking concrete steps...

In strengthening their relations with citizens, governments must ensure that:

- Information is complete, objective, reliable, relevant, easy to find and to understand;

- Consultation has clear goals and rules defining the limits of the exercise and government's obligation to account for its use of citizens' input;

- Participation provides sufficient time and flexibility to allow for the emergence of new ideas and proposals by citizens, as well as mechanisms for their integration into government policy-making processes.

...to build commitment and capacity

Governments must invest adequate time, resources and commitment in building robust legal, policy and institutional frameworks, developing appropriate tools and evaluating their own performance in engaging citizens in policy-making. Poorly designed and inadequate measures for information, consultation and active participation in policy-making can undermine government-citizen relations. Governments may seek to inform, consult and engage citizens in order to enhance the quality, credibility and legitimacy of their policy decisions...only to produce the opposite effect if citizens discover that their efforts to stay informed, provide feedback and actively participate are ignored, have no impact at all on the decisions reached or remain unaccounted for.

This PUMA Policy Brief No. 10 describes a range of concrete measures and suggests ten guiding principles for strengthening government relations with citizens and civil society.

Why strengthen government-citizen relations?

Several driving forces have led OECD countries to focus attention on strengthening their relations with citizens, including the need to:

- *Improve the quality of policy,* by allowing governments to tap wider sources of information, perspectives, and potential solutions in order to meet the challenges of policy-making under conditions of increasing complexity, policy interdependence and time pressures.

- *Meet the challenges of the emerging information society,* to prepare for greater and faster interactions with citizens and ensure better knowledge management.

- *Integrate public input into the policy-making process,* in order to respond to citizens' expectations that their voices be heard, and their views be considered, in decision-making by government.

- *Respond to calls for greater government transparency and accountability,* as public and media scrutiny of government actions increases, standards in public life are codified and raised.

- *Strengthen public trust in government,* and reverse the steady erosion of voter turnout in elections, falling membership in political parties and surveys showing declining confidence in key public institutions.

Defining government-citizen relations in policy-making

Government-citizen relations cover a broad spectrum of different interactions at each stage of the policy-making cycle: from policy design, through implementation to evaluation. In reviewing this complex relationship, the OECD survey used the following working definitions:

- *Information: a one-way relation* in which government produces and delivers information for use by citizens. It covers both 'passive' access to information upon demand by citizens and 'active' measures by government to disseminate information to citizens.

- *Consultation: a two-way relation* in which citizens provide feedback to government. It is based on the prior definition by government of the issue on which citizens' views are being sought and requires the provision of information.

- *Active participation:* a relation based on partnership with government, in which citizens actively engage in the policy-making process. It acknowledges a role for citizens in proposing policy options and shaping the policy dialogue – although the responsibility for the final decision or policy formulation rests with government.

Main trends

Policy-making in all OECD countries rests on the foundation of representative democracy. Within this framework, many OECD countries have long-standing traditions of extensive citizen involvement. All are looking for new, and complementary, ways to include citizens in policy-making.

- *Information* for citizens is now *an objective shared by all OECD countries.* The scope, quantity and quality of government information provided to the public has increased greatly over the past decade.

- *Consultation and* opportunities for citizens to provide feedback on policy proposals is also on the rise, but at a slower rate. *Large differences remain between OECD countries.*

- *Active participation* and efforts to engage citizens in policy-making on a partnership basis are rare, undertaken *on a pilot basis only and confined to a very few OECD countries.*

Building legal, policy and institutional frameworks

Information is a basic precondition

Access to information requires sound legislation, clear institutional mechanisms for its application and independent oversight institutions and judiciary for enforcement. Finally, it requires citizens' to know and understand their rights - and to be willing and able to act upon them.

- *Laws:* the trend in adopting access to information laws has clearly gathered pace in recent years. In 1980, only 20% of OECD countries had legislation on access to information (also known as freedom of information, or FOI, laws). In 1990, this figure had risen to just over 40%, and by the end of 2000, it had reached 80%. In several OECD countries, access is the rule and secrecy is the exception. All provide access to documents held by public authorities and appeal mechanisms in cases of refusal.

- *Policies:* basic legal rights are given substance through government commitment to provide objective and reliable information. Policies on both 'passive' (e.g. response times or charging) and 'active' access to information (e.g. government communications policy) are needed.

- *Institutions:* Access to information laws generally apply to all administrative units. Implementation may be co-ordinated (e.g. by central government) and subject to external oversight (e.g. by the Ombudsman).

All OECD countries must reconcile the citizen's right to know with the individual's right to privacy and the need to preserve confidentiality where disclosure of information would be against the public interest. Balancing rights of access, protection of privacy and limits to official secrecy is a significant challenge – especially given the rapid evolution of information and communication technologies (ICTs).

Consultation is central to policy-making

Consultation has only recently been recognised as an essential element of public policy-making in the majority of OECD countries, and legal, policy and institutional frameworks are still under development.

- *Laws:* Legislation on public consultation may be broad (e.g. establishing petition rights or consultative referenda) or restricted in scope (e.g. requiring consultation with trade unions, professional associations or indigenous peoples during policy-making).

- *Policies:* Some OECD countries rely on rules (e.g. cabinet orders, guidelines, standards) and informal practice when conducting public consultation. Several require public consultation on new regulations (e.g. under regulatory impact assessment procedures), in line with the 1995 OECD Council Recommendation on Improving the Quality of Government Regulation.

- *Institutions:* Several OECD countries have long-standing institutional arrangements for consultation (e.g. tripartite forums of government, business and labour). Many have established permanent or ad hoc advisory bodies and commissions which include civil society organisations (CSOs).

Active participation is a new frontier

Active participation recognises the capacity of citizens to discuss and generate policy options independently. It requires governments to share in agenda setting and to ensure that policy proposals generated jointly will be taken into account in reaching a final decision. Only a few OECD countries have begun to explore such approaches and experience to date is limited to a few pilot cases.

- *Laws*: Citizens in some OECD countries have the right to propose new legislation (e.g. under laws on popular legislative initiative or on citizen-initiated referenda). These usually require the prior collection of signatures from a proportion of eligible voters within a specific timeframe.

- *Policies*: A few OECD countries have policies to support new and more flexible approaches to ensuring a greater degree of active participation by citizens in policy-making (e.g. policy statements).

- *Institutions*: There is no single institutional interface. The few examples that exist to date are drawn from different levels of government and policy sectors (e.g. central policy units engaged in collecting good practices, raising awareness, and developing guidelines).

Matching tools to objectives

The first step in the design of successful information, consultation and active participation in policy-making is to clearly *define the objective* of the exercise - on the basis of which the *target group* (e.g. all citizens, rural communities, youth) may be identified and an appropriate tool chosen.

No single tool or approach will be suitable for every country or situation. Often a *mix of tools* will be required, and these may need to be adapted to local traditions and practices. The choice of tools will also depend upon the resources (e.g. financial and human), time and skills available.

- *Information*: Even 'passive' access to information requires tools to enable citizens to find what they are looking for (e.g. catalogues and indexes). When governments engage in the 'active' provision of information, they may use a range of different products (e.g. annual reports, brochures, leaflets) and delivery mechanisms, which may be either direct (e.g. information centres, toll-free phone numbers) or indirect (e.g. media coverage, advertising, civil society organisations as intermediaries).

- *Consultation*: Governments use different tools to seek feedback on policy issues (e.g. opinion polls and surveys) or on draft policies and laws (e.g. comment and notice periods) from a broad range of citizens. They may also use tools for consultation that provide greater levels of interaction (e.g. public hearings, focus groups, citizen panels, workshops) with smaller groups of citizens.

- *Active participation*: Engaging citizens in policy deliberation requires specific tools to facilitate learning, debate and the drafting of concrete proposals (e.g. citizens' fora, consensus conferences, citizens' juries).

Unlocking the full potential of ICT

All OECD countries regard new information and communication technologies (ICTs) as a *powerful tool* and are making significant efforts to bring their administrations and their citizens 'on-line'. While many believe ICTs have great potential, today they remain complementary to traditional tools. Most OECD governments are working to bridge the 'digital divide', and recognise the need to ensure that all citizens, whether on-line or not, continue to enjoy equal rights of participation in the public sphere.

- *Information*: All governments in OECD countries provide an increasing amount of information on-line (e.g. via government Web sites and portals), although the quantity, quality and range varies greatly.

- *Consultation*: The use of ICTs for feedback and consultation is still in its infancy in all OECD countries (e.g. e-mail addresses on government Web sites, e-mail lists, on-line chat events).

- *Active participation*: Only a very few OECD countries have begun to experiment with on-line tools to actively engage citizens in policy-making (e.g. on-line discussion groups, interactive games).

- *Integration* with established, 'off-line' tools and approaches is needed to make the most of ICTs.

Evaluating performance

All OECD countries recognise the *need to develop tools* and to improve their capacity for evaluation. The survey shows a striking imbalance between the amount of time, money and energy that OECD countries invest in strengthening government-citizen relations and the amount of attention they pay to evaluating effectiveness and impact on policy-making.

No OECD country currently conducts a systematic evaluation of government performance in providing information, conducting consultation and engaging citizens in policy-making.

Guiding principles

The survey suggests the following guiding principles for successful information, consultation and active participation in policy-making:

Commitment

Leadership and strong commitment to information, consultation and active participation in policy-making is needed at all levels - from politicians, senior managers and public officials.

Rights

Citizens' rights to access information, provide feedback, be consulted and actively participate in policy-making must be firmly grounded in law or policy. Government obligations to respond to citizens when exercising their rights must also be clearly stated. Independent institutions for oversight, or their equivalent, are essential to enforcing these rights.

Clarity

Objectives for, and limits to, information, consultation and active participation during policy-making should be well defined from the outset. The respective roles and responsibilities of citizens (in providing input) and government (in making decisions for which they are accountable) must be clear to all.

Time

Public consultation and active participation should be undertaken as early in the policy process as possible to allow a greater range of policy solutions to emerge and to raise the chances of successful implementation. Adequate time must be available for consultation and participation to be effective. Information is needed at all stages of the policy cycle.

Objectivity

Information provided by government during policy-making should be objective, complete and accessible. All citizens should have equal treatment when exercising their rights of access to information and participation.

Resources

Adequate financial, human and technical resources are needed if public information, consultation and active participation in policy-making are to be effective. Government officials must have access to appropriate skills, guidance and training as well as an organisational culture that supports their efforts.

Co-ordination

Initiatives to inform, request feedback from and consult citizens should be co-ordinated across government to enhance knowledge management, ensure policy coherence, avoid duplication and reduce the risk of 'consultation fatigue' among citizens and civil society organisations. Co-ordination efforts should not reduce the capacity of government units to ensure innovation and flexibility.

Accountability

Governments have an obligation to account for the use they make of citizens' inputs received through feedback, public consultation and active participation. Measures to ensure that the policy-making process is open, transparent and amenable to external scrutiny and review are crucial to increasing government accountability overall.

Evaluation

Governments need the tools, information and capacity to evaluate their performance in providing information, conducting consultation and engaging citizens in order to adapt to new requirements and changing conditions for policy-making.

Active citizenship

Governments benefit from active citizens and a dynamic civil society and can take concrete actions to facilitate access to information and participation, raise awareness, strengthen citizens' civic education and skills as well as to support capacity building among civil society organisations.

About this Policy Brief

This Policy Brief is designed to support policy-makers in building effective frameworks for information, consultation and active participation by citizens in public policy-making. It draws heavily upon the experience and insights of national experts and senior officials from the centres of government in OECD countries, whose deliberations have provided the Secretariat with broad comparative perspectives and concrete examples of good practice. The Policy Brief is based on the main findings of two OECD surveys carried out in 1999-2000 on "Strengthening Government-Citizen Connections" and "Using Information Technology to Strengthen Government-Citizen Connections". The surveys were based on self-reporting by OECD countries: central governments provided information on current provisions for, and practice in, providing information, opportunities for consultation and active participation of citizens in policy-making.

Promoting good governance

The OECD supports its Member countries in building and strengthening effective, efficient, transparent and accountable government structures. Access to information, consultation and active participation in policy-making contributes to good governance by fostering greater transparency in policy-making; more accountability through direct public scrutiny and oversight; enhanced legitimacy of government decision-making processes; better quality policy decisions based on a wider range of information sources; and, finally, higher levels of implementation and compliance given greater public awareness of policies and participation in their design.

More information

The OECD publication "Engaging Citizens: Information, Consultation and Public Participation in Policy-making", on which this Policy Brief is based, is a unique source of comparative information on measures for strengthening citizens access to information, consultation and participation in policy-making. It does not attempt to evaluate or rank countries in terms of their progress in strengthening government-citizen relations. Rather, it offers an overall framework within which to examine a wide range of country experiences, identify examples of good practice and highlight innovative approaches.

In doing so, the report takes into account the great diversity of country contexts and objectives in strengthening government-citizen relations to be found among OECD countries.

The report is accompanied by a "Handbook on Strengthening Government-Citizen Relations" designed for use by government officials in OECD Member and non-member countries. The handbook offers a practical guide in building robust frameworks for informing, consulting and engaging citizens during policy-making.

The report and accompanying handbook will be published in early October 2001 and may be purchased from the OECD Online Bookshop (*http://www.oecd.org/bookshop/*).

Next steps

The OECD report and policy brief will be the subject of public discussion and debate with representatives of civil society organisations (CSOs). Events planned include: national workshops organised by participating governments, an international roundtable event and an on-line electronic discussion forum hosted on the PUMA web site.

PUMA's future work programme on E-government will also focus on two key aspects of government-citizen relations, namely: a) the use of new ICTs in consulting citizens and civil society for policy-making and b) on-line service delivery with the publication of a brief report in late 2001.

For further information on OECD work on government-citizen relations please contact Joanne Caddy

E-mail: *joanne.caddy@oecd.org*
Fax: +33-1-45.24.17.06 / 87.96
OECD Public Management Web site: http://www.oecd.org/puma/

OECD PUBLICATION, 2, rue André-Pascal, 75775 PARIS CEDEX 16
PRINTED IN FRANCE
(42 2002 08 1P) — No. 52617 2002